POST-THEORY

POST-THEORY

NEW DIRECTIONS IN CRITICISM

Edited by

Martin McQuillan, Graeme Macdonald,
Robin Purves and Stephen Thomson

EDINBURGH
University Press

Edinburgh University Press
22 George Square, Edinburgh

Typeset in Bulmer
by Pioneer Associates, Perthshire, and
printed and bound in Great Britain by
The University Press, Cambridge

A CIP record for this book is available from the
British Library

ISBN 0 7486 1066 9 (hardback)
ISBN 0 7486 1065 0 (paperback)

CONTENTS

Part II   Inter

Part III   The Post-Theory Condition

PREFACE

The destiny of theory in our century is a peculiar one. On the one hand we are certainly witnessing the progressive blurring of the classical frontiers which made 'theory' a distinctive object: in an era of generalised critique of the metalinguistic function, the analysis of the concrete escapes the rigid straitjacket of the distinction theoretical framework/case studies. But, on the other hand, precisely because we are living in a *post*-theoretical age, theory cannot be opposed by a flourishing empiricity liberated from theoretical fetters. What we have, instead, is a process of mutual contamination between 'theory' and 'empiria' – the former having abandoned its aspiration to constitute a 'superhard transcendality' and the latter having lost the innocence associated with pure 'data'. So, although we have entered a post-theoretical universe, we are definitely not in an a-theoretical one. The deconstructive tradition, approaches such as Foucault's genealogic method, the logic of the signifier in Lacan and the various currents emerging from the Wittgensteinian opening have contributed a new sophistication in the analysis of the concrete, which can no longer be conceived in terms of an unproblematic empiricity. We could in some sense speak of a new transcendentalism – or, rather, quasi-transcendentalism – which illuminates the complex discursive strategies through which social relations take shape.

The various chapters in this volume reflect, in one way or another, this general intellectual trend. Drawing from developments which have taken place in various disciplines, they attempt to give the reader a comprehensive panorama of how theory has entered into a post-theoretical terrain.

Ernesto Laclau

ACKNOWLEDGEMENTS

The editors would like to acknowledge the help of the Graduate School of Arts and Humanities at the University of Glasgow and the British Academy whose financial assistance made this book possible. We would also like to thank Willy Maley, Dick Hebdige and Pierre Bourdieu for their enthusiasm and support during this project.

Chapter 10, by Robert Smith, first appeared in full in *Common Knowledge*, 5:1 (Spring 1996), 59–76. Chapter 8, by Catherine Belsey, first appeared in *Dedalus*. We are grateful to the editors of these journals for granting permission to republish this material.

This book is dedicated to all those who chose to spend three days with us in Glasgow between 4 and 6 July 1996. Many thanks.

THE JOY OF THEORY

Martin McQuillan, Graeme Macdonald,
Robin Purves and Stephen Thomson

This is not the first time that Theory has been reported dead.
This is not the first time that Theory has been reported dead.
This is not the first time that reporting the death of Theory has been reported dead.
This is not the first time that reporting the death of Theory has been reported dead.

However, we believe we are the first to call for an end to reporting the death of reporting the death of Theory.

It will come as no surprise to learn that the 'post' in 'post-theory' is not to be taken unequivocally – which immediately begs the question of how it *is* to be taken. Common Sense is only too happy to witness the passing of Theory. It was only a matter of time before we outgrew what had only ever been an irritating fad, just a phase we were all going through. Theory has no shortage of opponents waiting for the chance to say I told you so. Not that this distresses Theory. If resistant Blimps did not exist, Theory would have to invent them. The monolith of Common Sense has always been a fantasy of Theory, and a gratifying and sustaining one at that. Relegating resistance to an external reactionary force is always a profoundly comforting strategy.

In any case, Theory itself is only too happy to witness the passing of Theory. Nothing stimulates the production of Theory like the proclamation of its own death, regardless of who makes the proclamation. On the one hand, attacked by hostile voices, it reacts with righteous indignation and redoubles its efforts to prove the doubters wrong. On the other, the death of Theory is a persistent theme *in* Theory. Theory has been troubled by futures, ends and limits for some time. In effect, what is at stake is the right to write its own epitaph.

One reason why Theory has found it necessary to construct the bogey-man of Common Sense (a too-easy formulation which fails to take account of Theory's complex relation to Rationalist traditions) is in order to justify its own self-perception as 'radical'. Theory is 'radical' in that it affects fundamentally the relation one has to the processes and conventions of a given discipline. Theory changes the very conditions of reading literature, experiencing a painting, or sociological investigation. It goes to the root of those 'essential' and 'fundamental' operations and terminologies which function as disciplinary study. Theory 'revolutionises' these unquestioned foundations. If this is the sense in which Theory can be said to be radical, then it is also the sense in which Theory is political. However, the radicality of political praxis and the radicality of Theory might not be of the same order. To take literature as an example, Theory brings to academic criticism a way of thinking and a reason for existing which has more integrity and purpose than debating the minutiae of authorial biography and the impressionistic beauty of babbling brooks. Theory may challenge institutional traditions and liberal/bourgeois/humanist/empiricist (delete as applicable) fancies, and enable the reader to question their approach to a reception of given *a prioris*. However, this does not mean that Theory should be applied universally and mechanistically as a set of techniques, procedures and operators to every book ever written, exposing them one by one as vile inscriptions of reactionary western logomachy. Theory as sausage machine, pouring texts in at one end, producing 'new' readings at the other. Nothing could be less 'radical' or more depoliticising than the closing-off of questioning in an endless repetition of predetermined textual exegesis. Theory should not be a stick to beat a canonical tradition on which it has always relied, in one form or another, but an experience of critical reading which imbricates itself in the text it reads. Ask not what Derrida can do for Jane Austen but what Jane Austen can do for Derrida.

Theory wants more than anything to be thought of as 'Radical'. This desired radicality is firstly a response to its institutional critics, who are in fact only adopting a position Theory has created for them as a precondition of its own existence. It is also a wished-for Political activism. Undoubtedly Theory challenges institutional norms and canonical authority where their effects are most assuredly determined. It may disrupt relations of knowledge, but can Theory *qua* discipline claim that it has ever affected the material processes of history? How many reported cases are there of a Governor of the Bank of England emerging from a Theory reading group, arms raised with a white flag in one hand and a copy of Baudrillard in the other?

Few practitioners of Theory would argue over the merits of introducing students to the thoughts of Marx, Althusser, Fanon or Foucault, but is political commitment (implied by Theory's claims of radicality) as painless as an honours option or special topic choice? What encourages Theory to dress itself in this radical retro-chic, as if poststructuralism were as sexy as a lava lamp? The rise of Theory as an institutional practice is contemporaneous with the 'decline' of the political left. The retreat of the ambition of left-wing political parties and the advance of the radical claims of Theory are not coincidental. The hesitancy of the Political Left is in contrast to the certainty of the Theoretical Left, and the certainty of the Theoretical Left is in contrast to the undecidability which Theory proposes. In a discipline where meanings are endlessly questioned, are we sure we know what we mean when we talk of such difficult terms as 'politics' or 'the Left'? Furthermore, an inquiring mind might be led to the conclusion that there is some connection between 'market-led' educational reforms and the eminence of Theory within the academy. At a time when only the most popular courses survive and institutions compete for student numbers, Theory proves itself to be a crowd-pleaser which puts bums on seats. Accordingly, Theory does very well for itself in a *laissez-faire* university system which is prepared to promote it as an attractive option to students alongside Golf-Course Management and Tourism Studies.

If Theory's claims of radicalism are greatly exaggerated, then by the same token the radical effects of Theory are greatly undervalued. Certainly, general elections are not fought over the question of aesthetic self-reflexivity, but social activity is always influenced by the unlimited effects, in the field of ideology, of the academic apparatus. Not only is the university itself a site of political contest both in terms of what is taught and in terms of the struggle for control of access to education and 'academic freedom', it is the university in its production and demarcation of the limits of knowledge which defines the possibilities of any institutionalised, or otherwise, activity of thinking. It is in this sense that the way of thinking and reason for existing which Theory introduces to literature, sociology, art-history and so on is of profound importance and its radical effects are unlimited. Of course, any research institution is not free of a compromising relation to the state which sponsors intellectual life. Mark up the first double-bind; Theorists also have mortgages.

'Post-Theory', for Geoffrey Bennington (see Chapter 7), means a falling-off-from-theory (theory, for Bennington, being the *practice* of 'thinking hard'). 'Post-Theory', for Nicholas Royle (see Chapter 1), is the possibility of the hitherto unthought. In their opposition, each definition assumes a certain impatience with Theory at this stage in the theoretical game. If the collection entitled *Post-Theory* can be said to represent something, then it might represent this impatience, and the effort to revise it (the impatience, the theory) in productive directions. There are a number of resistances which this effort has to at least recognise, if it is to stand a chance of making headway.

Post-Theory rejects the dead hand of a self-satisfied and hypostasised

'Theory', a theory in love with and, finally, indistinguishable from its own rhetoric. It rejects the sclerosis of theoretical writing, the hardening of Theory's lexical and syntactical arteries. The words and phrases which are combined in over-familiar ways and thereby banalised, degraded, wielded like a fetish (the 'always already' whose precise and critical function has been reduced to a vacuous and impotent gesture of would-be mastery, a yawn-inducing yawn; the paronomasia which was once deployed as a strategy in a wider argument but which now appears to make puns for puns' sake, the text as a kind of Brownian motion for phonemes, and so on) in order to semaphore that 'Theory' is taking place are the surest sign that anything worthwhile just *is not*.

But there are problems more pressing than the laziness or decadence of individual theorists.

> It is impossible, now more than ever, to dissociate the work we do, within one discipline or several, from a reflection on the political and institutional conditions of that work. Such a reflection is unavoidable. It is no longer an external complement to teaching and research; it must make its way through the very objects we work with, shaping them as it goes, along with our norms, procedures and aims.[1]

Given the 'political and institutional conditions' within which 'Post-Theory' took shape, *Post-Theory* has its theoretical work cut out. The most visible manifestation of the current conditions must be the Research Assessment Exercise and its related *machins-bidules*. The impact of the RAE on the Humanities is only beginning to be analysed with any rigour. Sean Sayers has discussed the 'obsession with "research" dictated by the present system' and concluded that much of it 'is pointless . . . its main *raison d'être* [being] to gain a research rating and/or promotion'.[2] The system which is conceived as a way of ensuring and promoting quality tends to accelerate the process of banalisation. Research is often conducted for research's sake, not in the sense of some putatively disinterested pursuit of knowledge, but to secure funding to finance a place in which research (if, by now, it still deserves the name) is allowed to happen. The sclerotic 'Theory' outlined above could have been, *might have been*, made for such a scenario. 'Theory', its rhetoric, is *that which can be applied*, without having to bother *applying itself*.

A consideration of the constraints of the institutional context, however, does not start and finish with major events like Research Assessment. Whatever shape it comes in, the institution will always comprise certain banal, that is to say irreducible, features. If the university has one universal constant, it is that there are always fresh students to be taught.

Teaching, in effect, is where even theorists have to get vulgar. It is the point where they have to get their hands dirty, to risk showing their feet of clay, where the endless, circular agonising has to stop and give way to action. The point is not just that it is Theory's day job, but also that it is its destination. Teaching implies, more or less, packaging; material *must* be selected, presented, portioned in some way or other. Supposing a piece of Theory attempts to make itself resistant to this process, it may only be opening itself to a particularly brutal dismemberment. The spirit of out-and-out instrumentalism is, then, the path of least resistance. Conscious or unconscious, declared or undeclared, it might go something like this. I am quite happy with the theories I have, and there are classes to be taught. Do I really want to have to rethink my Theory all the time? To avoid embarrassment, I'll keep on churning out the same stuff about Theory being a constant revision of our conceptual frame, an unflagging vigilance, and so on. So the urgencies of teaching already tend to sclerosis.

The point, then, is not just to be snide at the expense of those for whom Theory has become canonical, a new orthodoxy, with the level of unconscious assumption that that entails. Nor, on the other hand, should one simply side with praxis (in the guise of teaching), the need to act, and so deride High Theory for excessive abstraction. For one thing, these represent two modalities that are necessarily always present in Theory. It is hardly a matter of choosing one, and discarding the other since the highest and purest Theory depends, for its institutional life, on some ultimate critical yield. To be read, accepted, digested is the inevitable fate of any œuvre. If reduction to a set of manageable tenets is an accident that befalls a text, then it is a peculiarly necessary accident.

Why necessary? That is, within what bounds? If there is a good reason for using some imagined teaching–research divide to express this difference in theoretical practice, it lies in the double form of the institution. Research Assessment and Quality Assurance did not impose this doubleness; they merely gave it a new formal rigour. For the time of research – let's say three years – is *not* the time of the undergraduate essay – one or two weeks. There follows a whole series of constraints on how far, and in what form, undergraduate students can ever be expected to engage with Theory, which in turn have some influence on the production of research. And yet, by the same token, a complete divorce between the methodology sponsored in teaching, and that pursued in research, could only be effected by bodily segregating staff. Indeed, a stark drone–queen division remains a possible option for the academic beehive. Yet even this, in turn, would only beg the question once more: what is Theory for? The answer would have to be: to produce books to which undergraduates, and lecturers devising courses, will refer, however obliquely, and from which they will derive knowledge. Resistance is futile; there are children to be taught. Otherwise we risk falling into a supplementary impatience – usually thought of as Victorian – that sees uncivilised elements not just as that-which-must-be-civilised, but as a wilful blight on the achievement of civilisation.

At any rate, kids want their Theory, and if they don't get it at school they'll get it somewhere else.

Theory, then, cannot afford to ignore its own institutionalisation and consecration. We are perhaps at a stage where its very pre-eminence has opened up real concerns about how it wants to proceed (which of course it must). Theory has itself become doxa, the very state it set out to subvert. This may be where a sociological examination of the state(s) of Theory might be helpful, if only to (re)confirm Theory's disruptive potential and, perverse as it might seem, its autonomy. There can be no doubt that Theory's strength has always been its awareness of its own instrumental apparatus and analytic procedures, its ability to snap at its own heels. What the reflexive turn has led to, or at least may be helpful in leading towards, is (somewhat paradoxically) the realisation that we can never be reflexive enough, we can never quite get there.

The confrontation over the uses of the various 'post-'theories in the social or 'human' sciences perhaps provides an example here. The debate over Theory in a discipline such as Sociology, traditionally mandated and committed to the double orientation of its pragmatic, situated practice, illuminates the debate over the orientation of Theory itself. Bourdieusian theory, as well as other material historicisms, in its attempt to get 'meta' over Theory, has been somewhat hampered by its inability to be reflexive enough about its own position. Attention to the positionality and perspectives of ethnographic observation and the position of the researcher-theorist *within* the institutional framework of practice would allow us to recognise the limits of reflexivity. Theory must always involve a negotiation of the aporia of reflection which holds the reflective in abeyance while remembering reflexivity as a condition of Theoretical production. In effect, the undecidability of this double-bind means that we can never be too reflexive; knowledge through self-reflection will always be endlessly deferred. What we might do in response to this impossible condition of Theoretical possibility is to acknowledge the Anthropology already implicit in Theory. There can be no doubt that there are strategies, rituals, taboos and totemic customs abundant in the Theory jungle. They are there to be uncovered and challenged by Theoretical means. For example, we might ask, what would a theoretical model of teaching look like? The industry of theory therefore is to reassess the Theory Industry. Derrida comments:

> The time for reflection is also the chance for turning back on the very conditions of reflection, in all the senses of that word, as if with the help of a new optical device one could finally see sight, could not only view

the natural landscape, the city, the bridge and the abyss, but could view viewing.[3]

In this sense, the 'post' in *Post-Theory* must refer to the doubleness of that adjective. As Nicholas Royle, following Robert Young, points out in Chapter 1, the ambiguities of 'post' point to both 'its temporal sense (where it signifies "coming after") and its spatial sense (where it can mean "behind")'. 'Post-Theory' must be a Theory which comes before and after itself, taking its own postness in the sense that Lyotard considers the post in postmodernism, by which Theory would be 'constitutionally and ceaselessly pregnant' with the reflexive double-bind of Post-Theory.[4] In other words, the temporospatial effects of a 'postness' which disrupts and challenges the sclerotic and the unquestioned must be an effect of *différance*, the differed space of the post and the deferred time of postness. Post-Theory then is not just a Theory which is not present but is potentially so, rather it is a theory (an experience of thought) which cannot be fully activated even potentially. Post-Theory is a state of thinking which discovers itself in a constant state of deferral, a position of reflexivity and an experience of questioning which constantly displaces itself in the negotiation with the aporias of Theory. Post-Theory speaks to the Other to whom it must be addressed. Even if the position of thought we are calling Post-Theory does not reach and leave its mark on its institutional other, it still makes its call, address takes place. The deferral of this experience of thought does not relegate the possibility of such a position to an ateleological future. On the contrary, if theory itself (as an experience of thought) is that which is deferred by the practice of Theory (as a series of institutional aporias), then it is an obligation placed upon every practitioner of 'Theory' to attempt to approach the Post-Theory condition through the rigorous discipline of thought from within Theory. The engagement with Theory is the experience of the endless promise. Post-Theory promises that 'Theory' will only take place when one can 'finally see sight'.

In a certain sense, then, 'Post-Theory' is a Theory 'yet to come'. If *Post-Theory* as a text were to claim a distinctive approach to the problematic of the institutional fate of Theory (the 'new direction' promised in the subtitle), it might be found in its desire to make an intervention in the here-and-now of the academy. The chapters in this book fall into two categories. Part I, '*Déjà Vu*', responds to the situation described above, by pausing to reassess the state of Theory the morning after the party. Theory is the cure to its own hangover, the hair of the dog that bit us. Part III, 'The Post-Theory Condition', offers signposts for the directions Theory might take. Part II, Geoffrey Bennington's Chapter 7, 'Inter', is the hyphen (*trait d'union*) that links and separates these sections. The collection brings together three

generations of theorists. There are those 'Young Turks' whose work introduced modern French thought to the English-speaking world and whose
commitment and courage (sometimes in the face of implacable opposition)
helped to establish the anglophone discipline of Theory. They are joined by
a generation of thinkers who have both consolidated Theory's position within
the academy and expanded the horizons of Theory into a poststructuralist
diaspora which crosses disciplinary borders and continents of thought.
Finally, there is a generation of academics who have grown up with Theory
and who cannot remember a time when they did not have it. The future
lies with them, and theirs is the greatest responsibility. It is their task not
to re-enact old paradigms and operations, no matter how comforting and
familiar. They must be in a state of constant rediscovery of the conditions
of Post-Theory: thinking through the aporias of the institution and resisting
a disengagement with theoretico-political events. As such, we are already in
the Post-Theory condition.

In Chapter 1, '*Déjà Vu*', Nicholas Royle examines the destabilising role
which the 'concept' of *déjà vu* plays in several essays by Freud. *Déjà vu* is
shown, through rigorous exposition of each particular context, to be 'undecidable' and even to resist the possibility of a psychoanalytic theory and
practice. Royle suggests that *déjà vu* and 'post-theory' are 'concepts' which
'fundamentally unsettle the "first time" of an experience', and he offers them
as points of departure for a new generation of academics into new, newly
self-reflexive, theoretical potentials. If the 'Post' in 'Post-Theory' implies a certain return to the already-seen for Royle, Christopher Norris's 'Deconstruction
and the "Unfinished Project of Modernity"' (Chapter 2) might be said to
offer a response to the *déjà lu*. Norris presents a reading of Kant's three
Critiques through an examination of two essays by Derrida ('Parergon' and
'Mochlos'). He argues that so-called postmodern theory has tended to promote a cultural and moral relativism which is at odds with the post-Kantian
enlightenment project of critical-emancipatory thought. Norris offers an
attentive reading of Derrida's essays to demonstrate that, in spite of what is
often believed, it is not Derrida who authorises a turning away from the
conditions of truth and the rigour of philosophical inquiry. In this respect,
Norris makes a claim for the impossible autonomy of philosophy as a critical
resource in the 'post-Theory' university.

   In Chapter 3, 'Post-Gender: Jurassic Feminism Meets Queer Politics',
Patricia Duncker suggests that there is an important sense of *déjà vu* about
contemporary Queer Theory. Duncker calls the feminist politics of the 1960s
and 1970s in which she participated 'Jurassic' because of its attachment to
certainties and to a limited appreciation of the 'political régime of gender'. In
contrast, she finds a new subversive energy in a Queer politics of demand.
Queer Theory might be said to offer a more complicated understanding of

the gender system in its insistence upon the dismantling not only of patriarchal authority but also of heterosexual 'normality'. However, Duncker
suggests, what is potentially revolutionary about Queer Theory is merely a
re-presentation of the strategies and demands of 'Jurassic Feminism': namely,
a rejection of essentialism, an emphasis on political organisation, and the
destruction of the myths of gender. Antony Easthope could also be said to
revisit important theoretical sites of the 1970s and 1980s as a way of thinking
through a space for Post-Theory. In Chapter 4, 'The Pleasures of Labour:
Marxist Aesthetics in a Post-Marxist World', Easthope considers the crisis of
faith surrounding the possibility of a dialectical history. He asks what future
there might be for Marxist literary theory, and addresses the problem of the
possibility of a Marxist aesthetic operating beyond a functionalist paradigm.
By reassessing the attempts (and failures) of the Frankfurt School, *Screen*
and Derrida, Easthope argues for an ongoing assessment of the problem and
proposes a more rigorously reflexive approach. What is at stake is the possibility of theorising the unalienated labour which art has always offered. In
conclusion, Easthope suggests that Lacan's theory of the alienation of the
subject might suggest a possible direction for Marxist theory.

Eric Woehrling, like Christopher Norris, is critical of the tendency to
identify deconstruction with a Utopian free play of the signifier on the one
hand, or cultural relativism on the other. In Chapter 5, 'Is the Novel Original?
Derrida and (Post-)Modernity', Woehrling argues that deconstruction might
be more usefully thought of as 'post-postmodern' and uses a deconstructive
understanding of time to rethink deconstruction's ethical relation to tradition. Part I concludes with Chapter 6, Jeremy Lane's 'Pierre Bourdieu and
the Chronotopes of "Post-Theory"'. Lane offers a reading of the current
upturn in interest in the work of Pierre Bourdieu, as a symptom of a nostalgia on the part of certain critics who are suffering from Theory fatigue. To
explore this longing for an after of Theory (which is paradoxically a return
to the past certainties of the before of Theory), Lane looks at the play of the
idea of doxa throughout Bourdieu's œuvre. Lane argues that, while we
should not reject the possibility of a sociological approach, we should be
suspicious of a critical tendency which wants to find there that perversely
seductive thing, a doxic theory.

Chapter 7, Geoffrey Bennington's 'Inter', tolls the bell for Theory, with a
capital T, the science of interpretation as it is practised today in the Anglo-
American academy. Bennington argues that, having carried the entire
theoretical field, difference has effectively become carried away with itself.
Henceforth it confounds itself with the classic themes of respect for persons;
we can all agree to disagree. When this happens, Theory has thrown off its
problematic element; it ceases to question itself and is content to promote
some self-satisfied historicism. Bennington wants to shake up this smugness
of a History that would like to think that it has got past the challenge of

Theory. He meets this return to History head-on with what is indeed a return to Hegel, to the text of Hegel, so as to see what is irreducible therein. Bennington's contribution could be taken as a call to reading against a certain culture of potted history and the silliness of second-hand philosophy.

For Catherine Belsey in Chapter 8, 'English Studies in the Postmodern Condition: Towards a Place for the Signifier', we are witnessing the end of literary criticism, even the best examples of which are no longer enough. This will be the case as long as we limit ourselves to the traditional terms of Lit Crit (author, work, inspiration and so on) which, although worn out, are still in use. For although Theory has been questioning these practices for some years now, there is no lack of resistance and reaction. Furthermore, the criticism that comes in the wake of Theory is too eager to winkle out its favourite themes and issues; it therefore tends to rush straight to the signified without pausing to consider the signifying process. Thus, what we must do is to give renewed attention to the signifier and its effects. Belsey engages with a recent strong instance of the return to tradition, the imposing *The Western Canon* of Harold Bloom. She points out how far Bloom depends upon the idea of the *Unheimliche*, the strange power of literature to bring us face to face with the secrets of life and death, to give shape to the return of the repressed. These are concepts which would require a theory of language capable of giving an account of the experience of the signifier as an experience of the Other. Without this, we are doomed to remain with Bloom gaping before an essentially theological mystery. A literary criticism that fulfilled its potential can still give us a particularly fruitful vantage point for the study of the constitution of the subject in language.

Chapter 9, Lorna Hutson's '*Ethopoeia*, Source-Study and Legal History: A Post-Theoretical Approach to the Question of "Character" in Shakespearean Drama', keeps the conversation of *Post-Theory* momentarily with Literary Studies. This is appropriate considering the historical importance of Literary Studies (and Shakespeare Studies within it) as a space for Theory in the Anglo-American academy. Hutson examines the resistance of the category of 'character' within Shakespeare criticism to poststructuralist and New-Historicist approaches. Hutson's response to this residual trace of Lit Crit is quite different from that offered by Belsey. Hutson makes a return to the analytic strategy of source-study, so quickly dismissed by Theory. Through a reading of *Measure for Measure* and contemporaneous legal documents on slander and sexuality, Hutson suggests that the liberal humanist notion of character may in fact be a consequence of the historical legacy of Shakespearean drama.

Chapter 10, Robert Smith's 'The Death Drive Does Not Think', starts with the question: if we are to follow Freud's *Beyond the Pleasure Principle* to its logical conclusion, is it ever possible to say that full conscious thought ever takes place? What is at stake is the economy of the psyche, the mechanisms whereby experience is expended in advance, delayed and exchanged. This broaches the metaphorical status of 'economy', which leads to the Enlightenment as a moment of speculation in thought as in commerce. Smith considers the challenges posed to ethical thought by psychoanalysis, where a death economy of low-risk investment in second-order reproductions might seem to be the norm rather than simply a failure of taste. Smith's chapter opens the collection out onto new theoretical territory. In Chapter 11, ' "Various Infinitudes": Narration, Embodiment and Ontology in Beckett's *How It Is* and Spinoza's *Ethics*', Alex Houen suggests that Spinoza remains the philosopher who provides the best model for thinking a plane of immanence. As Houen points out, however, this involves two distinct forms of infinity: on the one hand, a infinite quantity of finite bodies, modal forms of substance; on the other hand, truly transcendental essences without which substance as a quality common to all things would be unthinkable. What, asks Houen, is the relation between these two forms of infinity? Criticism faced with what looks like a doubling has tended to offer two distinct Spinozas: the one an idealist, the other a materialist, rarely both at the same time. What is more, it is precisely this classic partition of the spiritual and the bodily which regulates the relation between Theory and Literature. The former is called upon to give us an *idea* of the latter, which appears as an *object*, a phenomenon. Counter to this, it is to a novel, *How It Is* by Samuel Beckett, that Houen sends us for a more adequate response to this problematic.

Charles Forsdick outlines Edward Said's ambivalent relationship with Theory in Chapter 12, 'Edward Said after Theory: The Limits of Counterpoint'. On the one hand, Said has for a long time been critical of what he sees as a new orthodoxy and furthermore a factory for the production of western concepts which attempt to pass themselves off as universal. On the other hand, it is from within this western university that Said elaborates his own concepts. In response to his critics, Said has more recently proposed a criticism that would value counterpoint, the play of domination-resistance that is already at work *in* the colonial text. From this, one might have expected a more reflective project, more understanding of the nuances of contact and less given to apportioning blame along simple geographical boundaries. In spite of this admirable intention, or indeed precisely because of its grandeur, Forsdick suggests that Said can seem insensible to the possibilities of resistance presented by a reflective exoticist such as Victor Segalin. Seeing nothing but the exoticist, Said misses out on the *poète du métissage*. It is in its global ambition that counterpoint finds its limits. Chapter 13, Julian Murphet's 'Grounding Theory: Literary Theory and the New Geography', concludes Part III. In the light of the decline in prestige of the dialectic and the limits that the linguistic turn seems to have reached, Murphet proposes a reassertion of the production paradigm through space. Citing the burgeoning interest in Lefebvrian theory and the new geography, Murphet proposes the possibilities of its adaptation to the representation of space in literary works. The New Geography might also provide the materials for a more nuanced approach to the conditions of the production of texts. Murphet's interest in the theoretical productions of space might be thought of as being in dialogue with Jeremy Lane's consideration of the chronotope which concluded Part I.

In his 'Preface', Ernesto Laclau responds to the implications of Post-Theory and so sets the scene for *Post-Theory*. In this context, Laclau's text might be thought of as the opening move in the theoretico-political event of this book. As such, this preface is our first post, a marker which opens us out onto Post-Theory. The volume finishes with an extraordinary text by Hélène Cixous, eloquently translated by Eric Prenowitz. This 'Post-Word' is both fragmented and 'unfinished', and, in the light of all that has been said, and all that will necessarily have to be said, about the 'post', this is perhaps the perfect way to 'conclude' this book. The text presented here is a letter sent to the editors in response to a request for a brief epilogue of concluding remarks. In keeping with the logic of the post, Cixous's text exceeds the bounds of what might be thought possible in such a limited space. It also rejects the limits of that space as a possibility for thought. The 'Post-Word' is necessarily incomplete and, as such, compels us to follow a train of thought which steers and folds back along its own impossible way, back to Laclau's reasoned 'Preface', and asks us to make another return to Post-Theory.

NOTES

1. Jacques Derrida, 'The Principle of Reason: The University in the Eyes of its Pupils', *Diacritics*, 13 (1983), 3.
2. Sean Sayers, 'Who are my Peers? The Research Assessment Exercise in Philosophy', *Radical Philosophy*, 83, May/June 1997.
3. Derrida, op. cit., p. 19.
4. Jean-François Lyotard, 'Rewriting Modernity', in *The Inhuman: Reflections on Time*, trans. Geoffrey Bennington and Rachel Bowlby (Cambridge: Polity Press, 1991), p. 25.

PART I

Déjà Vu

Chapter One

DÉJÀ VU

Nicholas Royle

'Post-theory': this compound ghost gives me a feeling of *déjà vu*. I want to emphasise that this is a feeling, in the same way as Jacques Derrida insists on the feeling he has about Marx and ghosts in *Spectres of Marx*: as he puts it, 'everyone reads, acts, writes with *his or her* ghosts'.[1] I can attempt to ratio-nalise this feeling of *déjà vu*. It trails back at least fifteen years, to a conference in Southampton in 1981 (the proceedings of which were published the following year in the *Oxford Literary Review*) and in particular to a paper that Robert Young gave on that occasion, entitled 'Poststructuralism: The End of Theory'.[2] In announcing 'poststructuralism' as 'the end of theory', he noted the ambiguities of 'post' in its temporal sense (where it signifies 'coming after') and in its spatial sense (where it can mean 'behind'). He pointed to that 'uncanny antithetical doubling [which] is rather humbly embodied in the word "posterior"' (p. 4) before going on to claim that the word

'poststructuralism' suggests that structuralism itself can only exist as always already inhabited by poststructuralism, which comes both behind and after. It is always already unfolding as a repetition not of the same but as a kind of *Nachträglichkeit*, or deferred action. In this sense, poststructuralism becomes structuralism's primal scene . . . (p. 4)

In a more recent essay called 'Poststructuralism: The Improper Name', he reiterates the temporal and spatial strangeness of this theoretical posterior, paradoxically in terms of a certain historical continuity: 'no one has ever really agreed on a definition of poststructuralism, which remains to this day conceptually elusive'.[3] What Young says about poststructuralism could be said to apply to every and any postism. I want to explore here the time, space and experience of post-theory in terms of what, like poststructuralism, 'eludes definition because it cannot be defined through a certain conceptual content, but only through its insistently deranging pressure'.[4] More explicitly

3

perhaps even than poststructuralism or postmodernism, post-theory deranges concepts. The deranging force of post-theory, I want to suggest, might be traced through the figure of *déjà vu*. If (to adapt Young's phrase) post-theory becomes theory's primal scene, how might an understanding of *déjà vu* inflect the primariness of that 'primal'?

No doubt post-theory must entail an encounter with the conceptually elusive notions of poststructuralism and postmodernism: it must be at once theory about posts (about all kinds of sending and tele-phenomena) and about post-theories. But there is perhaps also something new, uncertain, exciting and even frightening that is intimated in the word 'post-theory', a sense perhaps that we are getting to a point where (to quote Young's more recent essay again) 'Suddenly it becomes apparent that poststructuralism's abstract theorising, apparently divorced from the social and from history, in fact catches most accurately the forms of certain contemporary political and social situations relevant to the new radical democratic movements' (p. 80), and where the energies or allergies of a new generation of academics are starting to announce themselves in the thought of other spaces and times: post-theory.

At first sight (if that phrase remains available to us), 'post-theory' may look like the opposite of '*déjà vu*'; it suggests something quite new, in contradistinction to the past and already familiar. But it can also be said that 'post' and '*déjà*' share a signalling towards the past, while (as their etymologies would indicate) 'theory' and '*vu*' both concern the experience of seeing, a relation between structure and vision, a question of the spectacle and even the spectral. One might say in fact that there is a sort of doubling-up, a diplopia or *déjà vu* effect inscribed within the term 'post-theory', in that the compound is a kind of compound ghost simultaneously designating what is still theory but at the same time *post* theory, what is at once post-theoretical and post-post-theoretical. It is as if each part of the compound were already seen (*déjà vu*) to have been repeated: post-post-theory-theory. My feeling (and it is perhaps only a feeling) is that no post, no postism, no post-theory can be sheared away from the question and experience of *déjà vu*, even if, or perhaps to the very extent that, the concept of *déjà vu* (if it is a concept) is still to be thought.

What is *déjà vu*? If one consults a dictionary, as Freud does at the start of his essay on 'The "Uncanny"',[5] one finds that the term '*déjà vu*' is defined in two broadly distinct ways. Thus in the *OED*, for example, we find:

a. An illusory feeling of having previously experienced a present situation; a form of paramnesia . . .
b. occas. The correct impression that something has been previously experienced; tedious familiarity . . .

The first recorded usage of the term in English in sense (a) is 1903; in sense
(b) 1960. This historical detail is provoking: it suggests that we are living in
the epoch of the double sense of '*déjà vu*' today. If post-theory has a time, it
would be the time of this phrase.[6] '*Déjà vu*' seems to figure as a kind of
primal word or phrase, one that carries an antithetical or contradictory sense
within it, a kind of verbal double. What would it mean to suppose that a
primal word is not only 'primal' but also '*déjà vu*'? '*Déjà vu*' signifies at once
the illusion of 'having previously experienced a present situation' *and* 'the
correct impression' of having really 'previously experienced' it. Given this
semantic duplicity, a duplicity that menaces or haunts the very possibility of
a dictionary (what could be called a *déjà vu* effect that necessarily makes
every definition tremble, doubling and contradicting it, dividing it within), it
is perhaps appropriate that dictionaries such as the *OED* and *Chambers*
should emphasise the earlier or 'original' sense in a definition of '*déjà vu*'
specifically and merely as 'illusion' or 'illusory'. *Chambers* thus gives its
equivalent of *OED* sense (a): '*déjà vu*': 'an illusion of having experienced
before something that is really being experienced for the first time'. This
definition rests on an opposition of illusion and reality, presupposing the
reality of what 'really' is 'being experienced' in a sense that is displaced and
even proscribed by the *uncertainties* that could be said to characterise '*déjà
vu*'. Both the *OED* and *Chambers* present '*déjà vu*' as a phrase whose meanings may be antithetical but can nevertheless be clearly distinguished and
categorised as such. Yet what is perhaps most striking about '*déjà vu*' is the
uncertainty, the deranging of definition that is, by definition, excluded by
these various definitions of the term. Both the *OED* and *Chambers* see to it
that '*déjà vu*' be defined as 'an illusion' or 'illusory' and both delegate the
authority for such a definition to the discipline of psychology and in particular to the psychological concept of paramnesia. Thus in *Chambers* one
reads: '*déjà vu*': 'a form of the memory disorder paramnesia (*psychology*)'. If
one then looks in *Chambers* for a definition of 'paramnesia' one discovers
with seemingly unremarked irony: 'a memory disorder in which words are
remembered but not their proper meaning'. (This is the first sense of
'paramnesia', according to *Chambers*, the second being 'the condition of
believing that one remembers events and circumstances which have not
previously occurred'.) The dictionary itself seems subject to some sort of
paramnesia.

What is the 'proper meaning' of '*déjà vu*'? If one goes back to one of the
earliest usages of the term '*déjà vu*', as specified in the *OED*, one finds a
reference to (whom else but?) Freud, to Chapter 12 of *The Psychopathology
of Everyday Life*.[7] Let us, then, return to Freud. (No post-theory without
that, still, again.) Here, in the chapter on 'Determinism, Belief in Chance and
Superstition – Some Points of View', in a series of paragraphs dating from
1907, Freud writes:

We must also include in the category of the miraculous and the 'uncanny' (*in die Kategorie des Wunderbaren und Unheimlichen*) [the English translator, Alan Tyson, puts the word 'uncanny' in quotation marks, as James Strachey does in translating the title of Freud's essay on this topic, i.e. 'The "Uncanny"': why? Might the implicit logic of quotation as duplication here signal something more intimate about the rapport between the 'uncanny' and *déjà vu* and, correspondingly, between the uncanny and 'post-theory'? We shall return to this . . .] the peculiar feeling we have, in certain moments and situations, of having had exactly the same experience once before or of having once before been in the same place, though *our efforts never succeed* in clearly remembering the previous occasion that announces itself in this way (*das sich so anzeigt*). I am aware that I am merely following loose linguistic usage when I call what arises in a person at such moments a 'feeling' (*eine Empfindung*) [without any explanation 'feeling' too, then, joins the 'uncanny' as a word apparently always already 'in' 'quotes', at least in the English translation]. What is no doubt in question is a judgement (*es handelt sich wohl um ein Urteil*: 'it is probably a matter of a judgement'), and, more precisely, a perceptual judgement; but these cases have nevertheless *a character quite of their own*, and we must not leave out of account the fact that what is looked for is *never remembered*. (pp. 328–9/294, emphases added)

What must be remembered is that what is looked for is never remembered: so Freud, in effect, says. With that lucidity and fixity of purpose that is so grave and yet also sometimes so comical and affecting in his writing, Freud then goes on (at least on one level) to contradict his own thesis. For it turns out that, thanks to psychoanalysis, our efforts to remember at least in principle *can* succeed and what is looked for *can* be remembered: with the experience of *déjà vu*, he declares,

> something is really touched on which we have already experienced once before, only we cannot consciously remember it because it has never been conscious. To put it briefly, the feeling of '*déjà vu*' corresponds to the recollection of an unconscious phantasy. (*Die Empfindung des 'déjà vu' entspricht, kurz gesagt, der Erinnerung an eine unbewußte Phantasie.*) (p. 329/295)

(Freud then goes on to give an analysis of 'a single case', in which a woman's experience of *déjà vu* is explained as a sort of substitute for 'recalling', as if for the first time – *déjà vu* at the origin, one might say – a repressed or unconscious phantasy about wishing or expecting her brother's death.) It is in this context, then, that Freud is able to put forward a proposition that is also completely at odds with the dictionary definitions of '*déjà vu*', including the *OED* definition which refers to the Freud text for verification of the authoritative usage of the term! He states simply and categorically: 'It is in my view wrong to call the feeling of having experienced something before an illusion' (*Ich meine, man tut unrecht, die Empfindung des schon einmal Erlebthabens als eine Illusion zu bezeichnen*) (p. 329/295). But Freud makes a judgement here, and, in the very gesture of asserting that the feeling of *déjà vu* is not 'an illusion' and ascribing to it instead the seeming '"reality"' of 'the recollection of an unconscious phantasy', he arrests, forecloses, shuts off consideration of the 'feeling' of *déjà vu* as 'a judgement' (a 'perceptual judgement') (*ein Urteil, und zwar ein Erkennungsurteil*, pp. 294–5) that is *in question*.

The author of *The Psychopathology of Everyday Life* says that he 'know[s] that the subject [of *déjà vu*] would merit the most exhaustive treatment (*der eingehendsten Behandlung würdig wäre*)' (p. 329/295), but he declines to give it. Or so it may appear. It may appear that *déjà vu* is a minor concern in the writings of Freud, in other words, but perhaps one should look again. In this way, like the question of telepathy, *déjà vu* may come to 'reappear' at the very heart of psychoanalysis, always already there *as a question*, and as the experience of a question. What would be going on in such an experience, as seen at once again and anew? What would it mean to suppose that the theoretical edifice of psychoanalysis lies here, trembling in the question of *déjà vu*, of actual and false recognition, of what is or is not really being experienced for the first time, of when experiencing is not dreaming, of arresting a judgement on or doing justice to an experience that has (in Freud's own words) 'a character quite of its own' (*ein ganz eigentümlicher Charakter*, p. 295)? This, to repeat Freud's words, 'would merit the most exhaustive treatment'.

References to *déjà vu* are scattered across the Freudian œuvre.[8] I propose to concentrate here on two texts in which, it seems to me, the question of *déjà vu* is decisively at stake. First, a short piece which appears in volume XIII of the Standard Edition, immediately before 'The Moses of Michelangelo': it is an essay entitled '*Fausse Reconnaissance* ("*déjà raconté*")' in Psycho-Analytic Treatment', first published in 1914.[9] This essay focuses on the '*déjà raconté*', the already recounted or the '*But I've told you that already*' (*das habe ich Ihnen aber schon erzählt*) (p. 201/116). Freud observes that this situation 'not infrequently' (*nicht selten*, p. 116) arises in the course of an analytic treatment: the analysand believes, or claims to believe, that s/he has already told the analyst something or other. With the kind of amazing economy and precipitousness that is characteristic of certain passages of Freud's writing, this essay provides a sort of uncanny elliptical allegory or (one might say) *raconteurism* of psychoanalysis as a discourse about narrative and as a narrative about discourse. Thus the opening paragraph zooms into the notion of bearing witness as the foundation of the analytic experience. What happens if the patient insists on the idea that s/he has already told the analyst this or that, whereas the analyst does not believe it? Freud writes:

> To try to decide the dispute by shouting the patient down or by outvying him [*sic*] in protestations would be a most unpsychological proceeding (*ganz unpsychologisch*). It is familiar ground (*bekanntlich*) that a sense of conviction of the accuracy of one's memory has no objective value; and, since one of the two persons concerned must necessarily be in the wrong, it may just as well be the physician as the patient who has fallen a victim to a paramnesia. (p. 201/116)

'A most unpsychological proceeding': inadvertently perhaps, the comic scenario is evoked of analyst and analysand shouting at one another in a crazy agonistics. (But I've told you that already! No you haven't! I tell you I did! I swear this is the first I've heard anything about it! What's the point of analysis if you don't even listen to what I say? I *was* listening! Und so weiter, interminably.) 'It is familiar ground that a sense of conviction of the accuracy of one's memory has no objective value': thus Freud specifies the space of witnessing and self-witnessing. Although he does not say so, it is precisely this 'familiar ground' or sense of what is well known (*bekanntlich*) that we might regard as susceptible to becoming unfamiliar, unheimlich.

Focusing on those cases where it is supposedly the patient who is in error, and in a peculiar conceptual sliding, Freud equates the *fausse reconnaissance* (or false recognition) of having already recounted a particular memory or particular story (the *déjà raconté*) with the experience of *déjà vu*:

> The phenomenon presented by the patient in cases like this deserves to be called a '*fausse reconnaissance*', and is completely analogous (*durchaus analog*) to what occurs in certain other cases and has been described as a '*déjà vu*'. In these other cases the subject has a sponta-neous feeling such as 'I've been in this situation before', or 'I've been through all this already'. (p. 202/117)

Freud is then apparently in a position to go on to explore the '*fausse recon-naissance*' of the *déjà raconté as déjà vu*. But why does he say that the '*But I've told you that already*' is 'completely analogous' to the 'feeling' or 'phe-nomenon' of *déjà vu*? What is the basis of this analogy? What *is* 'analogy' here? Is it perhaps because the '*But I've told you that already*' is in some sense bound to give rise to a feeling *in the analyst* of having had this experi-ence before? The situation of being thus confronted, as he points out at the start of the essay, arises 'not infrequently' (*nicht selten*), after all. Is there not a suggestion here of a confusion of identities, the uncanny automatism of a kind of *déjà-vu*-finder, a certain transferential logic whereby the solitude of the patient's bearing witness is appropriated by the analyst and an effacement of the patient's experience is carried out through the very imposition of the 'analogy'? One might be tempted, on the basis of such apparent incoherence in his account, to consider dismissing Freud's essay as a piece of junk. He seems (or some part of him seems) to have already seen or foreseen such a possibility. 'A piece of junk' is how he describes the essay, in a letter to Ferenczi in February 1914.[10] It is not a question of dismissing the essay for this reason. Rather the reverse: junk can be crucial.

It would at least seem possible to suggest that what is going on in this parallelism between the *déjà raconté* and *déjà vu* is a peculiar metaphorics, a seemingly compulsive metaphorisation, a figurative transference or translation of the notion of *déjà vu*. Once *déjà vu* can be figured as a metaphor, transfer or translation (but was it ever anything else?), there is no limit to its applicability or replicability. *Déjà vu*: a concept of the recyclable and a recyclable concept. Why write or at least why choose to publish 'a piece of junk'? It is as if Freud is led on by the ghostly myrmidons of *déjà vu*.[11] In any event, it seems that what he wants to tell us about in this little essay called *'Fausse Reconnaissance'* is not *'fausse reconnaissance'* so much as *'déjà vu'* itself – even though he has (by his own admission) *already told us* about it, some seven years earlier, in *The Psychopathology of Everyday Life*. Embedded within this déjà raconteurism is an intriguing example of what Harold Bloom has called the anxiety of influence.[12] Freud refers to an essay by J. Grasset, published in 1904, which argues that 'the phenomenon [of *déjà vu*] indicates that at some earlier time there has been an *unconscious* perception, which only now makes its way into consciousness . . .' (p. 203) He then tells us about what he has supposedly already told us: 'In 1907, in the second edition of my Psychopathology of Everyday Life . . . I proposed an exactly similar explanation for this form of apparent paramnesia without mentioning Grasset's paper or knowing of its existence' (*ohne die Arbeit von Grasset zu kennen oder zu erwähnen*: 'without knowing of the work of Grasset or mentioning it') (p. 203/119). The hesitation, the index of anxiety in the final part of that sentence again generates, one has to say, a certain comedy, this time of Freud mentioning Grasset's paper *without* knowing of its existence.

On the one hand, then, Freud's theory of *déjà vu* has no priority; it is *déjà raconté*, in Grasset. On the other hand, and in keeping with the notion of *déjà vu* that I am trying to trace here, Freud's theory is not a theory as such. This is clear, again, from the disquieting need for quotation marks around the question of what Freud (or his precursor Grasset) 'believes'. There are two 'class[es] of explanation' for the 'phenomenon' of *déjà vu*, says Freud: one 'looks upon the feeling that constitutes the phenomenon as deserving of credence'; the other, 'far larger class' 'maintain[s], on the contrary, that what

we have to deal with is an illusory memory, and that the problem is to discover how this paramnesic error can have arisen' (p. 202). Freud then takes
up a position against, for example, Pythagoras, for whom 'the phenomenon
of *déjà vu* is evidence of the subject having had a former life' (pp. 202–3), and
instead allies himself with Grasset as 'one of the group which "believes" in
the phenomenon' (*Grasset hat in Jahre 1904 eine Erklärung des* déjà vu
gegeben, welche zu den 'gläubigen' gerechnet werden muß) (p. 203/118). The
word 'believes' ('*gläubigen*' ['believers']) is in quotation marks. In a way that
is strikingly similar (one might say, indeed, 'completely analogous') to the
case of telepathy, Freud presents himself as someone who '"believes"' in *déjà
vu*.[13] I 'believe' in telepathy, I 'believe' in *déjà vu*, says Freud. The quotes
around this word 'believes' point towards an experience of the undecidable.
To 'believe' in *déjà vu* can no longer be construed as the opposite of *not*
believing. *Déjà vu* can only ever be a question of belief but it is necessarily
belief in quotation marks, in suspense, a suspension of the very subject of
belief, a suspension which is moreover not a neutralisation but rather a
trembling of the 'I' in the very intimacy of its bearing witness.[14]

   And if one wanted to *believe*, let us say, that there were some pure, non-
metaphoric 'concept' or 'phenomenon' of *déjà vu*, and that this logic of an
experience of the undecidable could or should be confined to a specific kind
of context or situation, that its propensities for analogical application or
replication could and should be carefully controlled and restricted, the
conclusion to Freud's essay provides cold comfort. On the contrary, this
conclusion makes an extraordinarily daring and violent gesture of appropriation in order to suggest that, indeed, *fausse reconnaissance*, *déjà raconté* or
déjà vu is the very ground ('the familiar ground', we could say) on which
psychoanalysis comes to rest. Freud's final paragraph runs as follows:

> There is another kind of *fausse reconnaissance* which not infrequently
> [*nicht selten*: the same phrase that Freud has already used, coming back
> here as if recycled from the start of his essay] makes its appearance at
> the close of a treatment, much to the physician's satisfaction. After he
> has succeeded in forcing the repressed event (whether it was of a real or
> of a psychical nature) upon the patient's acceptance in the teeth of all
> resistances, and has succeeded, as it were, in rehabilitating it – the
> patient may say: '*Now I feel as though I had known it all the time*'. With
> this the work of the analysis has been completed. ('Jetzt habe ich die
> Empfindung, ich habe es immer gewußt.' *Damit ist die analytische
> Aufgabe gelöst*.) (p. 207/123)

Does Freud believe in this *déjà vu*? Or does he merely 'believe' in it? What
is psychoanalysis if its most satisfying and complete achievement consists in
the transference of an acredible *déjà raconté déjà vu*?

Déjà vu: the uncanny figure of that which is irreducible to the psychical or the real, an undecidable trembling that phantomises the possibility of 'belief'.

What Freud's essay '*Fausse Reconnaissance*' shows is finally, perhaps, the uncanny, protean power of *déjà vu* as an explanatory 'concept', 'analogy' or 'theory'. It is uncanny because it entails a logic that cannot be confined but rather operates as a kind of dangerous supplement. Not only does *déjà vu* work as a promiscuous term for 'analogy' with other feelings or experiences seemingly heterogeneous to it (for instance, the *déjà raconté* or the psycho-analytic experience itself), not only does this 'concept' serve as a means of describing both a symptom or affect and the experience of the cure ('*Now I feel as though I had known it all the time*'), not only does Freud use *déjà vu* as a 'theory' by which simultaneously to appropriate and to represent the patient's experience of psychoanalysis (the satisfaction provided at the close of a treatment, though also, it hardly needs be said, at the close of Freud's essay itself: the close of a narrative treatment, the apparent satisfaction of a narrative desire); but before and beyond anything else, *déjà vu* just *is* the experience of a supplement (and it is this, paradoxically, that gives cases of *déjà vu* 'a character quite of their own'): it is itself nothing other than supple-mentarity-as-experience, the experience of a supplement without origin, a disturbance of any sense of 'familiar ground'.

The second Freud text which I wish to discuss here is his essay on 'The "Uncanny"' (1919). This may appear to be a rather obvious choice of text. But here is a remarkable thing which, as far as I am aware, has not had attention drawn to it before: in Freud's essay 'The "Uncanny"', there is not a single reference to *déjà vu*. Freud never explicitly mentions the 'feeling' or 'phenomenon' of *déjà vu*, even though years earlier in *The Psychopathology of Everyday Life* he had specifically referred to *déjà vu* as something that 'we must . . . include in the category of the miraculous and the "uncanny"'. Why this omission? Why doesn't Freud discuss or even make passing ref-erence to what he himself elsewhere describes as something that *must* be included in the category of the uncanny and therefore in any *theory* of the uncanny? How might we construe this exclusion of what must be included, this strange theoretical supplement or post-theoretical figure called '*déjà vu*'?

Such questions lead us into strange fields of thought and feeling. If such spaces are in some sense speculative (theoretical, conjectural, risky, non-demonstrable and so on), they also engage a certain conceptual twist, entailing the curious cohabitations of speculation with a logic of *déjà vu* 'itself'. Where could speculation be said to begin, for example, if it is only initiated on the basis of a singularly spectral *déjà vu*?

To repeat: how to construe this exemplary 'Freudian slip', this uncanny exclusion of the feeling or phenomenon of *déjà vu* from 'The "Uncanny"'? It evokes, perhaps, a duplicitous sense, a double feeling: (1) for Freud to introduce the question of *déjà vu* in a categorical and systematic fashion into a theoretical account of the uncanny would be to introduce a sort of demonic logic capable of contaminating the entire project of the essay and of psycho-analytic theory in general; (2) *at the same time*, it will not have been possible for the question of *déjà vu* to be excluded in any case: it can be *already seen* to be in operation in Freud's essay. Like the supposedly normal 'abnormal' feeling called *déjà vu* (whereby one feels that one has experienced before something that is really being experienced for the first time), the 'place' of *déjà vu* in Freud's essay would be itself only thinkable in the light of the readerly experience of a sort of double-take. Excluded, *déjà vu* is more uncannily active in Freud's essay than if it were included. And it is because it is excluded that it is included. *Déjà vu* is present *and* absent in Freud's essay; and it is *neither* present *nor* absent.

Without ever being named as such, *déjà vu* haunts this great Freud text from start to finish. Indeed, from *before* the beginning and beyond its final words, *déjà vu* frames or supplements the text. One could multiply indefi-nitely the examples and possible rereadings of 'The "Uncanny"' as an essay about *déjà vu*. To conclude, I would like to focus on three instances of this uncanny supplement, this post-theoretical figure that haunts, that comes back without perhaps ever appearing.

First, *déjà vu* would be at once that which conditions and phantomises the possibility of 'belief'. There is no believing without the ghost of *déjà vu*. This ghost haunts Freud's argument that beliefs which have been surmounted have not entirely been surmounted. The uncanny, he contends, has to do with the revival of surmounted beliefs (belief in 'the prompt fulfilment of wishes' and in 'secret injurious powers', the belief in the 'omnipotence of thoughts', the belief in 'the return of the dead', p. 370). He writes:

> We – or our primitive forefathers – once believed that these possibil-ities were realities, and were convinced that they actually happened. Nowadays we no longer believe in them, we have *surmounted* these modes of thought (*wir haben diese Denkweisen überwunden*); but we do not feel quite sure of our new beliefs, and the old ones still exist within us ready to seize upon any confirmation. As soon as something *actually happens* in our lives which seems to confirm the old, discarded beliefs we get a feeling of the uncanny; it is as though we were making a judge-ment something like this: 'So, after all, it *is* true that one can kill a person by the mere wish!' or, 'So the dead *do* live on and appear on the scene of their former activities!' and so on. (pp. 370–1/262)

Freud effectively presents himself here as a double, and imposes on his reader the same structure of being-two ('we' as Freud and the reader, but also the reader, you or me for example, as already a double): we non-religious, non-primitive, non-mystical people do *not* believe; and yet these 'surmounted' modes of thought 'still exist within us ready to seize upon any confirmation'. Not believing is still believing. These phantom 'modes of thought' will have seen us coming. A feeling of the uncanny comes when 'something *actually happens* in our lives which seems to confirm the old, discarded beliefs'. Like junk, beliefs are discarded but hang around; belief is cryptic, the experience of a foreign body within oneself. And this scenario of when something '*actually happens*' is one of *déjà vu*. It entails a fundamental unsettling of the 'first time' of an experience. The moment when something '*actually happens*' is a moment of '*Now I feel as if I had known it all the time*'.[15]

Second, *déjà vu* leads us back to *The Interpretation of Dreams* and indeed into an encounter with the question of the very definition of dreams and thus the very possibility of an interpretation of dreams.[16] Without being named as such, *déjà vu* provides Freud with what he himself singles out as being 'the most beautiful confirmation' (*die schönste Bekräftigung*, p. 258) of his 'theory of the uncanny'. In 'The "Uncanny"', he writes:

> It often happens that neurotic men declare that they feel there is some-thing uncanny about the female genital organs. This *unheimlich* place, however, is the entrance to the former *Heim* [home] of all human beings, to the place where each one of us lived once upon a time and in the beginning . . . [W]henever a man dreams of a place or a country and says to himself, while he is still dreaming (*und wenn der Träumer von einer Örtlichkeit oder Landschaft noch im Traume denkt*): 'this place is familiar to me, I've been here before', we may interpret the place as being his mother's genitals or body. (p. 368/259)

There is a moment of apparent *déjà lu* here for Freud-readers, since this 'same' example is also considered years earlier in *The Interpretation of Dreams* (1st edn, 1900). What is uncanny about this example, however, may be in the way it provokes a sort of retroactive 'new' reading of *The Interpretation* itself. Far from being merely familiar (*déjà lu*), *The Interpretation of Dreams* is rendered suddenly unfamiliar by this ghost of *déjà vu* that hovers over Freud's essay of 1919. In *The Interpretation*, he had observed:

> In some dreams of landscapes or other localities, emphasis is laid in the dream itself on a convinced feeling of having been there once before. (Occurrences of '*déjà vu*' in dreams have a special meaning.) These places are invariably the genitals of the dreamer's mother; there is indeed no other place about which one can assert with such conviction that one has been there before. (p. 524: second sentence added in 1914; the remainder first published in 1909)

With his argument that *déjà vu* in dreams 'invariably' means that one (as a man or as a woman?) is dreaming of one's mother's genitals, it is perhaps impossible either to agree or disagree: it is haunted, at the very least, by an experience of the undecidable. If, as Freud maintains, 'there is indeed no other place about which one can assert with such conviction that one has been there before', it may be equally valid to maintain that there is no other place about which one can assert with such conviction that one cannot possibly know what one is talking about in supposing that 'one has been there before'.

But there is another question, another uncertainty that perhaps unsettles the ground of Freud's argument in advance, *viz.*: can one move so unfalteringly, as Freud implies one can, from talking about *déjà vu* in waking life to talking about *déjà vu* in a dream? Are they the same? Limiting ourselves to the sense of *déjà vu* as 'the peculiar feeling we have, in certain moments and situations, of having had exactly the same experience once before or of having once before been in the same place' (Freud 1907), we may wonder whether it makes sense to speak of '*déjà vu* in a dream' at all. In a dream, we might suppose, there is not the feeling of anguish, excitement or surprise identifiable with the experience of *déjà vu* in waking life. There is no 'reality-testing'.[17] *Déjà vu* in a dream is much more concretely a determined experience of repetition (and in this respect perhaps not an 'experience' at all, at least to the extent that 'experience' belongs with the possibility of the unprogrammed or unprogrammable) than it is the *surprising* of a dreamer's 'perceptual judgement' (to recall Freud's phrase). According to Freud, *déjà vu* in a dream involves the dreamer thinking or 'say[ing] to himself, while he is still dreaming: "this place is familiar to me, I've been here before"'. In the case of *déjà vu* in waking life, however, it is a question of an experience which (to use Freud's phrase in *The Psychopathology of Everyday Life*) 'announces itself' (p. 329). In waking life, *déjà vu* comes from the other: it may appear, in some sense, the very announcement of the other.

These distinctions are perhaps not insignificant. By talking about *déjà vu* in dreams at all and more particularly by asserting that the 'special meaning' of *déjà vu* in dreams has to do with men dreaming of intra-uterine existence,[18] Freud is no doubt concerned to promote the authority of psychoanalysis and to extend its empire as a science. But this appropriation of *déjà vu* in the context of dreaming perhaps generates more questions than it puts to rest. In speaking of *déjà vu* in dreams, Freud is, in effect, providing a further example of the necessary impurity, the dangerous supplementarity of the concept and proper meaning of '*déjà vu*'. His account might thus lead us to ask: When is a dream not *déjà vu*? How could we know? When or where would '*déjà vu* in dreams' begin or end? Here we might draw on a point made by Freud's precursor or 'double' in this field, Havelock Ellis, who remarks on the links between dreaming and suggestibility: 'some degree of suggestibility, some tendency to regard the things that come before us in dreams as familiar – in other words, as things that have happened to us before – is . . . one of the very conditions of dreaming. It enables us to carry on our dreams'.[19] And conversely, how might the uncertainty of *déjà vu* impact on the nature of the assumed boundaries between dreaming and waking experience? Is the 'peculiar feeling' of *déjà vu* the invasion of a dream-state or of a different wakefulness? Or is it perhaps irreducible to either? Paradoxically, in seeking to export *déjà vu* directly from the context of waking life into that of dreams, Freud effectively disavows the singularity of *déjà vu* experiences as having 'a character quite of their own'. In not respecting this singularity, he subordinates the notion of *déjà vu* to the theoretical indifference of dreaming or waking. *Déjà vu* cannot perhaps be so easily appropriated by Freud's or any other 'theory'.

Third, it is difficult to imagine a theory of the ghost or double without a theory of *déjà vu*.[20] The examples of the double and the ghost are central to Freud's attempt to provide a full and systematic account of the uncanny under the rubric of the 'theory of the qualities of feeling' (p. 339). Following Otto Rank, he explores the idea of the double as both 'an assurance of immortality' and 'the uncanny harbinger of death' (p. 357) and concludes: 'When all is said and done, the quality of uncanniness can only come from the fact of the "double" being a creation dating back to a very early mental stage [*seelischen Urzeiten*: i.e. an early time in human history], long since surmounted – a stage, incidentally, at which it wore a more friendly aspect' (p. 358/248). Freud sees the desire to invent the double as one which springs 'from the soil of unbounded self-love, from the primary narcissism (*primären Narziβmus*) which dominates the mind of the child and of primitive man' (p. 357/257).[21] Jacques Derrida has written at length, for example in 'To Speculate – On "Freud"', about the logic of the double in Freud's essay and in particular of its strange status as 'apparition', involving an experience of 'duplicity without an original'.[22] The double is always ghostly and cannot be dissociated from a sense of *déjà vu*. We might illustrate this, in a rather condensed fashion, with an observation about *déjà vu* made by Fouillée and discussed by Havelock Ellis: paramnesia or *déjà vu* is 'a kind of diplopia or seeing double in the mental field': the feeling of *déjà vu* involves 'the impression that the present reality has a *double*'.[23] *Déjà vu* is the experience of the double *par excellence*: it is the experience of experience *as* double. There can be no uncanny, perhaps, without some experience of this duplicity.

In the closing pages of his book *Spectres of Marx*, Derrida makes much of what Freud calls '*es spukt*' ('it ghosts', 'it comes back', 'it spooks') in 'The "Uncanny"'. In particular, Derrida elaborates on this '*es spukt*' as being where (by Freud's own admission) he could and should have begun his attempt to write a theory of the uncanny.[24] How should we try to conceive the *es spukt*? It is, Derrida suggests, a matter of becoming ready to welcome the stranger,

> a stranger who is already found within (*das Heimliche-Unheimliche*), more intimate with one than one is oneself, the absolute proximity of a stranger whose power is singular *and* anonymous (*es spukt*), an unnameable and neutral power, that is, undecidable, neither active nor passive, an an-identity that, *without doing anything*, invisibly occupies places belonging finally neither to us nor to it. (p. 172)

This leads perhaps to another sense of *déjà vu*: it is to be oneself *already seen*, watched (over). The ghost or double *is déjà vu. Déjà vu*: post-theory. This 'stranger within' has no name or finally assignable place, either in Freud or in Derrida or in ourselves. If (as Derrida stresses) Freud '*ought* to have begun' with 'the strongest example of *Unheimlichkeit*, the "es spukt", ghosts, and apparitions' (p. 173), one can equally well argue that Freud ought to have begun with *déjà vu* (*das Heimliche-Unheimliche*). And in a sense of course he does: he advances it initially some twelve years earlier, in 1907, in *The Psychopathology of Everyday Life*, as what 'must be included' in any account of the uncanny. Without saying or indeed perhaps realising that he is doing it, in 1914 he even writes an essay about it, a text that is at once a preface and postscript to 'The "Uncanny"', entitled '*Fausse Reconnaissance* ("*déjà raconté*") in Psycho-Analytic Treatment'.[25]

NOTES

1. Jacques Derrida, *Spectres of Marx: The State of the Debt, the Work of Mourning, and the New International*, trans. Peggy Kamuf (New York: Routledge, 1994), p. 139. Further page references are given in parentheses.
2. Robert Young, 'Poststructuralism: The End of Theory', *Oxford Literary Review*, 5 (1982), 3–15. Further page references to this text are given in parentheses.
3. Robert J. C. Young, 'Poststructuralism: The Improper Name', in *Torn Halves: Political Conflict in Literary and Cultural Theory* (Manchester: Manchester University Press, 1996), pp. 67–83: (p. 70).
4. Ibid., p. 70.
5. Sigmund Freud, 'The "Uncanny"', trans. James Strachey, *Pelican Freud Library*, vol. 14 (Harmondsworth: Penguin, 1985), pp. 339–76. Further page references are given in parentheses. References to the German text of this Freud essay are taken from *Gesammelte Werke*, vol. 12 (London: Imago, 1947), pp. 229–68, and page references are given in parentheses, following the English-translation page reference and preceded by a slash. For help with Freud's German in this chapter I would like to record my gratitude and indebtedness to Peter Krapp and Julia Lang.

6. Cf. Derrida's discussion, near the beginning of *Spectres of Marx*, of the 'troubling effect of "*déjà vu*"' (p. 14) whereby the question 'Whither Marxism?' can be posed in the 1990s, as if it had not been *the question* confronting so-called western intellectuals for 'at least forty years'. Derrida's specific inflection of the term is worth noting: it is a 'troubling' sense of *déjà vu*, even if '*déjà vu*' here is taken as *OED* sense (b).

7. Sigmund Freud, *The Psychopathology of Everyday Life*, trans. Alan Tyson, *Pelican Freud Library*, vol. 5 (Harmondsworth: Penguin, 1976); *Gesammelte Werke*, vol. 4 (London: Imago, 1941).

8. For Freud, it may appear, there is a point at which one has to stop: *déjà vu* may be a *question* of a 'perceptual judgement', but judgement on this predicament must be passed. Yet his relation to this subject is that of an uncanny double-bind: he never finishes with the question of *déjà vu*, or, perhaps one should say, it never finishes with him. Freud returns (still, again) to the subject in a late (1936) essay: see 'A Disturbance of Memory on the Acropolis', trans. James Strachey, *Pelican Freud Library*, vol. 11 (Harmondsworth: Penguin, 1984), pp. 447–56; *Gesammelte Werke*, vol. 16 (London: Imago, 1950), pp. 250–7. Here he speaks of *déjà vu* as a 'positive counterpart' (*die positiven Gegenstücke*, vol. 16, p. 255) of the phenomenon of derealisation and depersonalisation. It would be, in some sense, a 'positive' experience of the situation in which, he says, 'the subject feels either that a piece of reality or that a piece of his [*sic*] own self is strange to him' (*entweder erscheint un sein Stück der Realität als fremd oder ein Stück des eigenen Ichs* (vol. 11, p. 453/vol. 16, pp. 254–5). He writes:

> derealizations and depersonalizations are intimately connected. There is another set of phenomena which may be regarded as their positive counterparts – what are known as '*fausse reconnaissance*', '*déjà vu*', '*déjà raconté*' etc., illusions [*sic*] in which we seek to accept something as belonging to our ego, just as in the derealizations we are anxious to keep something out of us. A naively mystical and unpsychological attempt at explaining the phenomena of '*déjà vu*' endeavours to find evidence in it of a former existence of our mental self. Depersonalization leads us on to the extraordinary notion of '*double conscience*' [in French in original: 'double consciousness'], which is more correctly described as 'split personality'. But all of this is so obscure and has been so little mastered that I must refrain from talking about it any more to you. (*Das ist alles noch so dunkel, so wenig wissenschaftlich bezwungen, daß ich mir verbieten muß, es vor Ihnen weiter zu erörtern.*) (PFL, vol. 11, pp. 453–4/vol. 16, p. 255)

This fascinating passage provokes numerous questions. Do we necessarily 'seek to accept something as belonging to our own ego' in the experience of *déjà vu*? How is 'double consciousness' distinct from the notion of 'a former existence of our mental self'? According to what criteria and authority should 'double consciousness' be '*more correctly* described as "split personality"' (my emphasis)? Freud stops himself, apparently, from saying any more: 'I must forbid myself to expound it any further in front of you (*ich mir verbieten muß, es vor Ihnen weiter zu erörtern*)'. Who is forbidding whom here? In refraining from saying any more about this subject that is so resistant to scientific mastery, Freud paradoxically puts himself on the very stage of *déjà vu*, onto the scene, that is to say, in which the 'I' trembles *in secret*. As I hope will become clearer as I go on, the sense of '*déjà vu*' as it emerges in Freud's work is in some ways strangely similar to deconstruction (*das Heimliche-Unheimliche*). Like deconstruction, *déjà vu* can be described as the experience of a trembling which is the trembling of experience itself. It is concerned with an absolute past, a past that was never present. It has to do with an experience of the undecidable that may be erotic and 'positive' as well as strange and frightening. It is not 'mystical' (cf. PFL, vol. 11, p. 453). It is the experience of the being-promise of a promise in all its disruptive perversity *and* affirmation. It 'announces itself', it is the announcement of the other, it says 'come' to a future that cannot be anticipated. How long will it last? Is this an event? To whom is it happening? Post-theory would be the experience of these questions.

9. Sigmund Freud, '*Fausse Reconnaissance ("déjà raconté")* in Psycho-Analytic Treatment', trans. James Strachey, *Standard Edition*, vol. 13 (London: Hogarth Press and the Institute of Psycho-Analysis, 1955), pp. 201–7; *Gesammelte Werke*, vol. 10 (London: Imago, 1946), pp. 116–23.

10. See *The Correspondence of Sigmund Freud and Sándor Ferenczi: Volume 1, 1908–1914*, ed. Eva Brabant, Ernst Falzeder and Patrizia Giampieri-Deutsch, trans. Peter T. Hoffer (Cambridge, MA: Belknap Press, 1993), p. 540. Freud writes: 'The paper about déjà vu that you asked about is a piece of junk.'

11. It is with the sense of these myrmidons that one might begin to consider the possible uncanny rapport between *déjà vu* and what Freud calls the repetition compulsion: how would one distinguish between such conceptual ghosts? Would the repetition compulsion be a form of *déjà vu* or would the latter be merely an 'analogy' for the irruptive yet inaccessible character of the former?

12. Is the anxiety of influence not in some sense an anxiety of *déjà vu*? If one tracks off here to another of the precursor texts to which Freud specifically refers (see '*Fausse Reconnaissance*', p. 202, n. 1) in his own account of *déjà vu*, namely Havelock Ellis, *The World of Dreams* (London: Constable, 1911), and in particular Chapter 9, 'Memory in Dreams' (pp. 212–60), one finds the following Bloomian observation: 'We may read a new poem with a vague sense of familiarity, but such an experience never puts on a really paramnesic character, for we quickly realise that it is explainable by the fact that the writer of the poem has fallen under the influence of some greater master' (pp. 242–3). Alongside this conception of the anxiety of influence, however, one might also set the figuration of *déjà vu* implicit in a remark Geoffrey Bennington makes about the writings of Plato and Derrida: 'from a certain point of view the whole of Derrida is already "in" Plato (for those who read . . . like Derrida, and therefore do not believe that we really know what "in Plato" means), as his ghost or double'. See Bennington and Derrida, *Jacques Derrida*, trans. Bennington (London and Chicago: Chicago University Press, 1993), p. 273.

13. For a fuller account of Freud and telepathy, see, for example, Jacques Derrida, 'Telepathy', trans. Nicholas Royle, *Oxford Literary Review*, 10 (1988), 3–41; and permit me to refer also to 'The Remains of Psychoanalysis (i): Telepathy', in my book *After Derrida* (Manchester and New York: Manchester University Press, 1995), pp. 61–84.

14. Cf. Jacques Derrida, *The Post Card: From Socrates to Freud and Beyond*, trans. Alan Bass (Chicago: Chicago University Press, 1987), where he describes a similar process or interruption of process at work in the logic of Freud's *Beyond the Pleasure Principle*: 'A certain *I*, the same but immediately an other, does not know to what extent *I* believes in them [i.e. in Freud's hypotheses]. It is not only belief, but the relation to belief which finds itself suspended, the relation of science or of consciousness' (p. 379).

15. Our primitive forefathers are ghosts within us, it may seem. Yet it is impossible to remember what our forefathers felt: come back as if from nowhere, it is belief itself that is ghostly. This temporal phantom-effect is perhaps evident in a slightly different way in an observation made by Havelock Ellis at the end of his essay on paramnesia and *déjà vu* ('the best known form of paramnesia', p. 230). These phenomena, he says,

> are of no little interest since, in earlier stages of culture, they may well have had a real influence on belief, suggesting to primitive man that he had somehow had wider experiences than he knew of, and that, as Wordsworth put it, he trailed clouds of glory behind him. (p. 260)

Rather than, as Freud suggests, the beliefs of our primitive forefathers providing a rationalisation for understanding why we have 'uncanny' experiences, might we not just as well suppose (following the line of Ellis's proposal in what could nevertheless be called a Freudian spirit) that in some sense everything comes back to *déjà vu*, in other words that every belief (whether hypothetically 'primitive' or not), belief *in general*, passes by way of a *déjà vu* structure?

16. Sigmund Freud, *The Interpretation of Dreams*, trans. James Strachey, *Pelican Freud Library*, vol. 4 (Harmondsworth: Penguin, 1976). Further page references are given in parentheses.

17. Cf. Freud, 'An Outline of Psychoanalysis', trans. James Strachey, in *Pelican Freud Library*, vol. 15 (Harmondsworth: Penguin, 1986), where he suggests that '*reality-testing*' is an 'institution . . . which is allowed to fall into abeyance in dreams on account of the conditions prevailing in the state of sleep' (p. 435). From a different perspective, see Lacan's remarks about the 'ambiguous phenomenon of déjà vu' in *The Seminar of Jacques Lacan: Book I Freud's Papers on Technique, 1953–1954*, ed. Jacques-Alain Miller, trans. with notes by John Forrester (Cambridge: Cambridge University Press, 1988), p. 59. Lacan claims that 'Freud is talking of nothing other than [déjà vu] when he tells us that any experiencing [*toute épreuve*: John Forrester suggests the connotation here of *épreuve de la réalité*, "reality-testing"] of the external world implicitly refers to something which has already been perceived in the past'.

18. See 'The "Uncanny"', p. 367, and cf. *The Interpretation of Dreams*, p. 525, n. 2.

19. Havelock Ellis, *The World of Dreams*, p. 232.

20. I borrow the style of this formulation from Jacques Derrida who makes an analogous claim with respect to telepathy and a theory of the unconscious: 'Difficult to imagine a theory of what they still call the unconscious without a theory of telepathy. They can be neither confused nor dissociated.' See 'Telepathy', p. 14.

21. But what would be the 'primary' of 'primary narcissism'? What self would

indulge in a self-love that was not love of an other? Can one love one's self, one-self, without loving one's double? It would perhaps accord with the drift of this chapter to supplement these questions with another: what might it mean to suppose that primary narcissism is a *déjà vu* concept? The sense of such a supposition may present itself in encountering the following passage, for example, from 'On Narcissism: An Introduction' (1914) (*Pelican Freud Library*, vol. 11, pp. 65–97):

> The primary narcissism of children *which we have assumed*, and which forms one of the postulates of our theories of the libido, is less easy to grasp by direct observation than to confirm *by inference from elsewhere*. If we look at the attitude of affectionate parents towards their children, we have to recognise that it is a *revival and reproduction* of their own narcissism, which they have long since abandoned. (p. 84, my emphases)

22. 'To Speculate – on "Freud"', in *The Post Card*, pp. 257–409: see p. 270.
23. Quoted by Ellis, p. 252.
24. Freud notes that 'Many people experience the feeling [of uncanniness] in the highest degree in relation to death and dead bodies, to the return of the dead, and to spirits and ghosts . . . [S]ome languages in use today can only render the German expression "an *unheimlich* house" by "a *haunted* house" (*ein Haus, in dem es spukt*)' (p. 364/255). He then goes on, oddly, to say: 'We might indeed have begun our investigation with this example . . . of the uncanny, but we refrained from doing so because the uncanny in it is too much intermixed with what is purely gruesome and is in part overlaid by it' (p. 364). It is this odd admission that Derrida picks up on in *Spectres of Marx*.
25. The ascription of 'The "Uncanny"' to 1919 is, of course, contentious in various ways. As Neil Hertz puts it: 'Even the simple facts concerning the writing and publication of "The Uncanny" seem designed to raise questions about repetition. The essay came out in the fall of 1919, and a letter of Freud's indicates that it was written in May of that year, or, rather, rewritten, for the letter speaks of his going back to an old manuscript that he had set aside, for how long it isn't clear – perhaps as long as a dozen years.' See Neil Hertz, 'Freud and the Sandman', in Josué V. Harari (ed.), *Textual Strategies: Perspectives in Post-Structuralist Criticism* (London: Methuen, 1979), pp. 296–321: here p. 297.

Chapter Two

DECONSTRUCTION AND THE 'UNFINISHED PROJECT OF MODERNITY'

Christopher Norris

I

Commentaries on Derrida tend to divide very sharply when it comes to assessing the relationship between deconstruction and what Habermas calls the 'unfinished project' of post-Kantian critical thought.[1] For some – post-modernists and Rorty-style 'strong' textualists among them – this relationship is not so much a matter of continuing critical engagement as a straightforward rejection, on Derrida's part, of all those 'enlightened' truth-claims and values that once made up the philosophic discourse of modernity.[2] Thus Derrida is interpreted as taking the view that philosophy is just one voice in the 'cultural conversation of mankind', or again, just another 'kind of writing' (Rorty's phrase) whose chief merit is to move the conversation along by inventing new language-games, metaphors, narratives, modes of self-description and so forth.[3] On this account it is merely unfortunate – the last thing for which his writings should be valued – when Derrida reverts to certain forms of argument in the 'quasi-transcendental' (or conditions-of-possibility) mode which betray a lingering Kantian influence. For others – most notably Rodolphe Gasché – it is just those elements in Derrida's work that constitute its chief philosophical merit, its claim both to *conserve and to radicalise* the critical impulse of modernity.[4] The third main tendency in Derrida exegesis is that represented by thinkers such as Habermas who interpret him pretty much in Rorty's fashion – as a gadfly rhetorician bent upon levelling the 'genre-distinction' between philosophy and literature – but who draw very different conclusions as to the value and desirability of carrying that project through.[5]

Thus, according to Habermas, deconstruction can best be seen as a further stage in the history of irrationalist or counter-enlightenment thought which first took hold very soon after Kant and which harked back to an earlier (pre-Kantian) phase when thinking had not yet accomplished the passage to a critical awareness of its various constitutive powers and limits. What Rorty most likes about Derrida – his supposed indifference to the standards of 'serious', 'constructive' philosophical inquiry – is what Habermas finds most reprehensible. Indeed he takes it as evidence enough of the close link between deconstruction and the wider postmodernist retreat from any notion of progressive or emancipatory thought. This complaint is taken up – albeit in a different (broadly 'analytic' or Anglo-American) key – by opponents of Derrida such as John Searle who profess to see nothing in deconstruction but a wilful desire to play mischievous games not only with the texts of philosophers from Plato to Austin but also with those 'ordinary-language' codes and conventions that allow philosophy its claim to treat issues of shared human concern.[6] Hence the bad name that deconstruction has acquired – whether by hearsay or (less often) through direct acquaintance with the texts – among mainstream philosophers on both sides of the notional rift between 'continental' and 'analytic' lines of descent.

That this rift is more a product of short-term professional interests than deep-laid philosophic differences is a case that has been argued with considerable force by recent commentators, Michael Dummett among them.[7] Indeed Derrida himself voices some perplexity – in the course of his response to Searle – concerning the hybrid derivation of those various arguments brought against him by critics who supposedly speak for the two philosophical cultures.[8] At any rate, Searle and Habermas have this much in common: that they charge deconstruction with illicitly collapsing certain cardinal distinctions, as for instance between philosophy and literature, reason and rhetoric, or language in its various (e.g. constative and performative or factual-informative, ethico-evaluative and 'world-disclosive') aspects. Moreover, they both see Derrida as refusing to engage in rational debate and embracing what amounts to a nihilist outlook – or an attitude of 'anything goes' – with regard to crucial issues of truth, meaning and interpretation. For Searle, this results from Derrida's failure to grasp the basic principles of speech-act theory, or rather (more likely) his perverse desire to make trouble by wilfully misreading texts and creating all manner of pseudo-problems. For Habermas, it is more a matter of placing deconstruction in the wider present-day cultural context of philosophies that have given up too soon on the 'unfinished project' of modernity, and which continue to rehearse issues that belonged to an earlier, subject-centred discourse of epistemology and ethics.[9]

Thus Derrida's obsession (as Habermas sees it) with the predicament of 'logocentric' reason – with the aporias created by a so-called western 'metaphysics of presence' – is one that by now should have ceased to exert such a hold with the turn towards language (or communicative action) as the best way forward from those false dilemmas. In short, Habermas agrees with Rorty when he interprets Derrida as (1) out to demolish the philosophic discourse of enlightenment, and (2) subject to a backward pull that prevents him from exploring the alternative resources now offered by a speech-act theory (a 'universal pragmatics') with strongly normative validity-conditions. Where they differ is on the question of whether anything is to be gained by recasting those typically Kantian issues in a somewhat updated or 'linguistified' form. Rorty sees this as just another sad example of the way that philosophers strive to hang onto their old delusions of grandeur by periodically scaling down their epistemological claims while inventing some new technical idiom that smuggles those claims in again by the back door.[10] This is why he treats Derrida's 'philosophical' writings as symptomatic of a backsliding tendency which we can safely ignore once we have taken the point of his other, more liberating 'textualist' performances. On Habermas's reading, conversely, the trouble with deconstruction is that it skips straight across – in typical post-modernist style – from disillusionment with that old, subject-centred episte-mological paradigm to an attitude of all-out hermeneutic licence where there exist no constraints upon the range of interpretative options, whether in the sphere of 'ordinary language' or in various more specialised branches of inquiry.

Searle is less concerned with these long-term genealogical issues, speaking as he does from a briskly (not to say brusquely) 'analytic' standpoint that assumes all genuine philosophic problems to be capable of solution simply by applying certain straightforward speech-act precepts. Thus for him it is just a matter of Derrida's lacking the most basic competence in these matters, rather than a case calling for treatment in the large-scale historical-philo-sophico-diagnostic mode.[11] Still, he concurs with Habermas in viewing deconstruction as a product of the drive to conflate different aspects of language, aspects which need to be distinguished not only for the sake of philosophical clarity but also in order to explain how linguistic communica-tion is possible in various (standard and non-standard, e.g. fictional) contexts. Moreover, he shares Habermas's belief that Derrida has muddied the waters by taking the latter sorts of case – metaphor, fiction, poetry, 'deviant' utter-ances of various kinds – as somehow (absurdly) prior or prerequisite to language in its normal, everyday-communicative role. As Habermas describes it, this amounts to a massive overemphasis on the aesthetic, the rhetorical or 'world-disclosive' dimension of language and a consequent failure to make room for those other (truth-related or ethico-evaluative) dimensions which are thereby consigned to a merely derivative and ancillary status.

So it is – on this account – that Derrida betrays the unfinished project of modernity and opens the way to a postmodern notion of endless interpreta-tive 'free play' where there is no longer any place for such typecast Enlightenment values as truth, reason and critique. In short, Habermas agrees point for point with Rorty that the most significant aspect of Derrida's

work is its desire to have done with those antiquated values and its idea of
philosophy as just another another 'kind of writing', on a par with other (on
the whole more inventive and entertaining) kinds such as fiction, poetry and
literary criticism. But where Rorty thoroughly approves this turn in the present-day 'cultural conversation', Habermas views it as one more sign of the
widespread failure of moral, political and intellectual nerve that goes under
the blanket name of postmodernism. Unlike Searle, he shows some awareness of the complex and intricate character of Derrida's arguments, especially
as regards their relationship to Kant and to episodes in the post-Kantian
history of thought from Fichte, Schelling and Hegel to recent, sharply
polarised debates in the wake of Nietzsche and Heidegger. But on the main
point at issue – Derrida's supposed irrationalist retreat from the sphere of
intersubjective understanding or shared communicative norms – Habermas
and Searle can properly be seen as making common cause.

  I have written elsewhere at some length on the various distortions and
misunderstandings that have given rise to this prevalent notion of Derrida
as a counter-Enlightenment thinker deploying all the means at his crafty
disposal to subvert or discredit the philosophic discourse of modernity.[12]
What I want to do now is approach the same topic from a slightly different
angle, one that takes in the question of deconstruction's bearing vis-à-vis the
claims of Enlightenment critique, but which treats that question in a wider
institutional context. For it is clear that both Derrida and his opponents see
a strong connection at this point, that is to say, between relatively specialised
questions concerning the powers, the scope and limits of critical reason in its
various modes of deployment, and on the other hand primarily ethical questions concerning the comportment of critical intellectuals in the wider social
sphere. Of course Derrida's writings on Kant are the obvious place to go if
one wishes to grasp the issues at stake in this current, much-publicised
debate about the ethics and the politics of deconstruction.[13] I shall therefore
focus my discussion on two of his texts from the 1980s: 'Mochlos: or, The
Conflict of the Faculties' and 'The Parergon'. (*Mochlos* and *parergon* are
Greek words meaning 'lever' and 'frame', a pair of terms whose significance
I hope to make clear.) There is no denying that Derrida maintains a complex,
ambivalent, at times distrustful attitude towards the philosophic discourse
of modernity. All the same there is no warrant – prejudice aside – for counting
him among the postmodern enemies of reason or those who (as Habermas
charges) wish to revoke the unfinished project of critical-emancipatory
thought.

II

In 'Mochlos: or, The Conflict of the Faculties', Derrida takes his subtitle
from an essay by Kant which addresses various issues having to do with the

intellectual division of labour between various academic disciplines and the order of priority that governs their relationship.[14] What is in question here is a certain idea of the modern university, an idea that has come down to us principally from Kant and from other philosophers (Humboldt among them) in the broadly 'Enlightenment' tradition. For it is not just a play on words to point out the link between Kant's 'system' of the faculties – pure (or speculative) reason, cognitive understanding, practical reason, aesthetic judgement and so on – and the various faculties (namely, university departments, disciplines or subject-areas) that we have largely taken over from that same tradition.

To be sure, the division of labour has changed in some respects, as for instance through the development of new, more specialised fields of scientific research or new interdisciplinary ventures. (These are not opposite trends, by the way, but very often go closely together, as with the emergence of molecular biology as a specialised discipline that unites physics with the life sciences.) But essentially we are working with the same ground-plan, the same disciplinary 'map', so to speak, which one could use as a guide to find one's way around the modern university campus. So there are the sciences, the natural or physical sciences (both 'pure' and 'applied') whose different branches and sub-branches would each have its campus location. Then there are the various 'humanities' or 'social sciences' departments – history, anthropology, sociology, economics, philosophy, literature, languages ancient and modern – which would probably occupy rather less space, or perhaps (some of them nowadays) just an office with a part-time secretary and a small supply of headed notepaper. In some cases – for example, sociology and economics – the exact location and amount of room might depend on their perceived standing vis-à-vis the natural sciences, that is, the extent to which they adopt properly 'scientific' (empirical or quantitative) methods and techniques. So there are shifts of alignment going on all the time, brought about by pressures 'internal' and 'external', insofar as one can actually distinguish those two sorts of pressure. This is indeed one of the questions that Derrida raises with regard to the modern post-Kantian idea of the university as an autonomous institution where certain intellectual pursuits – such as philosophy – should properly be subject to no forms of 'external' interference or control. Still, there is a sense in which all these disciplines – and the various relations (not to mention the rivalries) between them – have their model in Kant's seemingly rigid but in fact quite flexible schema. Here we might recall Gilles Deleuze's happy metaphor of the system of 'rotating chairmanship' whereby the different faculties (pure reason, understanding, practical reason and judgement) take up a prominent or subsidiary role according to the case in hand.[15]

What interests Derrida, in his writings on Kant, is the extent to which this can still be thought of as a model – albeit an idealised model, a regulative 'idea of reason' in the Kantian sense – for the conduct of debate in or upon the modern university. Up to a point, he shares the postmodernist outlook of scepticism with regard to its continuing relevance or validity. Thus, as might be expected, Derrida sets out to deconstruct the various oppositions between 'pure' and 'applied' research, between (on the one hand) disinterested, speculative or purely truth-seeking disciplines, and (on the other) areas of research whose interests are dictated by 'external' incentives such as commercial funding or government contracts. For Kant, in his essay 'The Conflict of the Faculties', it is important – indeed a vital condition for academic freedom in the modern university – that these distinctions be constantly borne in mind.[16] Moreover, Philosophy is the subject-area where reason asserts its right to pursue such inquiries without hindrance, restraint or the threat of censorship. It can legitimately assert that right, Kant argues, since it does not (or should not) exert any claim to influence people – people outside the university – in matters of political, moral and religious belief, as distinct from raising speculative issues in politics, ethics and theology. There are other disciplines (law, theology, medicine – the so-called 'higher' faculties) which do have that kind of extramural influence on account of their closer relationship with the state and with the offices of state-administered power. These are the disciplines that possess some *leverage* in matters of executive decision-taking and policy-formation – whence one meaning of the 'mochlos' metaphor, as Derrida deploys it. In exchange for this privilege, they can and should be held accountable for upholding whatever the state rightfully decrees with regard to political, social and religious obligations. And if they overstep the limit in this respect – as, for instance, by pursuing speculative questions that might have a dangerous (subversive) impact on the beliefs or conduct of people outside the university – then their published opinions may properly be subject to censorship.

Philosophy is therefore a 'lower' faculty in the sense that it lays no claim to executive power. Furthermore, Kant says, it is very important that philosophers should not seek to arrogate such power, because if they did then they could have no legitimate complaint when their writings and teachings were censored or suppressed. Thus 'the freedom of the lower faculty, though *absolute*, is a freedom of judgement and intra-university speech, a freedom to speak out on *that which is*, through judgements essentially theoretical'.[17] And again, in Derrida's words:

> [t]his freedom of judgement Kant takes to be the unconditioned condition of university autonomy, and that unconditioned condition is nothing other than philosophy. Autonomy is philosophical reason insofar as it grants itself its own law, namely the truth. Which is why the lower faculty is called the philosophy faculty; and without a philosophy department in a university, there is no university.[18]

However, that prerogative is granted only on certain mutually agreed terms and conditions. If philosophers presumed to tell people what they should believe or how they should act – setting up, in effect, as an arm of the executive – then they would be breaking the contract (or the unwritten concordat) that guarantees their freedom of thought and expression. For philosophy has to do with the exercise of reason in a mode quite distinct, or in a sphere quite separate, from the interests of church and state. It can discuss theology but it must not instruct people as to just what religious beliefs they should hold; it can raise important issues about God, about the immortality of the soul, about the possibility (or impossibility) of proving God's existence, but should exercise a due caution lest those issues stir up public controversy. In the realm of politics likewise, philosophers may question all manner of received (or state-sanctioned) beliefs with regard to freedom, democracy, human rights or the scope and limits of legitimate state power. However, it should do so always in its proper ('theoretical') mode, and without seeking an influence beyond the sphere of 'disinterested' philosophical inquiry. For these are issues that could have quite explosive or incendiary effects upon the population at large if they were discussed, say, in the popular press or in books of wide public appeal. However, Kant advises, there is a bargain to be struck, or – to put it less crudely – an 'enlightened' compromise solution. This will help to prevent any damage either to the interests of philosophy (through unwarranted restrictions on its freedom of thought and speech) or to the interests of legitimate state power (through forcing it to act beyond its proper remit in such delicate matters). Philosophers will not tell people what to think, they will not stray beyond their appointed domain, they will confine their speculation to the learned (not-too-accessible) books and journals. And in return for that agreement the politicians, theologians and guardians of the public peace will refrain from intervening in issues that should scarcely be cause for official concern.

No doubt we have to do some charitable reading-between-the-lines in order to avoid the impression of hypocrisy or moral cowardice. At this time, Kant had serious problems with state and church censorship, after a fairly long period of relative freedom.[19] Certainly he is making (or implying) some much higher claims for philosophy – for its bearing on matters of moral, religious and political conscience – than he can safely express straight out. He is *not* just taking a line of least resistance, caving in under pressure, and requesting that philosophers be left free to pursue their harmless speculations, just so long as they treat of religious questions 'within the limits of reason alone' (another of his nicely judged titles) and agree not to meddle with politics.[20] On the contrary, it is hard to imagine any reader of Kant – except perhaps the most gullible of state censors – who would fail to perceive the ironic subtext of a work like 'The Conflict of the Faculties'. For if there is one Kantian precept that demands to be heard – not only in these occasional writings but also throughout the three *Critiques* – it is the principle enshrined in his famous watchword 'Sapere aude!', that is, 'have the courage to think for yourself!' In other words, it is Kant's paramount belief that human beings achieve autonomy (or 'maturity') in matters of scientific, intellectual, ethical and religious judgement only to the extent that they accept nothing on trust – or in blind faith – and hence claim the freedom to exercise their powers of enlightened critical reason.

Now Derrida is sceptical about all this, though only up to a point. He thinks it an illusion – though also, one might say, a vital and necessary illusion – that philosophy can somehow rise clean above the various interests that bear in upon it from 'outside' the university, or from other disciplines 'inside' the university which more or less directly represent those interests. Thus it is no longer possible in good faith – or in good intellectual conscience – to accept this idea of the Philosophy faculty as representing in itself, by some special dispensation, the good conscience of the modern (enlightened) university system. For there is, as Derrida pointedly remarks elsewhere, no discipline or subject-area nowadays that is so remote from the interests of state power or the imperatives of 'applied' research that it might not receive government support or funding by the US Navy.[21] After all, it is hard to tell what might be the pay-off – the long-term strategic yield – of a research programme in (say) translation studies, or in literary theory, or even in the deconstructive reading of texts. Deconstruction might just turn out to be useful in devising some new and well-nigh unbreakable code for the communication of military secrets, or perhaps for cracking such a code should the need arise. At this point, Derrida says, we can no longer have much faith in the Kantian distinction between 'pure' and 'applied' research, or the interests of knowledge and the interests of power, or those disciplines (philosophy chief among them) that pursue truth 'for its own sake' and those that adopt a pragmatic, instrumentalist approach.

Kant considered it vital to preserve this distinction since only thus, he believed, could philosophy be saved from the threat of state-sponsored interference. In Austinian terms, it is the distinction between *constative* and *performative* modes of utterance, that is to say, between speech-acts with assertoric force (those to which criteria of truth or falsehood apply) and speech-acts – such as promises, threats, requests, imperatives and so on – whose truth is not at issue but rather their aptness in some given situation or context of utterance.[22] With performatives, the sole criterion is whether or not they meet the various 'felicity'-conditions that decide what shall count as a proper or genuine sample of the kind. If those conditions are met – if it is the right form of words, uttered in the right context, and by a speaker with due authority or qualifications – then the speech-act carries the intended performative (or 'illocutionary') force. Beyond that, it may also have 'perlocutionary' effects, as for instance by securing the desired result when an order has been issued or a request properly made and duly acted upon. Hence the analogy that Derrida draws between speech-act theory and the Kantian division of the faculties. It is the idea of philosophy as a 'constative' discipline concerned with matters of theoretical truth (matters that lie 'within the limits of reason alone'), and claiming no right to exercise power in the 'performative' or politico-juridical domain. For there is then less danger that the censors or guardians of the public peace will take it upon themselves to cross that line (so to speak) in the opposite direction and presume to legislate on matters of a purely philosophical or speculative nature.

In his well-known essay on Austin ('Signature Event Context'), Derrida produces a variety of arguments to show that this distinction between constative and performative speech-acts is highly unstable or hard to maintain in any rigorous, philosophically adequate way.[23] It is subject to effects of undecidability which result from the problem of defining what should count as a genuine speech-act, whether in terms of speaker's intention (sincerely meaning what one says) or with reference to various circumstantial factors (appropriate context of utterance). I shall not go further into these issues here since they have already received a good deal of critical commentary.[24] My point is that Derrida finds similar problems with Kant's attempt – his perhaps rather less than sincere attempt – to keep philosophy safely apart from the realm of public-political affairs. Thus:

> Kant needs, as he says, to trace, between a responsibility concerning truth and a responsibility concerning action, a linear frontier, an indivisible and rigorously uncrossable line. To do so he has to submit language to a particular treatment. Language is an element common to both spheres of responsibility, and one that deprives us of any rigorous distinction between the two spaces that Kant at all costs wanted to dissociate . . . Kant speaks only of language when he speaks about the 'manifestation of truth', or 'influence over the people', or the interpretation of sacred texts in theological terms, or, conversely, philosophical terms, etc. And yet he continually effaces something in language that scrambles the limits which a criticist critique claims to assign to the faculties, to the interior of the faculties, and, as will be seen, between the university's inside and its outside.[25]

In part, this is a matter of the problems that arise with any attempt to hold the line between 'pure' and 'applied' research, or truth pursued for its own sake – in the mode of disinterested speculative reason – and knowledge pursued with certain predetermined ends in view, be they techno-scientific, military-strategic, sociopolitical, or whatever. This is why, as Derrida says, he has 'let himself be guided' in his reading of Kant by the discourse of speech-act theory and – more specifically – the kinds of complication that can be seen to affect the constative/performative dichotomy. The connection is brought out in the following passage which modulates between Kant's doctrine of the faculties (in both senses of that term) and Austin's approach to the classification of speech-act forms, genres or modalities.

> The pure concept of the university is constructed by Kant on the possibility and necessity of a language purely theoretical, inspired solely by an interest in truth, with a structure that one today would call purely constative. This ideal is undoubtedly guaranteed, in the Kantian proposal as such, by pure practical reason, by prescriptive utterances, by the postulate of freedom on the one hand, and, on the other, by virtue of a de facto political authority supposed in principle to let itself be guided by reason. But this in no way keeps the performative structure from being excluded, in principle, from the language whereby Kant regulates both the concept of the university and what within it is purely autonomous, namely . . . the 'lower' faculty, the faculty of philosophy.[26]

Thus the chief problem with speech-act theory – that of distinguishing clearly between constative and performative modes of utterance – is also the problem that afflicts any doctrine, like Kant's, aimed towards establishing a guaranteed space within the university for the exercise of reason in its pure theoretical mode, unbeholden to the interests of executive power and laying no claim to such power on its own behalf. Besides, this doctrine goes clean against what Kant had to say elsewhere about the 'public' as opposed to the 'private' uses of reason, and the duty of enlightened intellectuals not only to 'think for themselves' but to think on behalf of humanity at large, that is, with reference to a public sphere of shared ethico-political values and concerns.[27] So there is strong *prima facie* warrant to suppose that Kant cannot really mean what he says in thus restricting philosophy – or the purest, most essential interests of philosophy – to a realm where the privilege of free thought is purchased at the price of willing acquiescence in the dictates of authorised public belief.

This reading finds additional support if one looks more closely at Kant's 'doctrine' of the faculties as developed throughout the three *Critiques*. For it then becomes clear just how many and various are the linkages, exchanges or relations of mutual interdependence that exist between them. This applies especially to the *Critique of Judgement* where Kant addresses a number of issues that were left unresolved – or inadequately treated – in its predecessor works.[28] They include, as exegetes have often noted, the epistemological issue (taken up from the First *Critique*) of just how sensuous intuitions can be 'brought under' corresponding concepts, and – with regard to the *Critique of Practical Reason* – the question of how generalised ethical maxims apply to particular cases of situated moral judgement.[29] But there is also the problem of accounting for that exercise of free, 'disinterested' judgement which, according to Kant, transcends all merely self-motivated ('pathological') tastes and inclinations. This is why aesthetics – improbably enough – assumes so prominent a role in Kant's philosophy: as the sphere of thought where judgement attains a maximal distance from the promptings of unregenerate desire or self-interest. In the case of the beautiful, this condition comes about through the harmony achieved between the two 'faculties' of understanding and imagination. In the case of the sublime, it results, more paradoxically, through the failure of understanding to grasp what lies beyond its utmost scope of comprehension. That is to say, it transpires through the mind's suddenly confronting images of awesome power or violence in nature (the dynamical sublime), or ideas of reason, such as those of the infinite or the infinitesimal, which yet remain devoid of conceptual-intuitive content (the mathematical sublime). For it is precisely at this point where understanding despairs of bringing intuitions under adequate concepts that we are somehow made aware of a higher realm – a realm of 'suprasensible' ideas – which allows us the glimpse of a moral law (that of 'pure practical reason') transcending the confines of creaturely existence.[30]

So the Third *Critique* is the text where various lines of thought are taken up and developed more fully – redeemed, so to speak, like promissory notes that Kant had held over from his previous works on epistemology and ethics. Indeed, it is the text where his entire project comes under critical review, since everything depends upon Kant's being able to bring the various 'faculties' into some kind of overarching order, some system of complex yet harmonious interdependence. For it is not only in the ethical or 'suprasensible' sphere – that of practical reason – that Kant seeks to draw this suggestive analogy with aesthetic judgement in its twofold (beautiful and sublime) aspects. The analogy is also of crucial importance for his attempt to explain how our knowledge of the world (everyday or scientific knowledge) presupposes the existence of an order in nature which corresponds to the various forms or processes of human understanding and reflective inquiry. This is Kant's theme in the second part of the *Critique of Judgement*, the part where he discusses nature under its teleological aspect as a regulative idea – an Idea of Reason – in the absence of which such knowledge would be wholly unattainable. For there could then be no means of bridging the gulf between concepts and sensuous intuitions, or intuitions and the realm of natural (real-world) objects, processes and events to which those intuitions must be thought to correspond. In other words, there is a certain image of nature which is the condition of possibility for everything we can claim to know or understand concerning the natural sciences or indeed our most basic forms of perceptual and cognitive grasp.

Once again, commentators are deeply divided on the extent to which Kant is successful in carrying this argument through. In fact, one could argue that the two main traditions of modern Kant commentary, 'analytic' and 'continental', part company on just this question of whether the issues raised in his First *Critique* are in any way resolved – or need to be resolved – through a teleological doctrine of nature and the faculties of human judgement. Analytic philosophers mostly take the view that this whole aspect of Kant's thinking should best be passed over in tactful silence, or treated as merely an unfortunate lapse into the kind of speculative whimsy that has got post-Kantian 'continental' philosophy its well-deserved bad name. From the latter viewpoint, conversely, there are problems left outstanding in the First *Critique* – problems such as that gulf between concepts and phenomenal intuitions – which cannot be addressed except through the turn towards a more reflective, hermeneutic or aesthetically oriented approach.[31] Thus the difference works out, very often, as a 'continental' tendency to read Kant backwards, starting out from ideas developed in the *Critique of Judgement*, as opposed to a broadly 'analytic' stress on the primacy of Kant's epistemological concerns. The former line of argument is one that runs from Heidegger's *Kant and the Problem of Metaphysics* to Lyotard's reflections on the Kantian sublime as a mode of judgement that disrupts or disarticulates the entire 'system' of the faculties.[32] And one could also suggest – as does Pierre Bourdieu in his brilliant short study of Heidegger – that the division reaches back into treatments of the First *Critique*, with commentators tending to lay chief stress *either* on the relatively clear-cut arguments that Kant puts forward in the 'Transcendental Analytic', *or* on those problematic passages in the 'Transcendental Aesthetic' which in turn give a hold for Heideggerian reflections in the depth-hermeneutical manner.[33] At any rate, there are clearly some large issues bound up with this particular 'conflict of the faculties' as it takes shape among Kant's exegetes of differing philosophical persuasion.

III

Let me now return – not before time – to Derrida's deconstructive reading of Kant on the relation between philosophy and politics, or (more precisely) between the various faculties of 'pure' and 'applied' knowledge. As I have said, he offers various reasons to doubt that any such distinction could ever be firmly maintained, whether in Kant's time (when philosophers were subject, like everyone else, to numerous 'external' pressures and incentives) or, again, in the present-day university context (where this argument applies with yet greater force). Thus:

> Kant . . . wanted to make a line of demarcation pass between thinkers in the university and businessmen of knowledge or agents of government power, between the inside and the outside closest to the university enclosure. But this line, Kant certainly has to recognize, not only passes

along the border and around the institution. It traverses the faculties, and this is a place of conflict, of an unavoidable conflict.[34]

However this is *not* to say that we should give up altogether on the Kantian attempt to secure a space for philosophical reflection – for the free exercise of critical and speculative thought – secure from intrusions of executive power. What is notable about Derrida's reading of Kant is its focus on the notion of aesthetic 'disinterest', or on the 'free play' of the faculties that is supposedly the hallmark of aesthetic judgement when released from precisely those same pressures and incentives. For if this case can be argued convincingly – that is to say, if philosophy can establish its claim for the existence of just such a purely contemplative, disinterested state of mind – then the way is open to distinguish elsewhere (in the natural and the human sciences alike) between 'pure' and 'applied' branches of research, or inquiries pursued for their own sake 'within the limits of reason alone' and inquiries pursued with some practical end in view. Thus aesthetic 'disinterest' becomes the very touchstone of a critical philosophy – and a doctrine of the faculties – premised on the freedom to 'think for oneself' without regard to such extraneous motives.

The most relevant text here is Derrida's essay 'The Parergon', an extended reading of the Third *Critique* that raises exactly these questions concerning aesthetic judgement and its status vis-à-vis the other Kantian faculties.[35] What Derrida finds especially interesting – or symptomatic – is Kant's desire always to draw lines, to establish boundaries or lay down limits for their exercise in this or that context as defined by his overall system of priorities. (That 'Kant' in German is a common noun meaning 'edge', 'border' or 'dividing line' is a nice coincidence that Derrida duly notes without pushing the point too hard.) Thus understanding has its own special interest, namely that of bringing intuitions 'under' concepts, an interest that *must not* be confused with the interests of pure (speculative) reason on pain of producing insoluble aporias such as those laid out for inspection in the 'Transcendental Dialectic' of the First *Critique*.[36] Then again, there are the interests of practical reason – and of 'pure practical reason' especially – which require an autonomous (freely willed) choice to accept the dictates of moral law, and should therefore *on no account* suffer confusion with the interests of cognitive understanding. And so it goes on: one must always exercise the greatest care to distinguish concepts from ideas, constitutive from regulative rules, determinate from reflective judgements, judgements of taste ('disinterested' taste) from judgements admitting some taint of self-interest, some extraneous motivation, and so on. This last distinction is closely related to that between 'free' and 'adherent' beauty, the one appreciated solely in and for itself, the other at least to some degree in virtue of its function or fitness of design for the purpose in hand. Thus the attitude of pure, disinterested aesthetic

contemplation, called forth by some suitable object, is for Kant the very epitome of what transpires between mind and nature when the faculties achieve
that state of harmonious balance or perfected internal adjustment that his
system ultimately requires.

For Derrida, conversely, these various distinctions are all marked by a
chronic instability – or lack of conceptual rigour – which leaves them open
to a critical reading in the deconstructive mode. His title for this essay ('The
Parergon') refers to the Greek word for 'frame', that is to say, whatever sur-
rounds and sets off the artwork itself (the *ergon*), and which therefore should
not be considered properly a part of the work or in any way integral to it.
Thus – to take the most obvious or literal case – the frame of a painting is
something that can always be changed without altering the various essential
qualities (of balance, composition, formal structure, the internal play of light
and shade) which belong to that work and no other. And this applies even
more to external factors beyond or outside the frame, such as the wall on
which the painting is hung, the surrounding decor, other paintings in the
same room, the architectural features of the building wherein the exhibition
has been mounted, and so forth. Yet of course these factors *do* have an influence
on the way that the painting is perceived or appreciated, whatever Kant's
steadfast formalist refusal to accept that they *should* have any such influence.
Thus it can scarcely be denied that aesthetic considerations play some considerable part in deciding what kind of frame best serves to set off or enhance
the painting's qualities. A wrong choice of frame may spoil the overall effect
by distracting one's attention, obscuring certain salient details, or disturbing
the 'internal' sense of perspective. Moreover, it is impossible to draw a line
at this point and decree that whatever lies *outside* the frame – wall, decor,
surroundings and so on – can safely be excluded from the realm of aesthetic
judgement. For when the formalist citadel has once been breached by what
Derrida calls this 'logic of parergonality', then such distinctions can only be
a matter of stipulative warrant, rather than pertaining to the very nature of
aesthetic judgement or experience.

Derrida finds numerous examples in the Third *Critique* which show Kant
attempting to hold that line, the line that should properly fall between work
and frame, or again, between the framing concepts of aesthetic philosophy
and whatever should lie either definitely inside or definitely outside its
proper domain. In each case, the example proves somehow recalcitrant, or
fails to make the point as intended. Some of them are plainly problematic –
even slightly absurd – as for instance when Kant asks whether the robes or
draperies adorning a statue can be considered integral to its form, or when
he cites such architectural features as the flying buttress and decides that
they serve a mainly functional purpose, and should therefore be counted as
mere outworks (or *parerga*) devoid of genuine aesthetic value. But these
examples point to a deeper problem which extends beyond Kant's aesthetic

philosophy to the entire project of the three *Critiques*. For that project depends, as we have seen, on the making good of certain cardinal distinctions which are held over for their most elaborate treatment in those passages of the Third *Critique* where Kant seeks to justify his claim for the exercise of judgement in its strictly impartial, purely 'disinterested' mode. And this claim depends in turn on his ability to show – to deduce from first principles but also with the aid of convincing illustrative cases – that one can indeed distinguish 'free' from 'adherent' beauty, or disinterested judgements from those that admit some degree of 'extrinsic' motivation. However, Kant's argument breaks down on both counts: through the fact that his examples regularly fail to make the intended point, and through the *impossibility* of drawing that prescriptive line between aesthetic and other modalities of judgement.

For this is not just a matter of Kant's having spoiled an otherwise strong philosophical case by offering some inept or ill-chosen illustrations along the way. Rather, it is a question of his not being able to offer any argument in support of that case – any argument on philosophic grounds – that would respect the conditions (or remain within the boundaries) which Kant has laid down for judgements concerning the aesthetic. For it is a characterising feature of all such judgements, according to Kant, that they cannot involve the application of determinate *concepts*, that is to say, the kind of understanding that is properly achieved – as he argues in the First *Critique* – by bringing sensuous or phenomenal intuitions under adequate or corresponding concepts. If this were the case with aesthetic judgements then, quite simply, the aesthetic would cease to exist as a distinctive modality of experience, one that in some sense transcends and reconciles the other 'faculties' and their various potential conflicts of interest. What enables it to do so, as Kant seeks to show, is precisely the *lack* of any governing concept – any rule of judgement laid down, so to speak, in advance of particular applications – whereby one could establish fixed criteria in matters of aesthetic taste. On the contrary: such judgements are *indeterminate* in the sense that they always start out from the particular (that is, from some unique item of experience) and only then go in search of generalised criteria or principles whereby to justify their claim. Thus with judgements of the beautiful there is always room for disagreement – for differences of view concerning what should count as a good, excellent or paradigm example of the kind – even if those disagreements must at last be referred to the *sensus communis* of educated public taste or informed participant debate.

This is why the beautiful figures, for Kant, as an image of what should ideally be attainable in the ethical and sociopolitical spheres. It is a realm of intersubjective exchange where there exist certain widely shared criteria – of competence, good taste, expert opinion, 'disinterested' judgement and so forth – but where nobody can or should claim the right to silence opposing views by coming up with some argument-to-end-all-arguments, or some determinate *concept* that would finally establish what counts as a beautiful landscape, painting, symphony, poem or whatever. It is for this reason that Kant keeps judgements of the beautiful firmly on the side of our aesthetic responses – in the 'free play' that beauty evokes between the two faculties of imagination and understanding – rather than seeking to locate it in this or that objectively existent feature of the artwork or the natural world. And it is also why he makes such a point of insisting that determinate concepts have no place in our appreciation of nature or of art under their strictly aesthetic aspects. For the result of applying (or attempting to apply) such concepts would be to close off discussion at just that point where judgements of the beautiful extend by analogy to the conduct of debate in other spheres, among them that of 'pure practical reason', or ethical judgement in its highest, most purely 'disinterested' mode. Here also it is the case – according to Kant – that these judgements can only be distorted or compromised if they suffer some admixture of desire, self-interest or other such 'pathological' motives. Thus aesthetic 'disinterest' is a highly precarious state, threatened on the one hand by encroachments from the realm of determinate (conceptual) knowledge, and on the other by various intrusive interests – whether privately self-seeking or partisan-political – that would leave it with no proper sphere in which to operate. And the same applies to those fields of intellectual inquiry – like philosophy itself, as Kant describes it in 'The Conflict of the Faculties' – which can rightfully claim an unrestricted freedom of thought and speech just so long as they observe the limits laid down for the exercise of judgement in its purely disinterested, speculative mode.

IV

So it is not hard to see why Derrida focuses on the Third *Critique* as providing some crucial points of leverage (the Archimedean 'mochlos' metaphor again) for deconstructing Kant's doctrine of the faculties. That is to say, the idea of aesthetic 'disinterest' is one that bears a considerable burden of argument, and whose further implications extend to every aspect of Kant's philosophical endeavour. If there are problems in maintaining that idea – as indeed there are, on Derrida's showing – then those problems can scarcely be kept from affecting the entire associated Kantian system of terms, distinctions, faculty-limits, proper spheres of competence and so on. Thus, for instance, it is vital that aesthetic experience should not be confused with the philosophic discourse *on* or *of* aesthetics, since the latter necessarily employs certain *concepts* (most often binary pairs: form/content, intrinsic/extrinsic, 'free' *versus* 'adherent' beauty and so on) whose application involves determinate judgements, and can therefore by very definition play no role in aesthetic experience. For there would otherwise be nothing distinctive or especially valuable about aesthetic experience, that is to say, nothing that could set it apart from the various theories and ideas held about it by aestheticians, philosophers, literary critics, art-historians, sociologists of taste, and so forth. Moreover, this argument would apply even to a doctrinaire formalist such as Kant, one who wants to draw a categorical line between qualities intrinsic to the work itself – to its unique or essential form – and everything else that might somehow affect our judgement of it, whether 'ornamental' features of no aesthetic value or extraneous factors of the kind mostly instanced by historians or sociologists. For it is just as much a problem with the formalist approach that it cannot help but use a conceptual discourse – a discourse of determinate judgements – when staking these claims for the autonomy of art and the strictly *sui generis* character of aesthetic experience.

In short, as Derrida might put it, the condition of possibility for Kantian aesthetics is also its condition of *im*possibility. It is the strictly paradoxical requirement that philosophy should speak of art (or of nature under its aesthetic-contemplative aspect) in terms that achieve a sufficient degree of conceptual rigour and precision, while at the same time acknowledging the impertinence of such terms where aesthetic experience itself is concerned. For if one lets go of this cardinal distinction, then aesthetics becomes – as some would have it, sociologists like Bourdieu among them – a wholly pointless or a merely self-promoting endeavour, one that might just as well be abolished forthwith or absorbed into some other, more productive and disciplined field of inquiry.[37] (For Bourdieu, that field is the sociology of taste as a sub-branch of cultural studies; for others it is history, anthropology, psychology, linguistics, critical theory, literary criticism and so on.[38]) And it is not just the aestheticians who would find themselves suddenly out of a job if the distinctive nature of aesthetic experience were subject to any such conceptual definition, their own favoured sorts included. For there would then be all manner of perfectly adequate substitutes for that experience, as for instance by reading a detailed catalogue-description rather than looking at a picture, or following a Schenker-type thematic depth-analysis rather than listening to a symphony, or perusing the various critics and commentators on *Hamlet* rather than reading the play or attending a performance. Then again: one might conclude that a thorough knowledge – a good conceptual grasp – of the issues raised in Kant's Third *Critique* and other such works was enough to offset a very limited acquaintance with art, music or literature.

Aesthetic 'disinterest' is thus the key idea on which Kant bases his claims for the autonomy of art and for the qualitative difference, as he sees it, between aesthetic experience and the various concepts that philosophers may use in their efforts to define or categorise that experience. It is also a crucial resource, by analogy, for his thinking about issues in ethics, politics and the structure of the modern (enlightened) university. This latter he conceives as a sphere wherein the various 'faculties' each have their own appointed domain, and where philosophy occupies a privileged place – most closely analogous to that of pure practical reason – such that its freedom to pronounce on 'theoretical' matters is guaranteed by its self-denying ordinance in matters of executive authority and power. Thus, if Kant is unable to make good his claims for the disinterested character of aesthetic judgement, then that failure can be seen to have large and highly damaging implications for his entire doctrine of the faculties. And this is precisely Derrida's point: that despite all his efforts to delimit the sphere of the aesthetic – to set it off from purposive interests on the one hand, and from determinate concepts on the other – Kant rather demonstrates the *impossibility* (the absolute and principled impossibility) of sustaining any such argument.

It is not just a matter of Kant's coming up with a range of ill-chosen examples (draperies on statues, flying buttresses, load-supporting pillars and the like) which are meant to uphold the formalist dichotomy of 'intrinsic' *versus* 'extrinsic' features, but which in fact render that distinction untenable. Nor is it simply on account of Kant's aversion to the sensuous qualities in art, whether colour and texture in painting, metaphor and imagery in poems, or just about everything in music that belongs to the 'intensive manifold' of sensations, as opposed to its formal or structural features. No doubt this bias can be explained up to a point by Kant's pietist distrust of the senses, his limited range of aesthetic appreciation, and – in particular – his idea of music as the lowest of the arts on account of its strong sensuous-emotional appeal and its supposed lack of intellectual content. But of course this raises a further problem with regard to Kant's insistence that aesthetic judgements should *not* be confused with determinate judgements, or subject to the same standards that apply in the realm of conceptual understanding. For if Kant has any principled (as distinct from merely personal) reason for preferring literature and the visual arts over music, it must be his belief that music is the art-form least amenable to treatment in precisely those terms, that is, as pointing beyond the merely sensuous to a higher realm of articulate meanings or significant forms. But in that case one might just as well argue (with Schopenhauer and Nietzsche) that music is the highest of the arts *precisely on account* of its resisting translation into any such conceptual terms. Moreover, this claim could be seen as following – ironically enough – from Kant's own emphasis on the non-conceptual character of aesthetic experience. Against this, it might in turn be argued (as by Mark DeBellis in his recent study *Music and Conceptualization*) that there is no good reason, aesthetic prejudice aside, for holding our experience of music to transpire in a realm quite apart from the various descriptive or analytic concepts that we may bring to bear *in the very act or process* of educated musical response. Thus:

> a trained listener, when asked to describe what she hears, is apt to respond – spontaneously, and without much ratiocination – in a way

that employs theoretical terminology: she hears a piece under a certain music-theoretic description and will give that description in describing what she hears. There is simply no principled basis on which to say that trained listeners do not hear chords as tonics and dominants in as full-blooded a sense as that in which ordinary perceivers see tables and chairs.[39]

This passage indicates a central problem with Kantian aesthetics, namely its self-contradictory commitment to a theory of judgement that finds no place for conceptual understanding in our experience of art, but which nonetheless deploys a whole battery of elaborated concepts in order to propound that same theory.

The point can be made more simply by asking: why should it not be the case that our knowledge of a work such as the Third *Critique* may decisively affect our experience of artworks or of nature as an object of aesthetic contemplation? Then again: by what right (the classic Kantian *quid juris* question) does Kant lay it down that aesthetic experience *must* be held distinct from any concepts gained through the reading of philosophical, theoretical or other such (presumptively) non-aesthetic works? For it can scarcely be denied that the concepts we bring to such experience – concepts like that of aesthetic 'disinterest' or of the beautiful as theorised by Kant, among others – *can and do* very often have a marked influence on our aesthetic responses and judgements. Thus, for instance, a knowledge of Kant's views might very well affect the way that we respond to such works as Picasso's 'Guernica', or Orwell's *Animal Farm*, or the final movement of Beethoven's Ninth Symphony, or Britten's *War Requiem*. These are all works that, in Keats's phrase, have a 'palpable design' on the viewer/reader/listener, a didactic intent – to convince or persuade – which cannot easily be reconciled with the Kantian doctrine of aesthetic disinterest.

Now we might wish to say that Kant was wrong and that there is just no reason why we should appreciate these works any the less for their carrying a strong political or moral charge. Or again, we might take a more conciliatory line by adopting what amounts to a double-aspect theory, one that allows us to switch at will between a 'properly' aesthetic attitude and a mode of response more attuned to their suasive purpose. On this view, we could have some sympathy with Orwell in his complaint that the reviewers of *Animal Farm* all latched onto its topical uses as a piece of Cold War propaganda and ignored its literary merits as a piece of carefully crafted allegorical fiction. At any rate, there would then be no problem with the Picasso and Beethoven examples since our aesthetic valuation would in no way depend on our judgement of events during the Spanish Civil War, or our present-day (affirmative or negative) response to Beethoven's outlook of Promethean humanism. Still, there is a sense in which all these responses *cannot but* be

affected by our knowledge of the issues raised in Kant's Third *Critique*. And
to that extent, it must be the case – *contra* Kant – that conceptual understanding is intimately involved with aesthetic experience and judgement. For
clearly, such notions as 'disinterest' or formal 'autonomy' are notions that
gain whatever pertinence they have from our ability to grasp and apply them
in accord with certain well-defined conceptual criteria.

It is at just this point – the point of conflict between Kant's aesthetic
principles and their governing logic – that Derrida locates all the problems
and aporias that emerge from a deconstructive reading of the Third *Critique*.
They are not the kinds of problem that could be cleared up by adopting one
or other of the above 'solutions', that is, by simply endorsing Kant's aesthetic
philosophy, by rejecting that philosophy outright, or by adopting what I have
called the double-aspect theory and switching criteria as and when required.
Least of all can they be made to disappear – shown up as merely illusory – if
one espouses a 'strong'-sociological outlook according to which they are just
the sorts of problem that result from the invention of pseudo-disciplines
such as philosophical aesthetics. Now this is an important point to grasp
about Derrida's work in general and, more specifically, his writings on Kant.
To be sure, those texts go a long way towards deconstructing Kant's doctrine
of the faculties and showing the entire system to depend upon a series of value-
laden terms and distinctions whose status is constantly called into question,
or whose logic turns out to be everywhere subject to a countervailing logic of
'parergonality', a logic of logical anomalies. And it is precisely the borderline
cases that cause all this trouble, whether artworks (or details of works) that
cannot be firmly located either 'inside' or 'outside' the aesthetic frame of
reference, or reflective judgements that are not conceptually determinate yet
require an appeal to determinate concepts, or, again, that mode (concept?) of
aesthetic experience for which Kant offers the oxymoronic phrase 'purpose-
less purposiveness'. All these are examples of the 'logic of parergonality' that
Derrida finds perpetually at work in Kant's Third *Critique*, and whose
effects are most pronounced whenever it is a question of placing a frame – a
conceptual frame – around that which cannot (or should not) be subject to
conceptual definition. But he is also, as I have said, very far from adopting a
pragmatic line of least resistance that would claim to solve these problems at
a stroke by treating them as mere relics of that old philosophical 'discourse'
of modernity which specialised in producing such pseudo-dilemmas. For
Derrida is no less insistent than Kant that these are real issues, that they have
a wider bearing beyond the 'strictly' aesthetic domain, and that they need to
be thought through with the utmost care and precision.

V

This claim is borne out, albeit in negative fashion, by the fact that a strong sociologist like Bourdieu devotes a long appendix (in his book *Distinction: A Critique of Taste*) to attacking Derrida's essay on Kant.[40] Bourdieu's chief complaint – academic turf-wars apart – is that Derrida perpetuates the elitist discourse of aesthetic 'values' and 'taste' by adopting a philosophical rather than a cultural or social-diagnostic approach. He is right, it seems to me, about Derrida's refusal to yield up aesthetics (and the rest of philosophy along with it) to a generalised sociology of culture – or a theory of 'cultural capital' – which levels not only dubious distinctions of 'taste' but also genuine differences of scope, interest, method and competence between the disciplines. However, he is wrong in attributing this to an 'elitist' desire, on Derrida's part, to uphold the various structures of privilege and power that are partly maintained through the unequal distribution of cultural and intellectual capital. For it is here that Derrida – like Adorno before him, in an essay on Karl Mannheim – holds out against the strong-sociological drive to reduce every discipline of thought (philosophy included) to a reflex product of vested interests or hegemonic sociocultural values.[41]

For Adorno, this entails a practice of 'negative-dialectical' thought which rejects any version of Hegel's appeal to a false (because premature) reconciliation between subject and object, mind and nature, concept and intuition, or things as they are and things as they might be in some different – radically transformed – order of social existence.[42] Hence his resolute critique of 'identity-thinking', the idea – prevalent among epistemologists from Kant to Husserl – that particulars (as given through sensuous intuition) can be somehow 'brought under' adequate concepts without resistance or remainder.[43] On the contrary: it is only through a vigilant awareness of the non-identity, the gap that opens up (so to speak) between these orders of thought and cognition, that dialectics can find some purchase for resisting the pressures of commodified mass-culture and ideological control. Now Adorno has sometimes been claimed as a 'postmodern' thinker, and up to a point the description is apt enough.[44] After all, it is a constant theme in his writing – and one that sets him apart from second-generation Frankfurt theorists like Habermas – that the Enlightenment project has so far miscarried from its original aims and values that it is now complicit with the drive towards total domination of the lifeworld through the forces of instrumental reason. However, this is a grossly one-sided characterisation, as will soon become apparent to anyone who reads Adorno's texts with adequate care and attention. For his thinking could scarcely be more opposed to that strain of facile postmodernist talk which blithely announces an end to Enlightenment and its associated values of truth, reason and critique. To be sure, Adorno questions those values and subjects them to relentless (even ruthless) criticism in the negative-dialectical mode. To some present-day defenders of Enlightenment thought – Habermas among them – this has seemed a gesture of outright rejection and betrayal.[45] Yet Adorno wrote always with an aim to redeem the 'unfinished project' of modernity by testing its limits, locating its blind spots of prejudice, and insisting that the project live up to its own highest standards of critical thought.

There is a similar misconstrual of Derrida's work which takes deconstruction to be merely a 'destructive' or a nihilist project, one that sets out to dismantle the entire structure of (so-called) 'western metaphysics' while having no useful alternative project to set in its place. This idea goes along with the notion of Derrida as a counter-Enlightenment or postmodern thinker whose intent is to deconstruct (for which read: subvert from within and destroy altogether) such presumptively obsolete values as truth, reason and critique. However, as I have said, it is a false and prejudicial reading which ignores the many passages – especially in his essays on Kant – where Derrida affirms the need to keep faith with Enlightenment thought precisely by taking nothing on trust, its own more doctrinaire values and assumptions included.[46] Thus philosophy plays and should continue to play a decisive critical role. It is possible – indeed, it is a prime moral and intellectual imperative – not to accept the necessity of compromise, at least the sorts of compromise typically endorsed by postmodernist thinkers who equate truth with what is currently good (or 'performatively' valid) in the way of consensus belief.[47] Philosophy, Kant says, occupies the left bench in the parliament of the faculties, the left bench having been – since the French Revolution when this custom was established – the locus of dissent, the seat of opposition, the place from which criticism comes. Of course this is not (or not simply) a party-political distinction as between right and left, conservative and socialist, 'republican' and 'democrat', or whatever. Rather, it has to do with Kant's idea of philosophy as a voice that is raised on behalf of no particular group interest or political faction, a voice of critical reason unbeholden to established structures of authority and power. Thus, according to Kant, 'in as free a system of government as must exist where truth is at issue, there must also be an opposition party (the left side), and that bench belongs to the philosophy faculty, for without its rigorous examinations and objections, the government would not be adequately informed'.[48] If we think of the Kantian system as Deleuze describes it, that is, as a system of constantly 'rotating chairmanship', then this role would be occupied in turn by those faculties with least direct involvement in the exercise of power, faculties such as pure practical reason and disinterested judgement of the kind aptly figured in aesthetic estimations of the beautiful.[49]

As we have seen, Derrida doubts very strongly whether any such line can be drawn between intra- and extra-philosophical interests, or between (on the one hand) disciplines concerned purely with the pursuit of truth 'for its own sake' and (on the other) disciplines that respond to 'outside' pressures and incentives. However, he is equally far from thinking that we should just let go of that Kantian distinction and embrace the current postmodernist wisdom according to which such talk is another kind of 'performative' rhetoric, one that adopts a high moral tone (a fine-sounding language of principle, 'disinterest', and so on) as a cover for its own self-interested motives. For the left bench is the side from which criticism comes and should at least strive for some degree of autonomy, of non-compliance with the dictates of instrumental reason or executive power. After all, as Derrida describes it (paraphrasing Kant), '[t]he concept of *universitas* is more than the philosophical concept of a research and teaching institution; it is the concept of philosophy itself, and is Reason, or rather the principle of reason *as an institution*'.[50] So Derrida is sceptical up to a point with regard to Kant's claims for the role of philosophy as an arbiter of truth and justice in the so-called 'parliament' of the faculties. But he does not lean over from scepticism into downright cynicism, as may be said of postmodernists like Lyotard for whom this idea of critical disinterest (or reflective detachment from power-seeking drives and interests) must be seen as just a relic of old-style 'Enlightenment' thought.[51] On this view, everything has to do with the interests of power, with the extent to which so-called 'critical' intellectuals (philosophers, sociologists, workers in the human and the natural sciences) plug themselves into various power networks, various ways of extending or enhancing their 'performative' capacity to make things happen, to convince other people, or to win the most lucrative research grants. As I have said, Derrida accepts all this as a simply undeniable real-world aspect of the situation in which many intellectuals – philosophers included – find themselves now. Moreover, it is the same sort of situation that they have always had to cope with, as can be seen very clearly from Kant's compromise 'solution' in 'The Conflict of the Faculties'. Nevertheless – and this is where Derrida differs most sharply with Lyotard – one can take due account of these obstacles to the exercise of 'free', 'disinterested' critical thought while still seeking *so far as possible* to keep a space open for it.

Of course, that space cannot be confined to the Philosophy Department of the modern (post-Kantian) university, or the humanities faculty, or those branches of the 'pure' sciences (like mathematics and theoretical physics) that are supposedly least subject to pressures from the commercial, the military-industrial, or the political-executive centres of power. On the one hand, this ignores the extent to which even those disciplines have to compete for funding, to prove their utility and establish their cost-effectiveness, their 'relevance' in terms of deferred benefits, job-market indicators and so forth. On the other, it implies a serene indifference, on the part of comfortably tenured 'critical' intellectuals, towards whatever goes on in the world outside the Philosophy seminar room or the institute for advanced scientific research. Hence the various boundary disputes – the conflicts of interest, internal and external – that arise as soon as one attempts to demarcate the various zones of disciplinary competence. These conflicts arise from what Derrida calls the

'paradoxical structure' of any limits imposed *either* on the exercise of speculative, truth-seeking thought *or* on the wielders of executive power – those
outside the university – insofar as they seek to curtail academic freedom by
dictating programmes of 'pure' as well as 'applied' research. After all, as Kant
is obliged to concede, that freedom depends upon a certain charter (written
or unwritten) whose guarantor is precisely the state or some other state-
sanctioned authority. Thus the modern university may indeed be founded
on a Kantian idea of Reason, more precisely an idea of Pure Practical
Reason, that is, the *de jure* postulate of freedom in matters of moral and intellectual conscience. However, this status is ultimately granted 'by virtue of a
de facto political authority', one that is 'supposed in principle to let itself be
guided by reason', but whose power to accord (or withhold) that privilege
rests with the executive branch.

I must here quote at some length so as to bring out the kind of supplementary (or 'parergonal') logic that Derrida perceives constantly at work in
Kant's doctrine of the faculties.

> Though destined to separate power from knowledge and action from
> truth, they distinguish sets that are each time somehow in excess of
> themselves, covering each time the whole of which they should figure only
> as a part or a sub-set. And so the whole forms an *invaginated pocket*
> on the inside of every part or sub-set. We recognised the difficulty of
> distinguishing the inside from the outside of the university, and then,
> on the inside, of distinguishing between the two classes of faculties. We
> are not done, however, with this intestine division and its folding parti-
> tion on the inside of each space. The philosophy faculty is further
> divided into two 'departments': the *historical* sciences (history, geography,
> linguistics, humanities, etc.) and the *purely rational* sciences (pure
> mathematics, pure philosophy, the metaphysics of nature and morals);
> pure philosophy, on the inside of the so-called philosophy faculty, is
> therefore still just a part of the whole whose idea it nonetheless safe-
> guards. But insofar as it is *historical*, it also covers the domain of the
> higher faculties . . . Due to this double overflowing, conflicts are
> inevitable. And they must also reappear inside each faculty, since the
> faculty of philosophy is itself divisible.[52]

Of course Kant is speaking of 'philosophy' in a much wider (more 'interdisciplinary') sense than one expects to find in present-day usage. However, it
is precisely Derrida's point that any attempt to restrict or delimit the scope
of what counts as philosophical inquiry will always run up against just those
problems that Kant confronts in his effort to confine such inquiry 'within the
limits of reason alone'. That is to say, there is a properly philosophical aspect

of any academic discipline (whether in the natural sciences, in mathematics, anthropology, jurisprudence, history, sociology, linguistics or literary theory) where issues are raised concerning the truth or validity of certain governing precepts. 'Philosophy' in this sense is the name for that discipline of thought which has no proper disciplinary home but which represents the interest of reason – of pure practical reason – as a conscientious arbiter of justice and truth. However, that interest is always tied up with various motivating pressures that come from outside the university precinct – or the sphere of pure practical reason – and which need to be taken into account by any critical discourse on the faculties, their scope and limits. Thus 'there may be no possible inside to the university, and no internal coherence to its concept'.[53] And again, in more practical terms: 'there can be very serious competition and border-conflicts between non-university centres of research and university faculties claiming at once to be doing research and transmitting knowledge, to be producing and reproducing knowledge'.[54]

So it is impossible nowadays – more so perhaps than in Kant's time – for the 'pure' disciplines (philosophy among them) to maintain their preferred self-image as a haven of disinterested truth-seeking thought. To uphold this ideal in its classical (Kantian) form would be the kind of illusion that Kant himself pinpoints in the First *Critique* when he imagines the metaphoric dove of pure reason thinking to soar high and free by escaping altogether from the earth's atmosphere. 'Is it not nowadays', Derrida rhetorically asks, 'for reasons involving the structure of knowledge, especially impossible to distinguish rigorously between scholars and technicians of science, just as it is to trace, between knowledge and power, the limit within whose shelter Kant sought to preserve the university structure?'[55] However, there is another side to this question, one that turns it around so as to ask *by what right* philosophy should be prevented from raising issues of truth and justice with regard to those applied disciplines (or those extramural interests) that threaten to encroach on its own domain. After all,

> [t]he university is there *to tell the truth*, to judge and to criticize in the most rigorous sense of the term, namely to discern and decide between the true and the false; and when it is also entitled to decide between the just and the unjust, the moral and the immoral, this is insofar as reason and freedom of judgement are implicated there as well.[56]

In short, it is idle to maintain the idea of Philosophy as a locus of free thought *within* the university system unless it is also assumed to reach out *beyond* the university, to engage with just those conflicts of interest that exist in the wider sociopolitical or public-administrative sphere. For otherwise there could be no point of contact, no critical purchase (so to speak) between the exercise of reason in its 'pure speculative' or ideally 'disinterested' mode and the kinds of issue that should properly concern intellectuals in their 'public' role as thinkers committed to furthering the interests of truth and justice.

Hence (to repeat) Derrida's idea of philosophy as a *mochlos*, a lever, a critical discourse that occupies the left bench in the parliament of faculties and which uses that position to exert a force outside and beyond its apparently very limited sphere. More straightforwardly: we have to be aware of the extent to which every academic discipline is compromised by 'outside' interests, by its sources of funding (direct or indirect), its relationship with other disciplines, or its possible long-term application in fields far beyond its original research domain. After all, Kant himself 'is in the process of justifying, in terms of reason, what was a de facto organization determined by the government of his day, as if by accident its king [i.e., Friedrich Wilhelm, who had expressed grave displeasure at certain of Kant's writings] were a philosopher'.[57] This is all the more the case nowadays when there exist so many complex relays of power or forms of indirect leverage, whether those exerted from outside the university or between its various component disciplines. Yet we still need to preserve a margin of freedom, a space where thinking can make good its claim to examine, to criticise and (if need be) to raise a dissenting voice without the threat of censorship by those who wield executive power.

This is why Derrida goes such a long and complicated way around in deconstructing Kant's doctrine or system of the faculties. His purpose is *not* to level the difference between (say) philosophy and literary criticism, or jurisprudence and speech-act theory, or sociology and narrative poetics, or again – pushing this argument all the way – between the human and social sciences on the one hand and the natural sciences on the other.[58] Each of these claims has its present-day advocate(s), often citing Derrida's texts by way of notional support. Richard Rorty is perhaps the best-known exponent of the view that deconstruction is most usefully employed in debunking our idea of the various disciplines as somehow corresponding to real differences of method, approach, subject-matter or knowledge-constitutive interest. Thus philosophy becomes, for Rorty, just another 'kind of writing' whose value is measured – as with other kinds of writing like poetry, fiction, literary criticism, ethnography, molecular biology or nuclear physics – by its capacity to yield striking new metaphors or bold (strong-revisionist) accounts of its own history to date.[59]

However, this is not at all Derrida's intention in drawing out the complex structures of relationship and interdependence that cut across Kant's already quite complicated ground-plan of the various faculty divisions. No doubt we need to recognise that the plan is incomplete or under-detailed; that there exist all manner of labyrinthine passages or short-cut routes between and within the different buildings. And the same applies to Kant's doctrine of the 'faculties' in its other, more familiar guise: to the system of self-regulating checks and limits whose function it is to prevent any conflict of interests between cognitive understanding and practical reason, or judgement in its twofold (determinate and reflective) modes. Here again there is no question – for Derrida any more than for Lyotard – of upholding this doctrine in anything like its original Kantian aprioristic form. But there is also no question, for Derrida, of taking the postmodern line of least resistance and hence denying the very possibility that reason might exert some critical leverage – some effective counter-pressure – against the weight of consensus thinking, of conformist ideology, or of vested interests within or outside the university. For if the various divisions, internal and external, are a deal more complex than Kant allows, still it is the case – for Derrida as for Kant – that the modern 'enlightened' university (like the modern 'enlightened' polity) stands or falls on its willingness to tolerate dissenting or critical views.

NOTES

1. Jürgen Habermas, *The Philosophical Discourse of Modernity: Twelve Lectures*, trans. Frederick Lawrence (Cambridge: Polity Press, 1987).
2. Richard Rorty, 'Philosophy as a Kind of Writing: An Essay on Derrida', in *Consequences of Pragmatism* (Brighton: Harvester Press, 1982), pp. 89–109. See also Christopher Norris, 'Philosophy as *Not* Just a "Kind of Writing": Derrida and the Claim of Reason', and Rorty, 'Two Meanings of "Logocentrism": A Reply to Norris', both in Reed Way Dasenbrock (ed.), *Re-Drawing the Lines: Analytic Philosophy, Deconstruction, and Literary Theory* (Minneapolis: University of Minnesota Press, 1989), pp. 189–203 and 204–16.
3. Rorty, 'Philosophy as a Kind of Writing', op. cit. See also his essays 'Deconstruction and Circumvention', *Critical Inquiry*, 11 (1984), 1–23, and 'Is Derrida a Transcendental Philosopher?', in David Wood (ed.), *Derrida: A Critical Reader* (Oxford: Blackwell, 1992), pp. 235–46.
4. Rodolphe Gasché, *The Tain of the Mirror: Derrida and the Philosophy of Reflection* (Cambridge, MA: Harvard University Press, 1986).
5. See Habermas, 'On Levelling the Genre Distinction Between Philosophy and Literature', in *The Philosophical Discourse of Modernity*, op. cit., pp. 185–210.
6. See Jacques Derrida, 'Signature Event Context', and John R. Searle, 'Reiterating the Differences', both in *Glyph*, 1 (Baltimore: Johns Hopkins University Press, 1977), 172–97 and 198–208; also Derrida, 'Limited Inc a b c', in *Glyph*, 2 (1977), 162–254.
7. Michael Dummett, *The Origins of Analytic Philosophy* (London: Duckworth, 1993).
8. Jacques Derrida, 'Afterword: Towards an Ethics of Conversation', in *Limited Inc* (Evanston, IL: Northwestern University Press, 1989), pp. 111–60.
9. Habermas, *The Philosophical Discourse of Modernity*, op. cit.
10. Rorty, *Consequences of Pragmatism*, op. cit.; also *Objectivity, Relativism, and Truth* and *Essays on Heidegger and Others* (both Cambridge: Cambridge University Press, 1991).

11. Searle, 'Reiterating the Differences', op. cit.; also 'Literary Theory and its Discontents', *New Literary History*, 25:3 (1994), 637–67, and 'The World Turned Upside Down', *New York Review of Books*, 30:16 (27 October 1983), 74–9.

12. See Norris, *Derrida* (London: Fontana, 1987); *Truth and the Ethics of Criticism* (Manchester: Manchester University Press, 1994); *Reclaiming Truth: Contribution to a Critique of Cultural Relativism* (London: Lawrence & Wishart, 1996); *Against Relativism: Philosophy of Science, Deconstruction and Critical Theory* (Oxford: Blackwell, 1997).

13. See especially the texts brought together in Derrida, *Du droit à la philosophie* (Paris: Galilée, 1990); also *Institutions of Reason*, ed. Deborah Esch and Thomas Keenan (Minneapolis: University of Minneapolis Press, 1992); 'Economimesis', *Diacritics*, 11:2 (Summer 1981), 3–25; 'The Principle of Reason: The University in the Eyes of its Pupils', trans. Catherine Porter and Edward P. Morris, *Diacritics*, 13:3 (Fall 1983), 3–20; 'Parergon', in *The Truth in Painting*, trans. Geoff Bennington and Ian McLeod (Chicago: University of Chicago Press, 1987), pp. 15–147; 'Mochlos: or, The Conflict of the Faculties', in Richard Rand (ed.), *Logomachia* (Lincoln, NB: University of Nebraska Press, 1992), pp. 1–34.

14. Derrida, 'Mochlos', op. cit.

15. Gilles Deleuze, *Kant's Critical Philosophy: The Doctrine of the Faculties*, trans. Hugh Tomlinson and Barbara Habberjam (London: Athlone Press, 1984).

16. Immanuel Kant, *The Conflict of the Faculties*, trans. Mary J. Gregor (New York: Abaris Books, 1979).

17. Derrida, 'Mochlos', op. cit., p. 24.

18. Ibid., pp. 25–6.

19. For some relevant historico-philosophical detail, see Frederick C. Beiser, *The Fate of Reason: German Philosophy from Kant to Fichte* (Cambridge, MA: Harvard University Press, 1987).

20. Kant, *Religion Within the Limits of Reason Alone*, trans. Theodore M. Greene and Hoyt H. Hudson (Chicago: Open Court, 1934).

21. See Derrida, 'The Principle of Reason', op. cit., and 'No Apocalypse, Not Now: Seven Missiles, Seven Missives', *Diacritics*, 20 (1984), 20–31.

22. J. L. Austin, *How to Do Things With Words* (London: Oxford University Press, 1963).

23. See n. 6 above.

24. See for instance Stanley Cavell, *A Pitch of Philosophy: Autobiographical Exercises* (Cambridge, MA: Harvard University Press, 1994); Jonathan Culler, 'Convention and Meaning: Derrida and Austin', *New Literary History*, 13 (1981), 15–30; Shoshana Felman, *The Literary Speech-Act: Don Juan with J. L. Austin, or Seduction in Two Languages*, trans. Catherine Porter (Ithaca, NY: Cornell University Press, 1983); Stanley Fish, 'With the Compliments of the Author: Reflections on Austin and Derrida', *Critical Inquiry*, 8 (1982), 693–72.

25. Derrida, 'Mochlos', op. cit., p. 18.

26. Ibid., pp. 19–20.

27. See especially Kant, 'What Is Enlightenment?', and other texts collected in Lewis W. Beck (ed.), *Kant: On History* (Indianapolis: Bobbs-Merrill, 1963); also Kant, *Political Writings*, ed. Hans Reiss (Cambridge: Cambridge University Press, 1976).

28. Kant, *Critique of Pure Reason*, trans. Norman Kemp Smith (London: Macmillan, 1964).
29. Kant, *Critique of Practical Reason*, trans. Lewis W. Beck (Indianapolis: Bobbs-Merrill, 1977).
30. Kant, *Critique of Judgement*, trans. J. C. Meredith (Oxford: Clarendon Press, 1978).
31. For a useful conspectus of these differing approaches, see Paul Guyer (ed.), *The Cambridge Companion to Kant* (Cambridge: Cambridge University Press, 1992).
32. Martin Heidegger, *Kant and the Problem of Metaphysics*, trans. James S. Churchill (Bloomington, IN: Indiana University Press, 1982); Jean-François Lyotard, *Lessons on the Analytic of the Sublime*, trans. Elizabeth Rottenberg (Stanford, CA: Stanford University Press, 1994).
33. Pierre Bourdieu, *The Political Ontology of Martin Heidegger*, trans. Peter Collier (Oxford: Polity Press, 1991).
34. Derrida, 'Mochlos', op. cit., p. 23.
35. See n. 13 above.
36. Kant, 'Transcendental Dialectic', in *Critique of Pure Reason*, op. cit., pp. 297–484.
37. Pierre Bourdieu, *Distinction: A Social Critique of the Judgement of Taste*, trans. R. Nice (Cambridge, MA: Harvard University Press, 1984).
38. See also Bourdieu, *Language and Symbolic Power*, ed. John B. Thompson, trans. Gino Raymond and Matthew Adamson (Cambridge: Polity Press, 1991).
39. Mark A. DeBellis, *Music and Conceptualization* (Cambridge: Cambridge University Press, 1995), p. 94.
40. See n. 37 above.
41. Theodor W. Adorno, *Prisms*, trans. Samuel and Shierry Weber (Cambridge, MA: MIT Press, 1981).
42. See especially Adorno, *Negative Dialectics*, trans. E. B. Ashton (London: Routledge & Kegan Paul, 1973).
43. Adorno, *Against Epistemology: A Metacritique*, trans. Willis Domingo (Oxford: Blackwell, 1982).
44. For the most perceptive and interesting version of this argument – albeit hedged about with numerous qualifications – see Fredric Jameson, *Late Marxism: Adorno, or the Persistence of the Dialectic* (London: Verso, 1990).
45. See Habermas, *The Philosophical Discourse of Modernity*, op. cit.
46. See entries under n. 13 above.
47. See Rorty, *Consequences of Pragmatism*, op. cit.; also *Contingency, Irony, and Solidarity* (Cambridge: Cambridge University Press, 1989).
48. Cited by Derrida, 'Mochlos', op. cit., p. 28.
49. Deleuze, *Kant's Critical Philosophy*, op. cit.
50. Derrida, 'Mochlos', op. cit., p. 26.
51. See especially Lyotard, *The Postmodern Condition: A Report on Knowledge*, trans. Geoff Bennington and Brian Massumi (Manchester: Manchester University Press, 1984).
52. Derrida, 'Mochlos', op. cit., pp. 26–7.
53. Ibid., p. 12.
54. Ibid., p. 14.

55. Ibid., p. 16.
56. Ibid., p. 17.
57. Ibid., p. 5.
58. See especially Rorty, *Objectivity, Relativism, and Truth*, op. cit.
59. Rorty, 'Philosophy as a Kind of Writing', op. cit.

Chapter Three

POST-GENDER: JURASSIC FEMINISM MEETS QUEER POLITICS

Patricia Duncker

I was brought up on slogans: slogans shouted in the streets, recreated on badges, painted on walls, political slogans of the radical left and feminist slogans. These varied from the obvious 1960s vintage versions: BLACK IS BEAUTIFUL, SOCIALISM OR DEATH and END THE VIETNAM WAR to the slogans of our sexual revolution: ANY WOMAN CAN BE A LESBIAN and I'M GAY, KISS ME GIRLS. The value of slogans is not obvious, but I want to defend their potency and their function within our historical memory. They are condensed, 'in-your-face' statements. They are uncompromising, unnuanced, bald, provocative, aggressive. For us they were often political affirmations not only of identity, but also of evil intentions. Above all, they represented certainties, the certainties of what I now think of as jurassic feminism. We know what we want and we want it now. Certainty is an aspect of political Utopianism.

Well, now we live in a time without certainties. A time when all identities and subjectivities are suspect, unstable. It is no longer clear what a lesbian is, let alone who is one. And the category woman has long since been dissolved into a splintered mass of possibilities. *'One is not born, but becomes a woman.'* Adding a gloss to de Beauvoir's famous statement, I would say that all women are not born straight, but have the experience of being socially constructed as heterosexual. Femininity is socially constructed to mean heterosexual femininity. And the possibility inherent in de Beauvoir's comment is that if we are not born women, but become women, then, either by hazard or by choice, we could become something else. Something other than, better than, different from woman, the subject sex, the second sex. We could become monsters, aliens, freaks, perverts, dykes. If we define ourselves in any sense as feminists, then we are in opposition to what the word *woman* has always been held to mean. Post-feminism may not be here yet, but in order to be a feminist in the first place you certainly had to be post-woman.

51

Monique Wittig represents a current of French feminist thought that has effectively been erased in the Anglo-American concentration on the work of the Holy Trinity, Kristeva, Irigaray and Cixous. It is no coincidence that the high theory produced by this triad can easily be assimilated into a postmodern politics of fragmented subjectivities in which all political categories, such as woman, lesbian and Black, are suspect, self-indulgent, essentialist. Wittig is a materialist as well as a radical feminist. For her, women and men are social categories; gender difference is a sex-class difference. If we regard gender divisions as a result of social, political and above all economic structures, then the so-called natural differences upon which the entire institution of heterosexuality is based collapse. This is Stevi Jackson's point: 'Patriarchal domination is not based upon pre-existing sex differences, rather gender exists as a social division because of patriarchal domination'.[1] We should not then be too preoccupied with trying to transform the prison of gender, but with planning an escape. Here is Wittig's suggestion: *'Les lesbiennes ne sont pas les femmes'*.[2] In German, this reads as: 'Lesben sind nicht Frauen'. Interestingly, although the ambiguity of this translates into German, it does not translate into English. 'Femme' in French means both 'woman' and 'wife', just as 'Frau' does in German. In English we have two words. Wittig's pun calls attention to the overlap in the straight mind between woman and heterosexual woman. Lesbian is the emergency exit from the category woman. But Wittig's position, seductive as it is, is a betrayal of that old radical slogan: ANY WOMAN CAN BE A LESBIAN, with its suggestion of ability, power and of becoming: ANY WOMAN CAN. Lesbian represents the decision to cease being a woman altogether, rather than becoming post-woman. And the definition of lesbian which evolved within lesbian feminism actually excluded many women who had always thought they were lesbians and who had loved other women all their lives.

We all used to believe, in those days of radical, transforming certainties, that the decision to become something else was boiling in every woman. Radicalesbians' 1970 manifesto produced a compelling definition of lesbian. *'What is a lesbian? A lesbian is the rage of all women condensed to the point of explosion'*.[3] Setting off that explosion was the name of the game. I wrote the slogan LESBIANS IGNITE over numerous lavatory walls. But this is a version of lesbianism that belongs to a unique moment in women's revolutionary history. Lesbianism is celebrated as far more than an expression of sexuality, more than a way of life. Here it is the revolutionary impulse to liberty, to freedom, a sexual politics that is engaged, committed, dangerous. This is in fact very close to Wittig's position. But it has ceased to be the escape route open to any woman. Lesbian is the chess move out of and away from the rest of the pack. Lesbian is the sexual passport into the vanguard, leaving the category woman to be occupied by fembots, victims, collaborators, wives, mothers, heterosexuals. The refusal to be a woman involves stepping across the 'deadly space between' the normal and the deviant, out of the cage and into freedom.

What does it mean to be a woman? The clichés are clear. Within heteropatriarchal discourse a woman is a wife and mother, submissive, conformist, familial, heterosexual. This is not how being a woman is always experienced, but this is what woman means within that discourse. These are men's myths. Women's lives seem to be made up of men's myths. There are other categories intersecting that discourse: slut, slag, dominatrix, whore, bitch, dyke. And what does lesbian mean within that discourse? Well, it means two things. Firstly, abnormal, deviant, bent, queer. But it also means sexy, titillating, asking for it. I worked on a recent study[4] of inexpensive non-violent pornography in France and found that lesbian sex was the most commonly represented sexual fantasy in a wide range of magazines. The scenarios, visual and verbal, were largely domestic, familial and everyday: the sexual scene was located at work, shopping, outside the school gates, on holiday, in lifts, at home. The message was always the same. Women like doing it with each other and men like to watch. Any woman can be a lesbian, and most women are. This was lesbianism as home entertainment. It is simply not true to suggest that male rule is threatened by lesbian sexual desire.

Wittig puts her finger on something important, however, when she argues that lesbians are not women. What makes a lesbian life radically different from a woman's life is that she plays a less significant role in the service industry. Women's lives are spent in service and servitude, learning to be superserviceable, being at the service of others, being serviced. We are a service industry, serving husbands, lovers, bosses, children, aged parents, families, colleagues. Few of us ever escape this entirely. Even if you love women, live with women, spend all your affective life with women, you will probably end up working for and with men. And that means working in the heterosexual ego service industry.

Outside the heterosexual category of woman lies one of the gender myths occupied by radical lesbians, that of the warrior woman. She is the Amazon, the queen, the woman with one breast, the woman who rules, fights, kills. She exists in male myth too, but she is not always under male control. The male myths reproduce the woman tamed, captured, married. Thus Hippolyta is married off to Theseus in Shakespeare's sex-war comedy *A Midsummer Night's Dream*.[5]

The gender system is the political system within which we are all born, within which we all live – whether we call ourselves women, wives, mothers, feminists, straights, queers, dykes. But it is a political system, or, as Adrienne Rich argues, a compulsory political institution, which affects us all differently.[6] Some of us are privileged within it, financially protected by the heteropatriarchal state, if we play our cards right and as long as our luck holds. We are never secure. Some of us are caged, controlled, destroyed. Some of us are marginal to the structures of the institution. It does none of us any good. Of course, there is a difference between heterosexuality as an institution and as lived experience. The two cannot be seen as identical. But neither can they be severed. Heterosexuality is not the only element in the gender system, but it is one of the key elements.

The initial animus of the 1960s feminist critique was directed against three things: men, femininity and heterosexuality. Men were then perceived to be our masters, our owners and often, in no uncertain terms, the enemy. Even homosexual men benefited from belonging to the sex class of men. And they often bought into the gendered constructions of femininity. Femininity merely amounted to men's constructions of women. The heterosexual gender system, with all its manifold ramifications of marriage, motherhood, the family, unequal pay, violence against women, was the political régime within which women were kept down. Heterosexuality was endorsed by patriarchal religions, all patriarchal religions. Heterosexuality promoted Noah's Ark, a great sea of happy couples. We cannot escape these patterns. Many homosexual couples, lesbian, gay and transgendered, reproduce similar heterosexual structures in their relationships and in their lives. But similar is not the same. The hetero-structures reproduced will never be identical to those of the 'real' heterosexuals, whose divisions and power hierarchies are based on sexual difference within the gender system. Some homosexuals, especially men, are busy trying to eradicate that critical difference. Why can't we have the right to marriage, service in the armed forces, respectability in church and at work? These are the arguments of the assimilationists, such as Andrew Sullivan,[7] for whom homosexuals are 'virtually' but not quite 'normal'. Love is love, he says, whoever you happen to love. Love is the same. And no one should be persecuted for loving someone else. This is a very attractive argument. But it is a counsel of defeat and capitulation to the gender system. There is nothing normal about heterosexuality and the gender system. It works to the advantage of a single gendered class. It cannot be in the interests of any sexual dissident, no matter how mild their dissent, to demand inclusion in a gender system that is constructed precisely in order to make their lives wretched and untenable.

The social construction of love is, I believe, one of the key elements of oppression in the gender system. For most of us, our first overwhelming experience of love is for our parents. Our love may not be returned. We may in fact have a harrowing experience of rejection and frustration in our first love. But our love for our parent, or parents, whatever their sex, or indeed their sexual orientation, is also a relationship of dependency and possession. They own us. We have no rights, no redress. Even if we have the good fortune to be loved in return, our first experience of overpowering love is of powerlessness, desire and demand. The love of a child for a parent is a profoundly unequal love. We are helpless in our desires. Hence the aggression which characterises the expression of most children's love for their parents. We are socialised into our heterosexual gender roles in infancy; and this process of socialisation will vary enormously from culture to culture, but this nexus of passion, anger and powerlessness seems to be universal – and dangerous.

Women are infantilised within heterosexuality. We are treated like children, or like creatures of diminished responsibility. Think of the belittling patterns of endearment: baby, child, doll, little one. Whores call their pimps Daddy. Marilyn Monroe declared that her heart belonged to Daddy. Even the coded structures of male homosexual love contain ritualised inequality. Greek love was that of the older man for the younger boy. Marguerite Yourcenar and Mary Renault, both life-long lesbians, wrote historical novels of classical antiquity which celebrated difference and inequality in same-sex relationships between men. It has always been unusual to insist on equality, or on sameness, even in homosexual love.

The traditions of courtly love (*amour courtois*), which apparently involved giving women power, also involved putting us on pedestals and fixing us firmly into men's myths. Even the religious expression of love for God means that men fake the feminine role within the heterosexual structure. God is their (masculine) master. They wait, as women are supposed to do, to be ravished, consumed, possessed. Men's fantasies of God are often homoerotic, even of penetration and rape, but the male poet takes the woman's place. The feminine role is associated with vulnerability, submission, lavish clinging desire. It is the woman's role within heterosexual gender ideology.

I believe that this obsession with difference, otherness, inequality in our sexual desires is rooted in childhood, parenting and in our first family relationships. Our primary learning of love is from our parents, or the people who parent us. The first body we love is usually a woman's body. The first passion we have is for another woman. In a lesbian relationship the mother–daughter bond is echoed rather than repeated. It is largely from our mothers that we learn how to be women. And for most of us this is also the first experience of lies and betrayal. For it is the mother who teaches us how to be feminine, second-class, second-rate. And even when she affirms us as agents, as empowered beings who can choose our own lives, it is rare that she will tell us the truth about heterosexuality, about patriarchy, about men. It is rarer still that she will tell us how not to be women, how to get out. The primary relationship between women within patriarchy is ambiguous: an ugly mesh of betrayal, truth and lies. Very often we cannot afford to tell each other the truth. Sometimes we don't dare.[8] No one reared within the gender system will be exempt from this particular sexual pattern, this ubiquitous eroticising of inequality and difference in sexual structures, this pattern of power within desire.

One is not born a Lesbian, one becomes one. I would like to query the existence of the lesbian, and indeed the heterosexual gene. However attractive it might be to imagine that we were 'born that way' and however fiercely some of us might feel that to be the case, I think it is a biological dead end. Heterosexuality is no more natural than lesbianism or any other kind of sexuality. Sexuality is fluid. Sexual identities are radically unstable. And I for one am glad that they are. BIOLOGY IS NOT DESTINY was one of my favourite slogans. I want to go on saying, EVERY WOMAN CAN.

It was for only a brief time, ten years perhaps, from the mid-1970s to the mid-1980s, or even barely ten years, that the two political gender categories *lesbian* and *woman* came into a radical conjunction within a public and political discourse. *Lesbian* and *woman* were united within feminism as theory and as praxis. To decide to be lesbian was to attempt a different way of thinking, behaving and being. It was in fact an attempt to create another gender that women could choose to inhabit. To decide to be lesbian was to choose women, not as we were, or as we are, but as we could become. Lesbian/woman was something other than woman: to be a lesbian/woman was to be an active creator of revolutionary change, a subversive, a rebel, a saboteur. FEMINISM IS THE THEORY, LESBIANISM IS THE PRACTICE. So the old slogan says. In that particular historical moment, the women's movement in Britain was supported by a broad front of left-wing activism, Greens, trade unionists, environmental campaigners, CND, anarchists, Rock Against Racism, Gay Liberation. Socialism was not a dirty word. Feminists were not the only ones demanding a society that was more free and more just.

There have always been lesbians and there have always been women's communities, but they have not always seen themselves as part of a revolutionary movement. Lesbians have not always identified with women, nor have they seen themselves as dissidents. To be different is not necessarily to be in a state of rebellion. In fact, you may long to mask your difference, be desperate to conform. Lesbians have, for centuries, existed peacefully within romantic friendships, bisexual arrangements or closet marriages. Sometimes we have taken risks, cross-dressed and lived as men.[9] Lesbians have evolved subtle parodies and masquerades of heterosexual structures in butch/femme lives, and have lived differently, either flaunting it or underground.

But the revolutionary moment of feminism, a moment of Utopian joy and possibility, was unique in asserting that there were no entry qualifications: that you did not have to cross-dress, be an invert, be different, cut your hair, be born dyke. '*A lesbian is the rage of all women condensed to the point of explosion.*' All you had to be was explosively angry at the way you were treated and the little that you got. All you had to want was freedom. All you had to love was women. Whatever that meant to you. And the meaning of woman was up for grabs. So was the meaning of lesbian. The prison of gender was apparently breaking down. We were making our own meanings. All you had to be was a woman in the process of becoming. 'Woman' was no longer a fixed point of closure, but a dynamic process. We were women in movement, a movement of women.

Over the last ten years, I have watched the gradual separation of lesbianism from feminism and, inevitably, lesbian from woman. Lesbian is now part of a single corporate entity: the new firm, LESBIAN 'n' GAY, or subsumed into that new product, QUEER. Lesbians choosing to identify themselves as queers in Britain are, in the main, young women. They are a post-feminist generation. And they see feminism as their mothers' politics, a politics which may once have had something going for it, but which is now, like the somewhat redundant patriarchy – not the monolith it once was – also outdated and smelling of lies, betrayal, prohibitions and taboos. Cherry Smyth explains:

> The attraction of queer for some lesbians is flavoured by a rebellion against a prescriptive feminism that had led them to feel disenfranchised by the lesbian feminist movement . . . the importance of identifying politically as a lesbian had obscured lesbianism as a sexual identity.[10]

And sex, indeed SEX, defiant, perverted, flagrant, on your backs, in your face, is the name of the queer game. Lesbian sex is, in itself apparently, a subversive, political act. Feminism has atrophied into boring politically correct rules, mother saying no. Queer dykes are the new radicals, the new sexual outlaws. Here is Spike Pittsberg explaining the new frontier:

> We pushed back the borders and talked about SM, fantasies, taboos, butch/femme, violence in relationships, non-monogamy, penetration, ass-fucking etc. . . .[11]

Doing anything with anybody in any position might well be fun, but, despite my generation's experience as sexual liberationists, I find it hard to see how sex can be the source of revolutionary change. It was never the right to screw ourselves senseless in private that was in question, it was the right to gather socially, organise politically and dispute the heterosexual hegemony that caused trouble.

But Queer also means 'to fuck with gender', and here I do see radical possibilities. The binary opposition between masculinity and femininity is fluid and unstable. It always was. That is why it is so carefully policed. The pastiche dress codes of queers signal an engagement with and refusal of heterosexual binary divisions. Gender is performance. The body becomes ambiguous. Therefore, power and knowledge cannot be so easily allocated to the masculine in queer discourses. Queer is a gender game. Direct action rather than lobbying is characteristic of queer politics, just as it was within the original revolutionary moment of feminism.

Here comes the good news. You do not even have to be born woman to become lesbian. The intriguing encounter between jurassic feminism and queer politics was dramatised for me this summer when I reread Janice Raymond's *The Transsexual Empire*, first published in 1979 when lesbian feminists were busy occupying the righteous moral high ground of identity politics, and Kate Bornstein's *Gender Outlaw* (1994) which, as the subtitle points out, is about 'men, women and the rest of us'. Bornstein was a male-to-female transsexual, but is now, as she prefers to describe herself, transgressively transgendered. She is endearingly upfront about her onion of identities:

> I write from the point of view of an S/M transsexual lesbian, ex-cult member, femme top and sometimes bottom shaman. And I wondered why no one was writing my story? . . . I write from the point of view of a used-to-be politically correct, wanna-be butch, dyke phone sex hostess, smooth talking telemarketing, love slave, art slut, pagan Tarot reader, maybe soon a grandmother, crystal palming, incense burning, not-man, not always a woman, fast becoming a Marxist.[12]

Well, no one can say that she hasn't tried everything, and I wish her good luck with the Marxism. Bornstein's thesis, which she has evolved from this process of social and sexual transitions, is actually very simple. Gender is a violent political system which is enforced upon us. Gender has nothing to do with sexual orientation or how we actually experience our identities. There are certainly many more genders than two. But two genders are privileged: male and female, and they operate throughout the world as a hierarchical and unequal system of power. This is the system which privileges men over women and turns the rest of us into freaks. Bornstein identifies one of the reasons for the peculiar alliances between right-wing heterosexual gender fundamentalists and radical lesbian separatists. They are gender defenders. The often religious Right are busy upholding heterosexual family values, and lesbian separatists often base their identity on the gender of their sexual partners. This means that they need to be absolutely certain that the lines of inclusion and exclusion are firmly drawn: women-born-women-only. Please check your chromosomes. According to Bornstein, the real radicals are the gender transgressors, the frontier freaks who insist on the endlessly fluid articulation of gender. Here, gender is perpetual mutability.

Bornstein herself once believed in gender. She must have done or she wouldn't have bothered with genital surgery and made such a determined effort to cease being a man. She charts her move from gender-defending – after all, you have to think that you know what a woman is, if you want to become one – to gender scepticism.

I'm supposed to be writing about how to be a girl. And I sure don't know how to be a boy. And after thirty-seven years of trying to be male and over eight years of trying to be female, I've come to the conclusion that neither is worth all the trouble . . . A lot of people think it is worth the trouble . . . And hey, I'm not just talking about transsexuals here. I'm talking about men and women, maybe like you.[13]

There are solid financial reasons for wanting to remain a man, and if naked power gives you a thrill there are plenty of reasons for wanting to pass as a straight, white male. Many biological 'women' pretend to be Real Women to avoid being killed. But this is playing the gender game as tactical, survival strategy. It doesn't necessarily mean that you believe in it. Bornstein no longer subscribes to the myths of gender. Jurassic feminists never did. BIOLOGY IS NOT DESTINY. And, interestingly, Bornstein recognises this in the work of Janice Raymond. One of the most telling sentences in *The Transsexual Empire* reads as follows:

Men, of course, invented the feminine, and in this sense it could be said that all women who conform to this convention are transsexuals, fashioned according to men's image.[14]

Exactly. I've spent a lot of time performing the transsexual role of feminine woman. There are considerable rewards attached to a good performance. Raymond argues that lesbian feminism recreates the female in opposition to the man-made invention of 'woman'. This is therefore an alternative gender. I agree. It only becomes prescriptive when lesbian feminists proclaim that it is the only authentic option for females on the run from the prison of gender. And how many of us experience gender not as playful performance, a sequence of costumes we can slip on and off, but as a sexual and behavioural code that is imposed and enforced? I don't want to be told any more what my gender is and how I should therefore conduct my life.

Bornstein had the cash and the medical industry on hand to buy herself another gender. She charts her history from transsexual to transgressively transgendered queer artist as a progressive conversion experience. She is now neither man nor woman. She is a gender performer, a post-feminist figure, a maker of queer theatre, both as live entertainment and life in the raw. She does all this with panache and charm. But I did ponder the significance of the fact that she had no real sense of what male privilege actually was until she lost her prick and balls, the penis and the phallus all in one. She is honest enough to say so. Is that going to be generally true before we can get to a post-gendered world? I wonder. Legitimate protest and rational argument, from Mary Wollstonecraft onwards, appear to have had remarkably few results. Who willingly dismantles their gender privilege?

But what gives me heart is the sense of *déjà vu* I had while reading

Bornstein's book. Yes, I have read it all before. Here, queer theory re-presents the central demand of jurassic feminism: the destruction of the gender system and the end to male privilege. We can only do that by ending the existence of the categories men/women. The post-gendered world, which has been the subject of so many fictional feminist Utopias,[15] would look very different to our world. Maybe Bornstein's dream of a multiplicity of genders, of each one of us giving radically different performances, in any register, whenever we like, could then come true.

Bornstein stresses the risks that the transgressively transgendered take in negotiating the gendered world. She's right. They do. But, and this is the one point which makes it utterly clear that a jurassic feminist did not write *Gender Outlaw*, if you are born into the gender class of woman you are neither safe nor free, not because you are radically questioning the structures of gender, but because of your assigned place within those structures.

The break with feminism is complete if 'queer theory ultimately displaces patriarchal gender hierarchy in favour of heterosexuality as the primary regulatory system. It is vitally important for feminism that we see heterosexuality as a gendered hierarchy and not just as a normative construction of cross-sex desire.'[16] Being queer may well be an alternative to femininity, to being woman within the heterosexual ideology, but we cannot escape the political régime of gender by wishful thinking, or even by wishful theory.[17] Unless we pack our bags and head for the greenwood, as some women have long since decided to do. Separatism is both an important strategy and a radical solution. But it can't be our only solution. Subversion is the other alterative.

The energy of queer politics is obvious. I would rather be surrounded by the slogans that proclaim SILENCE = DEATH and CHEERS QUEERS, the slogans which taste of opposition and dissent, than retreat into privacy and seclusion as many ex-radicals have done before me. And I am all for putting the sex back into sexual politics and the camp into campaigning. Queer theory has put Lesbian and Gay studies on the academic map, invaded cultural politics, advertising, television and cinema, and given homosexuals of both sexes a new visibility; and, with its suggestive politics of cross-dressing, theoretical and literal, queers of every gender have provoked new debates about essentialism and the gender system, which is all to the good.

But.

And here are my queer caveats.

Every revolutionary movement appears to pass through eerily similar phases: the first years of celebration and manifestos when the old order totters, or at least has the grace to appear to do so. Demands are drawn up and the Golden Age is at hand. Then come the darker times of impatience at the slowness or absence of change, the rigid imposition of what had once been the radical dream, then finally the brutal divisions into the pure and the impure with purges to prove the point. Then, if the movement is not defeated altogether, there are the years of underground struggle: long, slow years of hard work, disappointment and imperceptible change. And so it has always been with jurassic feminism. Political and sexual structures do not, unfortunately, exist only in the mind. And even lies that have been recognised as such take centuries to displace. Change need not be progressive. Women's movements and radical gender challenges have been obliterated and suppressed, have vanished – without trace.

Queer is a politics of demand. But all too often that demand ends with the group who makes that demand. Where else can we begin but with our own agendas? I believe, passionately, that the old Jewish saying is right: 'If I am not for myself, who will be for me? And even if I think of myself, what am I? And if not now, when?'[18] No one else will fight for us, unless we fight for ourselves. But I cannot desire my own freedom without desiring the freedom of every 'woman' who is not free. However she defines herself. I want a world in which ANY WOMAN CAN BE A LESBIAN. If we achieve this, it will automatically follow that ANYONE CAN BE ANY GENDER. And we are still very far from enjoying a post-liberation honeymoon with the heteropatriarchy. A large purple slogan in my study declares I'LL BE A POST-FEMINIST IN POST-PATRIARCHY. We're not there yet.

When I first called myself a radical feminist, I was – I still am – a privileged, educated, white woman. When we marched, campaigned, argued, took direct action, wrote books, we were not only championing ourselves, although that was our point of departure. Insane as this now sounds, twenty-five years on, we did it in solidarity with all the women of the world. We did it for women who were not like us, women of other races, nations, faiths, women whose difference was often unimaginable, women who would probably not have recognised their commonality with us, women who defined themselves in completely different ways. We could not speak for them, but we were on their side.

JURASSIC FEMINIST: DON'T FORGET US

NOTES

1. Stevi Jackson, 'Gender and Heterosexuality: A Materialist Feminist Analysis', in Mary Maynard and Jane Purvis (eds), *(Hetero)sexual Politics* (London: Taylor and Francis, 1995), pp. 11–26 (p. 13).
2. Monique Wittig, 'The Straight Mind' (1980), in *The Straight Mind and Other Essays* (Hemel Hempstead: Harvester Wheatsheaf, 1992), p. 32.
3. Radicalesbians, 'The Woman Identified Woman' (1970), in Julia Penelope and Sarah Lucia Hoagland (eds), *For Lesbians Only: A Separatist Anthology* (London: Onlywomen Press, 1988), p. 17.
4. See Patricia Duncker, 'Bonne Excitation: Orgasme Assuré. The Representation

of Lesbianism in Contemporary French Pornography', *Journal of Gender Studies*, 4:1 (1995), 5–15.

5. Gender is never simple or undisputed in Shakespeare's work, and in fact *A Midsummer Night's Dream* does have its queer moments. The object of Titania and Oberon's quarrel is a beautiful Indian boy. They both want him. But then, Shakespeare is a complicated case.

6. Adrienne Rich's classic essay, 'Compulsory Heterosexuality and Lesbian Existence', in *Blood, Bread, and Poetry: Selected Prose 1979–1985* (New York: W. W. Norton and Company, 1986), pp. 23–75.

7. Andrew Sullivan, *Virtually Normal: An Argument about Homosexuality* (Picador, 1995).

8. See Adrienne Rich, 'Women and Honor: Notes on Lying' (1975), republished in *On Lies, Secrets and Silence: Selected Prose 1966–1978* (New York: W. W. Norton and Company, 1979), pp. 185–94.

9. See Marjorie Garber, *Vested Interests: Cross-dressing and Cultural Anxiety* (New York and London: Routledge, 1992), and Emma Donoghue, *Passions Between Women: British Lesbian Culture 1668–1801* (London: Scarlet Press, 1993), especially Chapter 3.

10. Cherry Smyth, *Lesbians Talk Queer Notions* (London: Scarlet Press, 1992), p. 26.

11. Ibid., p. 27.

12. Kate Bornstein, *Gender Outlaw: On Men, Women and the Rest of us* (London and New York: Routledge, 1994), pp.143–4.

13. Ibid., p. 234.

14. Janice Raymond, *The Transsexual Empire* (London: The Women's Press, 1980), p. 106.

15. One of the most imaginative in the period of jurassic feminism was Marge Piercy's *Woman on the Edge of Time* (1976). Piercy imagined a society in which he and she did not exist, but we were all referred to as 'per'. Technology took care of reproduction and the role of mothering was undertaken by women and men alike. Piercy was trying to imagine the abolition of the gender hierarchy, rather than proposing a multiplicity of genders as Bornstein does.

16. Stevi Jackson, op. cit., p. 18.

17. I am indebted to Jonathan Dollimore for this expression, and I was much influenced by his essay 'Bisexuality, Heterosexuality, and Wishful Theory', *Textual Practice*, 10:3 (1996), 523–39.

18. This saying is attributed to Rabbi Hillel, but I first came across it as the title to Primo Levi's novel of Jewish resistance and survival, *Se nom ora, quando?* (1982), first published in English (1986) *If Not Now, When?* (London: Abacus, 1987).

Chapter Four

THE PLEASURES OF LABOUR
Marxist Aesthetics in a Post-Marxist World

Antony Easthope

THE MARXIST VISION

Through labour in its struggle with nature, the human species produces simultaneously itself and its world. Under private ownership, that production is appropriated by capital so that the human subject becomes alienated from its own objective realisation; under democratic public ownership, this externalisation will once more become free expression, annealing the gap between subject and object. Of life, including artistic life, in the communist future, Marx writes in note form:

> production based on exchange value breaks down, and the direct, material production process is stripped of the form of penury and antithesis. The free development of individualities, and hence not the reduction of necessary labour time so as to posit surplus labour, but rather the general reduction of the necessary labour of society to a minimum, which then corresponds to the artistic, scientific etc. development of the individuals in the time set free, and with the means created, for all of them.[1]

As I heard Raymond Williams say at a conference in 1976, with socialism there will be no need for art because people will become their own art.

Even before then, with capitalism, under the conditions of alienated labour, Marx imagines art as holding out the possibility of unalienated labour. At the same time, of course, art is an instance of ideology compromised by its entanglement with the present aims and purposes of capitalist society. Marxist aesthetics, like Marxism itself, offers the practitioner a double vision and a double engagement – both the opportunity for incisive critique of aesthetic forms in the present and the hope the present contradictions will be finally superseded, in that communist Utopia so like the ideal of the English country gentleman who hunts in the morning, fishes in the afternoon, rears cattle in the evening and criticises after dinner 'without ever becoming hunter, fisherman, herdsman or critic'.[2] Where (that is) an individual's identity can be lived to the full without conflicting with the identity of others.

Marxist aesthetics does not consist of a given doctrine but rather a varied and continuing tradition. However, I shall take this double aspect of art, both complicit with the norms of society and resistant to them, as a sufficient general characterisation and explore the tradition with that in mind.

POST-THEORY, POST-MARXISM

A Marxist aesthetic arose from and within classic Marxism. One might assume that its validity and continuing interest depends upon the validity of this foundation. The question, then, for a Marxist aesthetics in 1999, would seem to be how to assess classic Marxism. If that is so, the outlook for Marxist aesthetics is bleak indeed.

Leaving only Cuba and North Korea, the utter and unanticipated collapse in 1989 of Eastern European communism (whether previously condemned as Stalinist or naturalised as actually existing socialism) signalled the end of any possibility that the Marxist vision would be fulfilled in practice as socialism spread across the globe. Already before then, the renewed Marxism of the 1960s, which inspired a generation of western intellectuals, had come into profound theoretical crisis. The limitations of classic Marxism need to be faced directly and openly.

One might begin with two empirical objections to classic Marxism. (1) It is a fact that a modern, national economy cannot be run through centralised, state control, no matter how many computers are crammed together in the Ministry of Economics in the capital city. (2) Marx believed that within his lifetime the main form of collective identity would be class, in a world divided between bourgeois and proletarian, and stretching from Birmingham to Bangkok. History shows that this view was mistaken. Emerging into modernity, the world has chosen as its essential mode of collective identity not class (or, for that matter, race or gender) but, from France to the Philippines, the nation state and national identity.

There are objections in principle to classic Marxism. One is to its anthropology. Unlike its cousin, Darwinism, classic Marxism is founded upon an anthropology which privileges labour and the instinct for survival over the instinct for reproduction ('Eat first', as Brecht says). A better anthropology would have to recognise both survival and reproduction as necessary instincts for the species. Along with – and beyond – the instincts for reproduction and survival, the human species differs from other animals in that to perform as a speaking subject everyone must achieve a sense of his or her own identity through recognition from others. As G. A. Cohen argues, against the anthropology of classic Marxism, 'nothing is more essentially human' than 'the need for self-identity'.[3]

Classic Marxism is logocentric. It finds a centre for itself by means of a series of binary oppositions. Materialism/idealism, use value/exchange value and base/superstructure are to be held in place by a foundational opposition between the real and the apparent. Foundational or would-be foundational: for as Derrida indicates, referring to Marx's discussion of the mysterious, spectral unreality of commodity fetishism with such delicacy and wit that one might miss his critical intent,

> Marx does not like ghosts any more than his adversaries do. He does not want to believe in them. But he thinks of nothing else. He rather believes in what is supposed to distinguish them from actual reality, living effectivity. He believes he can oppose them, like life to death, like vain appearances of the simulacrum to real presence.[4]

(Since the question of Marx and Heidegger will come up later, let me digress to record how Althusser's revisions aimed to step aside from this binary opposition between real and apparent, to decentre Marxism by claiming that the lonely hour of economic determination in the last instance would never come. Derrida has indicated the difficulties with Marx's logocentrism even in Althusser's attempt to make it good, by asking 'If the economy as last instance can never appear as such, then to what concept of present, of nonpresence, of phenomenon or essence does one have recourse?',[5] and urging recourse to a Heideggerian account of Being-under-erasure.)

And classic Marxism is functionalist. Jon Elster writes in *Making Sense of Marx*:

> Intentional explanation cites the *intended* consequences of behaviour in order to account for it. Functional explanation cites the *actual* consequences. More specifically, to explain behaviour functionally involves demonstrating that it has *beneficial* consequences for someone or something.[6]

There is nothing wrong with functional explanation if a mechanism is specified which moderates the relation between behaviour and consequence. As Steve Rigby points out,[7] evolutionary biology has some very good functional explanations – the human species lost all its body hair except in places where it protects vital organs because that increases the species' chances of survival, and there is genetic machinery to ensure reproduction of this beneficial effect. Functional explanations are much more problematic when applied to society, yet they pervade classic Marxism and generally without providing an adequate account of a feedback mechanism.

For example, consider a Marxist account of the institution of literature-teaching in Britain. One can easily argue that Eng Lit promotes individualism at the expense of a social perspective; sets up a canon, an ideal tradition with a trans-class character; discriminates a liberal elite from the masses, and so on. The institution has these actual consequences and many others besides. Further, it would not be hard to demonstrate that at times certain groups (the Newbolt Committee, for example) have had explicit intentions in advancing Eng Lit. So far, no problem. The objection arises if someone names the consequences of the institution of Eng Lit and then goes on to argue that these work to the benefit of an agent (say, the ruling class) without specifying mechanisms by which those benefits are monitored and ensured. Classic Marxism relies on functional explanation whenever it lists actual consequences and then treats them as though they were *intended*.

In this respect, classic Marxism betrays a Hegelian residue. When Marx writes famously that 'mankind [sic] always sets itself only such tasks as it can solve',[8] he assumes that the real is rational (if only it were) and that in history there are no accidents, as if some ever-living brain controlled the universe from the centre of the ultraworld. It doesn't. As Heidegger writes, 'Man is not the lord of beings. Man is the shepherd of Being.'[9] And probably a bad shepherd at that: global warming may have already released enough frozen methane to terminate the species with extreme prejudice.

TRUTH OR PRACTICE?

In sketching out these criticisms of classic Marxism, I have been proceeding on the assumption that Marxist aesthetics depends on classic Marxism and that in some serious respects classic Marxism is just not true. If in this sense classic Marxism fails, there can be no future for an aesthetics claiming to operate in its name.

It is necessary to cancel or at least put into suspension the previous comments in critique of classic Marxism, for the situation is not that simple, and it is part of what has been called 'post-theory' to respond to this complexity. To approach Marxism by listing ways in which its account of the species and the social formation is not true (some of the history is wrong, the anthropology is doubtful, it is functionalist and logocentrist) is to assess Marxism on the basis of a presumed correspondence between Marxist theory and the world, between a discursive formation and the real.

Such an enterprise is fraught with epistemological difficulty. It is also one-sided and reductive, for the continuing importance of a discursive formation cannot be narrowly equated with what some Oxford philosophers call its 'truth values'. On this issue, there is a suggestive and striking moment of convergence between Foucault and Habermas. Foucault's project is dedicated to exposing how scientific practices introduced by the Enlightenment – notably for the asylum, the clinic and the prison – cannot be adequately understood in terms of the knowledge they promise to yield and which they profess as their justification. Such forms of scientific discourse are inseparable from the power they covertly exercise. Although Foucault's political aim is to analyse a deployment of power, the unmistakable implication of his account is that a discourse cannot be adequately understood and assessed simply in terms of whether it is true or not.

Working from the other end, as it were, Habermas reaches a similar conclusion. The Enlightenment originated in a movement of demystification, a passage from supernaturalist obscurantism and ignorance to the revelation of a truth behind appearance. In the example Marx liked to use, judging from appearance, people imagine the sun goes round the earth while the scientific truth is that really the earth goes round the sun.[10] But, Habermas argues (quietly letting the question of truth-claims slip away), the western discursive tradition, inherited from the Enlightenment, imposes certain values and effects quite apart from its local capacity to manage a passage from appearance to the truth concealed behind it. Exerting pressure on those positioned within it to listen to arguments instead of using force, the Enlightenment discursive tradition enacts protocols and a methodology privileging rational coherence and appropriate use of evidence. It has a power (for Habermas a good power) over and above the question of knowledge. In this respect it is – it should be – inescapable.

So is Marxism, as Derrida has proposed:

> Whether they wish it or know it or not, all men and women, all over the earth, are today to a certain extent the heirs of Marx and Marxism. That is . . . they are heirs of the absolute singularity of a project – or of a promise – which has a philosophical and scientific form.[11]

Marxism envisages the possibility of justice, which is justice for all in that all are, as St Paul said, 'members one of another', but it does so not in a mythological or mystical form but in an Enlightenment, scientific discourse. After Derrida's defence, there is not much left of Marxism – class has gone along with the opposition between base and superstructure and that between idealism and materialism – there is no teleology, no totality. What remains is the widely dispersed effectivity of a secular discourse which points to social amelioration and enforces the injunction that all aspects of human society and culture be thought together as far as possible.

The same rationale holds for Marxist aesthetics. It is better to attend to the strategies and effectivity of Marxist aesthetics as an inescapable inheritance, asking not so much 'Is it true?' but 'What can it do?' What kinds of analysis does it make possible? What does it let participants say and what does it inhibit? What are its *effects*? On this basis, I shall consider four examples as offering terms for the discussion of aesthetic texts, approaching each to see how it puts to work the double vision of Marxist aesthetics.

In doing so, I shall be alert to the question of functionalism. As considered already, functionalism as a mode of social explanation is eager to read consequences retrospectively in terms of supposed intentions. Applied to the aesthetic text, functionalism encourages writers to bypass the problem of the relation between texts and readers because they know in advance what texts do to people.

The problem is there in Marx. Art shows unalienated labour trapped inside ideology, but it is not clear how Marx would explain the relation between artwork and audience, text and reader. Does the reader respond to the image of unalienated labour cognitively or emotionally or in both ways at once? Is some other connection envisaged? The problem of how texts and readers work on each other is crucial to the understanding of Marxist aesthetics but has often been fudged. Brecht, for example, criticises bourgeois art on psychoanalytic grounds (it encourages identification and 'implicates the spectator') and then goes on to defend his radical alternative for essentially *cognitive* reasons (it 'turns the spectator into an observer').[12] In my examples, I shall watch out for the way each conceives the text/reader relation and will return to the topic at the end.

MARCUSE

In a far-sighted and succinct essay of 1937, 'The Affirmative Character of Culture', Herbert Marcuse picks up the double-sided feature of art from Marx but also from the Lukács of *History and Class Consciousness*. Art in the classical period pertained to a world beyond, an impossible and elite ideal, while, Marcuse says, in bourgeois society everyone is supposed to participate equally in a universal culture freely accessible to all – except, of course, that this notional freedom of access is contradicted by the inequalities of class society. Even so, Marcuse describes such culture as affirmative because it is spiritual and establishes 'an inner state', 'an independent realm of value . . . considered superior to civilisation'.[13]

Art and culture would escape the realities which are its condition of existence and make it desirable. If bourgeois society is coldly utilitarian, art is passionately useless; if it binds its subjects to objective necessity, restricting the body, art envisages subjective freedom and celebrates the body; if such society is unequal, art asserts perfect democracy. Culture, then, as Marcuse insists, exhibits a double character, both as evasion which would justify the reality it evades *and* as utopian promise furnishing a critique of the conditions which make it necessary:

> Affirmative culture uses the soul as a protest against reification . . . it anticipates the higher truth that in this world a form of social existence is possible in which the economy does not pre-empt the entire life of individuals.[14]

Writing under the immediate threat of fascism, Marcuse remarks that 'even keeping alive the desire for fulfilment is dangerous in the present situation'.[15] Against a Kantian aesthetic which defines art as useless in its address to the pure perception of the individual, Marcuse can give a coherent account from a social perspective of how that very uselessness makes it useful to bourgeois society.

English writers of the 1930s, such as Christopher Caudwell, derive much satisfaction from castigating art for the crime of being a bourgeois illusion (the sado-masochistic pleasures of the English will be mentioned again later); unlike these, Marcuse situates himself in a lived relation to the culture he analyses. My summarising comments do not do justice to the way the writing of the essay keeps doubling back on itself, exposing art as escapist other only to affirm its divided character as an other affording a position of critique, a critique which is itself only possible because of art's alternative status. A reader is left with the sense, undeveloped perhaps, that Marcuse's critique is established not on some absolute point outside and looking on but in actual relation to the critical feature of art he announces.

And yet Marcuse never asks about any mechanism or mediations by which art does and does not do all that he says. The essay remains locked into functionalism, abstaining from questions of why, even given the situation he analyses, anyone might come to desire such culture, or, equally, how bourgeois society knows such culture is good for it, in its long-term interests (and maybe it isn't, on Marcuse's showing).

ADORNO

Marcuse treats high and popular art in together, thinking the double feature of Marxist aesthetics as the ambivalent potential of culture. Writing 'On Popular Music' in 1941 in the same journal that published Marcuse's essay, Adorno takes the opposition between unalienated labour and ideology, and renders it as the split between high art and popular culture. Thus the potentially Utopian and critical side of culture is discovered 'in Beethoven and in good serious music in general'[16] whereas popular music is defined as complicit and escapist. In its formal properties, Adorno says, popular music exhibits standardisation while serious music resists such standardisation, constantly, through unanticipated moves, unsettling its listener. In this essay, Adorno is on his way to the uncompromising position he takes up in 1948 in *Philosophy of Modern Music*[17] where he rejects western Renaissance tonality represented by Stravinsky as symptom of an exhausted traditionalism, and asserts that the radical novelty of Schoenburg's avant-garde experiments with an atonal system are more fitting to modernity.

There are probably two ways to refute Adorno's formal contrast between 'classical' and popular music: either to reject the opposition standardisation/ non-standardisation by denying his formal analysis, or to argue that techniques he describes as non-standard do in fact occur in popular music (Adorno seems to have missed Duke Ellington, for instance, and quite a lot more). Nevertheless, musical standardisation, demanded by commodity production, correlates to what he names as 'pseudo-individualisation' and defines by saying that the effect endows 'cultural mass-production with the halo of real choice or open market on the basis of standardisation itself'.[18] It is this which lends popular music its hold on the masses.

What makes Adorno's essay exciting is not only its ability to frame culture in a social perspective but also its willingness to pursue discussion onto the traditional terrain of formalism, and this in the case of that art-form most notoriously resistant to conventional analysis, music. Adorno's sympathetic yet critical insight contrasts favourably with, say, the snooty attitudes of Queenie Leavis writing about popular fiction in 1932.

Here is Adorno's psychoanalytically informed account of the internal process with which standardisation produces the effect of pseudo-individualisation:

> when the audience at a sentimental film or sentimental music become aware of the overwhelming possibility of happiness, they dare to confess to themselves what the whole order of contemporary life ordinarily forbids them to admit, namely, that they actually have no part in happiness . . . The actual function of sentimental music lies rather in the temporary release given to the awareness that one has missed fulfilment . . . Emotional music has become the image of the mother who says, 'Come and weep, my child'.[19]

This maternal image is very tricky. According to the usual structure of melancholic fantasy, the intensity of dyadic union desired from the mother is expressed by the intensity felt at her loss; lost, along with the possibility of happiness, the mother is (impossibly) refound as she tells the child to come and weep precisely for that loss. The marvellously suggestive implication of the analogy seems to be this: just as the commodity form of popular culture recalls the social alienation it means to conceal, so the imaginary fullness of 'sentimental music' reinstates lack by insisting so coercively on that very plenitude.

Adorno's image of popular culture as promising to restore the nostalgic, melancholic, masochistic, dyadic moment between mother and child, though extraordinary powerful, is not developed. Yet it pulls Adorno off any serene pedestal and into identification with the listener to popular music. And it outlines a sense of a mechanism at work between the commodity and its subject. Adorno does not, however, risk extending the terms of his explanation to performances of Mozart, Beethoven and Stravinsky; these remain somehow exempt from the intense emotional effects of songs such as 'Deep Purple', 'Sunrise Serenade' and 'Alexander's Ragtime Band'. Like Brecht before him, psychoanalytic explanation is good enough for popular culture; high culture requires something more uplifting.

'SCREEN' AND CULTURAL STUDIES IN BRITAIN

In the 1970s, a group of writers associated with the film journal *Screen* worked out a development of Marxist aesthetics which has come to be called '*Screen* theory'. This in turn was hugely influential on cultural studies in Britain during the 1980s and beyond. Drawing on Brecht and Althusser rather than Adorno and Frankfurt, *Screen* took the double vision of Marxist aesthetics and gave it the full formalist treatment, mapping the distinction between everyday ideology and radical practice onto that between the textual modes of realism and modernism. Aiming, in the words of Stephen Heath, to stage a totalising theoretical 'encounter of Marxism and psychoanalysis on the terrain of semiotics',[20] *Screen* was determined to look beneath the surfaces of content analysis for a formalist analysis of what it called the specific 'ideological operation' of its chosen topic, film. And it addressed, via Lacanian psychoanalysis, the question of the mechanisms operating between reader and text (once again, like Brecht and Adorno, *Screen* was acute in suggesting the psychic effects of mainstream cinema but not able to say much about the radical text beyond claiming it interrogated or challenged the imaginary complicities of realism).

Even with its confident discussion of mechanisms, the *Screen* project remained implicated in unsatisfactory functional explanations. Capitalism, through its chosen film institution, Hollywood, secured its interests by promoting the smoothly realist text, leaving it to a politicised avant-garde to attack capitalism by making films (usually with government money) whose jagged modernism confronted the reading subject with their own constructedness. But *Screen* came up with a brave and inventive if finally unconvincing manoeuvre to make good its functionalism: it distinguished between two kinds of reader of the text, the implied and the actual.

When Colin MacCabe wrote in an essay published in *Screen* in 1974 that 'the classic realist text ensures the position of the subject in a relation of dominant specularity',[21] he is talking about the effect of the text on its reader as understood within the parameters of *Screen* theory (and of course there are no facts outside a particular theoretical interpretation). That implied effect of the text is ultimately a consequence of Hollywood as capitalist institution. Meanwhile, any other actual effects of the film text can be safely pushed off-stage since they are not visible under the spotlight of *Screen* theory.

Adorno discussing popular music warms to the listener seeking to refind his or her mother: *Screen* in contrast had nothing but icy contempt for readers trapped in the realist text, sunk in ideology, captured by dominant specularity and limply subject to all the narcissistic pleasures of the Lacanian imaginary. Meanwhile, high above the struggle, like Moses on Sinai, well-versed film theorists could see and judge everything except themselves, measuring exactly the degree to which a given text reproduced or subverted the dominant ideology, an ideology to which those positioned within theoretical practice were themselves happily immune.

In *Screen* theory, and in subsequent work in cultural studies in Britain, that ascribed position outside and looking on was justified by appeal to Althusser's opposition between science and ideology. In its disdain for ordinary people, however, it reveals something rather more familiar. Wonderfully un-English as *Screen* theory was in its theoretical rigour and its tenacity in pursuing history through and beyond formalism, it fixed an unbridgeable gulf between those who understood theory and could sit through the more extreme interventions of British Independent cinema, and, on the other hand, the ordinary punters who go to the movies. That pitiless and superior demarcation inhabited a traditional English moralism, bringing *Screen* into unconscious proximity with the aesthetic rectitude of F. R. Leavis.

DERRIDA

While Marcuse, Adorno and *Screen* theory fit snugly within Marxist aesthetics because of their adherence to the view of art as double-featured, Derrida, though he claims his project is as much a beneficiary of Marx as Young Hamlet is heir to his dead father, may not properly qualify as Marxist. For him, art has a single effect and is always radical.

Difference ('différance') 'instigates the subversion of every kingdom',[22] and for Derrida writing – and especially literature as the military wing of *différance* – has a crucial function in subverting kingdoms:

> Whether it is phallocentric or not (and that is not so easy to decide), the more 'powerful' a text is (but power is not a masculine attribute here and it is often the most disarming feebleness), the more it is written, the more it shakes up its own limits or lets them be thought, as well as the

limits of phallocentrism, of all authority and all 'centrism', all hegemony in general.[23]

Although officially committed to the view that 'No *internal* criterion can guarantee the essential 'literariness' of a text',[24] Derrida speculates that the potentialities of some texts 'are richer and denser' than others, embodying a performativity which, 'in some sense, appears the greatest possible in the smallest possible space'.[25] 'Every literary work', he says, '"betrays" the dream of a new institution of literature',[26] a unique institution; though if it really were unique, could anyone read the text at all? These are the views of the man who, when asked to lecture at the Ninth International James Joyce Symposium at Frankfurt in 1984, told his astonished and appalled listeners that theirs was an institution Joyce had done everything 'he could to make impossible'.[27]

Derrida's High Modernist aesthetic would attribute inherent properties to certain aesthetic texts – richer, denser – as much as any Kantian or Coleridgean aesthetic: some texts, he argues, are just more *written* than others. And it's all high art, for there is not a trace here of popular culture (there is little anywhere to suggest that Derrida has ever sat in a cinema or watched television). His aesthetic picks up Adorno's trust in the power of high art as an alternative cultural mode; in fact, via the opposition between logocentrism and writing, Derrida actually extends the radical force of Modernist textuality by proclaiming it as a threat to 'all authority' and 'all hegemony in general'.

Although there is clearly a conceptual opposition between presence and *différance*, logocentric power and the subversions of writing, Derrida does not otherwise offer an account of how writing menaces phallocentrism. And although Derrida knows perfectly well that writing doesn't do anything unless its process is enacted in and through human subjects, frequently (as in the passages cited here) he stakes out a position that cannot escape the accusation of functionalism: the effect of art is necessarily radical. Given the present field of forces, by instancing the violence of *différance*, writing in the Modernist mode operates not to the benefit of established power but always to its detriment.

Derrida owes this kind of functional explanation not so much to Adorno, Frankfurt and the Marxist tradition as to something quite different. In his discussion of 'The Origin of the Work of Art'[28] and elsewhere, Martin Heidegger also rejects a Kantian aesthetic, on the grounds that it supposes an epistemological relation between reader and text, that 'art works become the object of a form of human experience' and 'in accordance with that, art counts as an expression of human life'.[29] In contrast, Heidegger proposes an ontological conception of the artwork, beyond any merely cognitive or emotional appropriation, as one of the most important modes in which Dasein brings its own possibilities into existence by 'discovering what it is to be human'.[30]

If, as Heidegger repeatedly maintains, *every* question is posed from the start as a question in relation to the truth of Being, then, I think, something like Heidegger's analysis of the work of art arrives inevitably. Similarly, if every question is posed in relation to an opposition between presence and *différance*, speech and writing, then the argument drives in a fairly straight line to Derrida's view that literature in the twentieth century has a radical power to shake up the limits of 'hegemony in general'.

Perhaps it does. But the account leaves some queries unanswered. What are the mechanisms by which literature does this, or is one to accept that this question is sufficiently answered by indicating the opposition between presence and *différance*? How does literature establish what its effects are, that it is indeed threatening hegemony and not unwittingly consolidating it? And crucially: is art to be thought of as a social and cultural phenomenon without the introduction of any sense of agents, subjects and intentions *at all*? (To admit this worry is not to urge a return to humanism and the belief that subjects are freely constitutive.)

WITH AND WITHOUT THE MARXIST UTOPIA

Marcuse, Adorno, the *Screen* position and, yes, Derrida too (despite Heideggerian attachments) reproduce and rework the Marxist aesthetic tradition because they explore varying implications of Marx's conception of art as unalienated labour. (One might even think of claiming Heidegger as a cognate line of the same tradition, not only because of his enormous respect for Marx, but because for him too art has a progressive force insofar as it may recall being-there from its forgetting of Being). Yet a persistent reservation has been that the continuing discourse of Marxist aesthetics relies too much on inadequate functional explanation, this taking the place of a detailed and attentive concern with how readers and texts react upon each other.

There may be another take on that issue. Marx assumes that within the alienated forms of ideological production art keeps alive the hope of unalienated labour. Suppose one were to approach that idea not from the side of history and the social formation but from the side of subjectivity and the unconscious. Leaving aside the possibility that the reader's response to the idea of unalienated labour is cognitive, that from art he or she acquires a piece of knowledge, what fantasy pleasures might the reader find in that image? How might the figure of unalienated labour serve as an object of desire?

Jacques Lacan discusses a quite different conception of alienation and arrives at a rather more pessimistic conclusion. What Lacan names as the *vel* – the either/or – of alienation is represented by a Venn diagram in which being and meaning, the subject and the Other, the real and the rational, necessarily exclude each other. Choose being and you fall into non-meaning; choose meaning and you get it, but only because your being is eclipsed by its disappearance into the field of the signifier. It is, as Lacan remarks sardonically, '*Your money or your life!*'[31] Now if this is really something like the situation into which we are thrown, it would reveal the immense attraction of any representation promising escape from the alienation of the subject, any image promising to restore unity between subject and object, any sense of a dyadic relation in which being and meaning appear to be at one so that art beckons with the words 'Come and weep, my child'.

Marx's account of economic alienation and Lacan's theory of the alienation of the subject run at tangents to each other. However, the Lacanian thing would explain, in a way the Marxist tradition itself cannot, why art's representation of unalienated labour draws the imagination so seductively. But it provides this explanation at a price (your money or your life). For it asserts that no matter what might happen in a communist future and no matter how much it might be hoped that people become their own art (through the rendering of objective realisation as free choice, by closing the gap between subject and object), no one will ever elude the *vel* of alienation. The constitutive either/or between meaning and being generates all those self-cancelling, excessively embedded Lacanian sentences which always end up saying the same thing: that the signifier 'functions as a signifier only to reduce the subject in question to being no more than a signifier, to petrify the subject in the same movement in which it calls the subject to function, to speak, as subject'.[32]

Such Lacanian disabusement reads the more persuasively because a Marxist aesthetics now has to read without answering the call of its Utopian resonances. In compelling interrogation of the ambivalent social implications of aesthetic texts, the force of the tradition remains undiminished but can no longer invite readers to thrill to the idea that it will all come right in the end, when production based on exchange value breaks down, labour time becomes a minimum necessary, there is the free development of individuals. Post-theory, post-Enlightenment, post-Marxist, the situation is as Tom Nairn has recently described:

> The persisting spirit of the European Enlightenment has always been terribly disappointed by its firstborn, Capitalism. Its eldest son, Nationalism, remains even more of a nuisance. But it no longer has the faintest hope of getting rid of either of them. It was this hope which ended around 1989, not history. . . . One reaction to post-1989 events is a lucid pessimism, the abandonment of hope by all who have approached them via this particular intellectual portal.[33]

Some things, like cigarettes, have to be given up. But a feeling of 'lucid pessimism' consequent upon loss of Utopia is no reason to stop us trying to make the situation better in the meantime.

NOTES

1. Karl Marx, *Grundrisse* (Harmondsworth: Penguin, 1973), pp. 705–6.
2. Karl Marx and Frederick Engels, *The German Ideology*, ed. C. J. Arthur (London: Lawrence and Wishart, 1974), p. 54.
3. G. A. Cohen, *History, Labour and Freedom: Themes from Marx* (Oxford: Clarendon, 1985), p. 154.
4. Jacques Derrida, *Specters of Marx*, trans. Peggy Kamuf (New York and London: Routledge, 1994), pp. 46–7.
5. Jacques Derrida, 'Politics and Friendship', in E. Ann Kaplan and Michael Sprinker (eds), *The Althusserian Legacy* (London: Verso, 1993), pp. 183–231, (p. 208).
6. Jon Elster, *Making Sense of Marx* (Cambridge: Cambridge University Press, 1985), p. 27.
7. See Steve Rigby, *Engels and the Formation of Marxism* (Manchester: Manchester University Press, 1992), pp. 182–4.
8. Karl Marx, 'Preface' to *A Contribution to the Critique of Political Economy*, in Karl Marx and Frederick Engels, *Selected Works*, 2 vols (London: Lawrence and Wishart, 1950), vol. 1, pp. 327–31 (p. 329).
9. Martin Heidegger, 'Letter on Humanism', in D. F. Krell (ed.), *Basic Writings* (London: Routledge, 1993), p. 245.
10. See, for example, Marx in 'Wages, Price and Profit': 'It is also paradox that the earth moves round the sun, and that water consists of two highly inflammable gases. Scientific truth is always paradox, if judged by every-day experience, which catches only the delusive appearance of things' (Marx and Engels, *Selected Works*, vol. 1, p. 384).
11. Derrida, *Specters*, p. 91.
12. Bertolt Brecht, *Brecht on Theatre*, ed. John Willett (London: Methuen, 1964), p. 37.
13. Herbert Marcuse, 'The Affirmative Character of Culture', in H. Marcuse, *Negations* (London: Allen Lane, 1968), pp. 88–133 (p. 103, p. 95).
14. Ibid., pp. 108–9.
15. Ibid., p. 131.
16. Theodor Adorno, 'On Popular Music', reprinted in Antony Easthope and Kate McGowan (eds), *A Critical and Cultural Theory Reader* (Buckingham: Open University Press, 1992), pp. 211–23 (p. 214).
17. Theodor Adorno, *Philosophy of Modern Music* (London: Sheed and Ward, 1973).
18. Adorno, 'On Popular Music', p. 217.
19. Ibid., p. 222.
20. Stephen Heath, '*Jaws*, Ideology and Film Theory', in T. Bennett et al. (eds), *Popular Television and Film* (London: BFI/Open University, 1981), pp. 200–5 (p. 201).

21. Colin MacCabe, 'Realism and the Cinema: Notes on Some Brechtian Theses', in A. Easthope (ed.), *Contemporary Film Theory* (London: Longman, 1993), pp. 53–67 (p. 58).
22. Jacques Derrida, 'Difference', in Antony Easthope and Kate McGowan (eds), *A Critical and Cultural Theory Reader* (Buckingham: Open University Press, 1992), pp. 103–132 (p. 123).
23. Jacques Derrida, 'An Interview with Jacques Derrida', in Derek Attridge (ed.), *Acts of Literature* (London: Routledge, 1992), pp. 33–75 (p. 59).
24. Ibid., p. 73.
25. Ibid., p. 46, pp. 46–7.
26. Ibid., pp. 73–4.
27. Derrida, in Attridge (ed.), *Acts*, p. 268.
28. Martin Heidegger, 'The Origin of the Work of Art', in D. F. Krell (ed.), *Basic Writings* (London: Routledge, 1993), pp. 139–212.
29. Heidegger, cited by Joanna Hodge, 'Against Aesthetics: Heidegger on Art', *Journal of the British Society for Phenomenology* 23:3 (October 1992), 263–79 (p. 263).
30. Ibid., p. 264.
31. Jacques Lacan, *The Four Fundamental Concepts of Psycho-Analysis* (London: Hogarth, 1977), p. 212.
32. Ibid., p. 207.
33. Tom Nairn, 'Breakwaters of 2000: From Ethnic to Civic Nationalism', *New Left Review*, 214 (November/December 1995), 91–103 (p. 96).

Chapter Five

IS THE NOVEL ORIGINAL?
DERRIDA AND (POST-)MODERNITY

Eric Woehrling

'There is no "limit" to deconstruction', says Nick Royle,[1] and that is why the claim to be 'post-deconstruction', or even 'post-theory', is a questionable one. But the advantage to adopting the label 'post-deconstruction' is that deconstruction and postmodernism are commonly considered to be synonymous, which means that being post-deconstruction also involves being 'post-postmodernist'. I want to de-synonymise deconstruction and postmodern*ism*, and in so doing show that there is no limit to deconstruction because it is 'post-postmodern'. I make this claim with reference both to 'postmodernism' in its conventional sense, and to 'postmodern' in its literal one ('post-what's-in-the-present'). In common usage, postmodernism refers to a kind of self-conscious ethical and epistemological relativism, which is accompanied by a diacritical relativism that asserts the 'equal validity of all readings'. Historically, such concepts are associated with the postmodern period – the definition of which is of course much debated – and are generally formulated within that period with the catchphrases of denial of the difference between fiction and reality (as in Baudrillard), a privileging of interpretative surface over truthful depth, abolishing the divisions between high and low art and so forth. Such characteristics are also generally applied to deconstruction by those who do not or cannot read it. These accusations have already been exhaustively refuted; what I want to contribute to this refutation is the establishment of a connection between its ethical and epistemological manifestations, to argue that deconstruction's ethical duty towards the other is in fact seamlessly implicit in the double gesture with which it reads philosophy.

Both these aspects are themselves related to the understanding of time which makes deconstruction post-postmodern in the literal sense. That being even literally *post*modern is a kind of aporia is not in itself new, and in fact stems from an aporia within modernity, which itself derives from the familiar aporia of the ordinary concept of time. The aporia within modernity is encountered by Habermas when he writes that the 'avant-garde . . . understands itself as . . . conquering an as yet unoccupied future'.[2] 'But', adds Habermas, 'these forward gropings, this anticipation of an undefined future and the cult of the new mean in fact the exaltation of the present' (p. 128). The conceptual, historical and literal definitions of modernity combine here in its definition as the exaltation of the present. In a review of Habermas's paper, Giddens notices 'the temporal self-destructiveness of the *avant-garde* which is constantly implicated in the moment of its own dissolution'.[3] According to this view, the new can only be encountered in the present, as soon as it becomes *present*, and that present is constantly disappearing to be replaced by a new present which itself lasts for only an instant before being replaced by yet a newer present, and so on. This account depends on the metaphysical and problematic notion of the instant, to which we shall return in a moment.

According to this particular understanding of time, there can be no post- modern, because there cannot be anything more modern than modernity; every moment is consumed by modernity as it is born, only to be left behind as immediately to the past once it has passed. Even if one were to imagine the future, this imagined future, beyond the present, would be imagined in the present, and locate that imagination of the future (with)in modernity. Within a concept of time as linear progression of the present – 'as a series of nows' to use Heidegger's phrase – 'postmodern' is an aporia. Heidegger, in the famous note xxx to *Being and Time*, criticises Hegel precisely for understanding time as a series of 'nows', which is also what Hegel criticises in Aristotle's concept of time. In an excellent article, Karl Simms shows that Aristotle had already demonstrated that a moment in the present can be perceived *only after it has passed*, and that the present can therefore only be experienced from the vantage point of the future: 'We apprehend time only when we have marked motion, marking it by "before" and "after"; and it is only when we have perceived "before" and "after" in motion that we say that time has elapsed'.[4] Hegel uses this to demonstrate the inherent contradiction of the concept of time as a series of presents, and in so doing makes possible the 'postmodern' in its literal sense. Simms writes:

> As we have seen, 'now' does not exist, since it is always already in the past. The future does not exist, since it has not happened yet. Past events do not exist because they have happened – if you will pardon the necessary tautology, they are in the past. . . . It is considerations such as these which cause Hegel to consider time as nothing. (p. 195)

Hegel resolves this contradiction dialectically by arguing that the 'concrete present is the result of the past and is pregnant with the future'.[5] The present can only be understood as the becoming future, and as the becoming of the past; the future is latent within the present, and at the same time constitutes the present as such. Following Hegel following Aristotle, we can say that the modern can only be experienced from the vantage point of the postmodern. And, following Hegel, we can say that the modern is pregnant with the post-modern, and that the postmodern constitutes the modern as such.[6]

Heidegger writes that both Aristotle and Hegel take the now as a limit. But in both Aristotle and Hegel the beyond of the now acts as the limit of the limit. The postmodern as future is thus the limit of an uncritical concept of time as a series of nows, which the postmodern reintegrates by dialecticising it. This Derrida recognises in his meditation on the limit:

A discourse that has *called itself* philosophy . . . has always insisted upon assuring itself mastery over the limit . . . It has recognised, con-ceived, posited, declined the limit according to all possible modes; and therefore by the same token, in order better to dispose of the limit, has transgressed it. *Its own limit* has not to remain foreign to it. Therefore it has appropriated the concept for itself; it has believed . . . that it thinks its other.[7]

The postmodern is the limit of the modern which is *aufgehoben*[8] by the modern in the Hegelian concept of time.

Derrida's concept of time must thus attempt to be literally post-postmodern if it is not to remain within the transgressed limit of metaphysics. But what time is left over for deconstruction? There was no time left after the modern, and the nothing that was left over was dialectically reappropriated as post-modern, as that excess of time beyond the present necessary for its constitu-tion. Consequently, there is no time left over for deconstruction. Deconstruction situates itself in the aporetic space where there is no time left, taking its chance from Madame de Maintenon: ' "The King takes all my time; I give the rest to Saint-Cyr, to whom I would like to give all" '.[9] Derrida remarks: 'But as the King *takes* all her time from her, then the rest, by all good logic and good economics, is nothing. She can no longer *take* her time. She has none left, and yet she gives it' (p. 2). Derrida finds in Madame de Maintenon's sentence the aporia of deconstruction's concept of time. And this concept of time which goes beyond 'good logic' is intimately connected to the gift which goes beyond the circular economy of exchange:

And yet, even though the King takes it all from her, altogether, this time . . . , she has left, a remainder that is not nothing because it is beyond everything, a remainder that is not nothing but that *there is* since she *gives it*. And it is even essentially what she gives, *the very thing*. (p. 3)

Derrida's concept of the gift is itself paradoxical. He begins with the conventional definition of the gift as the opposite of exchange: a gift is only a gift if you give without receiving anything in return. But the minute a gift which the recipient wants is intentionally offered or received – the very conditions of the gift, which distinguish it from theft or accidental loss, or from giving someone something they do not want, for example – the donor becomes symbolically repaid by gratitude (by what in French would be called *reconnaissance*, meaning both recognition of the gift and gratitude for it), and the gift becomes part of an exchange and therefore ceases to be a gift. Derrida argues that the gift is possible only if time is divided by that time outside of time designated by the deconstructive reading of Madame de Maintenon's sentence.

The concept of time required by Derrida's analysis is a difficult one, and is discussed at length in 'Ousia et grammè: note sur une note de *Sein und Zeit*' (1968)[10] and *Aporias* (1993).[11] Derrida allows the contradiction which Hegel resolves dialectically to remain in contradiction, defining time as *différance*, as the non-self-identity and perpetual deferral of the present.[12] This suggests a means of understanding the perhaps even more difficult aporia of the gift. Derrida's concept of time describes a situation in which there is no time, time being always divided and deferred. Derrida elsewhere deconstructs the unity of the subject, of the subject as self-identical in the unfolding of time; deconstructs the disparate moments of subjectivity as resolved into a unity called the subject;[13] time (as *différance*) divides the subject. I would like to suggest on the strength of this, and in a provisional manner, a way in which the gift might be possible. If he who gives is not a subject, if the giver is not identical with the one who is repaid by the gratitude elicited by the gift, if, divided by time, the giver is not able retrospectively to recognise the one who gave as himself, then perhaps something may have been *given*, in accordance with the full rigour of Derrida's understanding of that term.[14] The gift in Derrida is also of course an ethical duty. Whereas the economy of exchange is what constitutes the subject (the subject who gives, the subject who receives), the gift involves a duty to the other as absolutely other, and a relation to one's self as other, which deconstitutes the subject. The gift exceeds the way philosophy, within the limit of a certain concept of time as limit, 'thinks its other' (and therefore itself) as a subject. The deconstructive concept of time is inseparable from an ethics of the gift.

We now turn from ethics to deconstruction's relationship to tradition and to Bakhtin's definition of the novel and the epic. Bakhtin defines the epic as representing a world absolutely in the past and alien to contemporary experience, and contrasts it to the novel, which is in a 'zone of maximal contact with the present (with contemporary reality) in all its openendedness'.[15] The epic as form and all epics are 'absolute and complete . . . closed as a circle; inside . . . everything is finished, already over' (p. 16). But the present, writes

Bakhtin, 'is in essence . . . inconclusive; by its very nature it demands con-
tinuation, it moves into the future' (p. 30). In order to fulfil its vocation of
describing the present, the form of the novel must itself be ever-changing,
and therefore always oriented towards the future. Already, the valorisation of
an ever-changing present which is accomplished in the future constitutes a
point of resemblance between Bakhtin and (post-)modernity.

Although defining novel and epic in opposition to each other, Bakhtin
suggestively argues that a productive relationship obtains between the two.
The novel is defined as taking *language* as its object of representation: it does
not just use language to represent the real world, but also (with parody for
example) dramatises the language which carries out that representation. And
the most plentiful source of languages for the novel to represent, according
Bakhtin, is the epic. The novel represents the style of the epic in 'intonational
quotation marks'.[16] In other words, the novel relates to the epic by citing it.
By contrast, the epic's use of language is non-citational and purely representational. And from this stems a further point of similarity between Bakhtin's
novel and postmodernity. The non-citational nature of epic language makes
it self-sufficient: it cannot recognise any other way of describing that which
it describes. And, as Bakhtin argues from a rigorously historicist position,[17]
the language used by the epic is intimately connected with what Bakhtin calls
its 'point of view' (p. 60).

The epic is thus a dogmatic form, which presents its object on a valorised
plane which is absolutely superior to the reader's, and which only admits one
point of view. Bakhtin argues that the *'boundary* . . . is immanent in the form
of the epic itself and is felt and heard in its every word' ('Epic and Novel',
p. 16; my emphasis). The novel, by contrast, is democratic, and transgresses
the boundary of the epic in a postmodern way: it mixes high style with low
('Prehistory', p. 58), and literary forms of language with non-literary ('Epic
and Novel', p. 33); it presupposes an equality between the reader and the
text (p. 27); it brooks no 'single unitary language', but instead 'is a *system* of
languages that mutually and ideologically interanimate each other'
('Prehistory', p. 47); it is 'multi-generic, multi-styled . . . reflecting in all its
fullness the heteroglossia and multiple voices of a given culture', and in it
'the dominant discourse is reflected as something . . . ageing, dying' (p. 60).
By placing the epic or dominant point of view alongside others, the novel
relativises its claims to absolute authority.

Bakhtin asserts that the different genres and viewpoints in the novel argue,
and that the argument is one in which historically progressive and democratic
points of view always triumph. We should not be hasty, however, to see the
relationship of novel to epic as simple progression. Indeed, it is by avoiding
this determination that Bakhtin gets closest to the deconstructive insight:
'The novelisation of other genres does not imply their subjection to an alien
literary canon; on the contrary, novelisation implies a liberation from all that

serves as a brake on their unique development' ('Epic and Novel', p. 39). In citing the epic, the novel does not merely go beyond it, but allows the realisation of the epic's potential. But we should not be hasty either to prise this sentence from the context of Bakhtin's argument. Bakhtin consistently argues as if it were possible for the epic to represent the world without being a citational use of language. It is on this condition that he can rigorously separate the epic from the novel. He is thus able to say of the Roman artistic sensibility that it considered the epic form as being complete *only* with the addition of its novelistic parodic counterpart ('Prehistory', p. 58), as if the novel were the truth of the epic, its *Rettung*, to borrow a phrase from Walter Benjamin.

Derrida argues that the idea of non-citational language involves (as it does in Bakhtin) positing an origin for language which is both cultural and linguistic, a belonging of non-citational language to the fullness of context of a national language. He addresses the opposition between non-citational and citational language in these terms:

> The possibility of . . . citational graft . . . constitutes every mark in writing . . . which is to say in the possibility of its functioning being cut off . . . from its 'original' *vouloir-dire* and from its participation in a saturable . . . context. Every sign . . . can be *cited*, put between quotation marks; in so doing it can break with every context . . . This does not imply that the mark is valid outside of a context, but on the contrary that there are only contexts without any center or absolute anchoring. This citationality . . . is neither an accident nor an anomaly, it is that (normal/abnormal) without which a mark could not even have a function called 'normal'.[18]

Derrida here critiques J. L. Austin's theory of speech acts precisely for considering citation as abnormal, as a parasite on normal language. The novel in Bakhtin functions like the parasite in Austin, except that the parasitism of the novel is valued and welcomed by Bakhtin. But Derrida's point implicitly demonstrates that the epic's representation of a world view is impossible without the citation which Bakhtin presents as the sole province of the novel, writing that an utterance could not succeed 'if its formulation did not repeat a "coded" or iterable utterance or [if it were] not identifiable as *conforming* with an iterable model, if it were not then identifiable as a "citation"' ('Signature Event Context', p. 18). The epic cannot be said to exist autonomously, and therefore cannot be saved by the subsequent addition of the novel, because it is already novelistic according to its conditions of possibility. The novel is not original then, in the sense of an original addition to a completed epic, but is original in the sense of being the origin of the possibility of the epic. And the blindness which accompanies Bakhtin's wonderful insight is what keeps his thought postmodern. For him, the novel escapes any charge of relativism, of 'nihilistic denial' ('Prehistory', p. 55) so long as it is the site of an argument with the epic. This argument gives it a positive determination; but, once the epic is taken away, there is no longer a 'point of view' for the novel as such, and it reverts to relativism.

I want to contrast Bakhtin's concept of the novel with Derrida's strategy of the double gesture. The citationality of language conditions for Derrida the way we read what Bakhtin might have described as epic:

> The writer writes *in* a language and *in* a logic whose proper system . . . his discourse cannot dominate absolutely. He uses them only by letting himself . . . be governed by the system. And reading [*la lecture*] must always aim at a certain relationship, unperceived by the writer, between what he commands and what he does not command of the patterns of the language that he uses. This relationship is . . . a signifying structure that critical reading should *produce*.[19]

Deconstructive reading begins within the divided text which it reads. That text is divided because of the citationality which is the condition according to which language is possible. Such reading goes beyond all the relationships to tradition which are exhausted by historical modernism. It is neither submission to the past, nor opposition in the name of a modern subject independent of tradition. What it must produce is both the rigorous coherence of the text, and the point at which that text ends in aporia. And in accepting as its starting point the always-already-there of the text, of the tradition within which it writes, deconstruction spurns any invention of an alternative tradition. It is also foreign to any relativism, demonstrating the limits of the text it reads precisely in order to achieve a more rigorous understanding of the problematic with which it grapples.[20] The deconstructed text therefore does not belong to its original author or deconstructive reader: its project is only possible because of the reading, but the reading is only possible on the basis of the always-already-there of the text. To understand this, we require a new understanding of originality:

> Geoff Bennington 's reading of Kant is, I am almost sure, a valid countersignature for Kant. It adds something new that is Geoff's gesture, Geoff's invention; but this invention is an interesting one only to the extent that it acknowledges an event that was already there, which is Kant's text. If you ask me why do you have to apply yourself to these things, it is because they are other and I cannot, and I should not, and I do not want to erase this otherness. And they are other to the extent that they were before me, which means that I am before them. I am before them as before the Law. They are the Law. So, in that case, my

duty, my obligation of being before them, is to countersign with my own blood, my own ink, my own work, countersign what they have done and in a way that their ghosts could not only approve or recognise something, but also be enriched by a gift; and accepting a gift means countersigning.[21]

In this respect, the T. S. Eliot who writes this sentence is close to Derrida: 'If we approach a poet without this prejudice we shall often find that not only the best, but the most individual parts of his work may be those in which the dead poets, his ancestors, assert their immortality most vigorously'.[22] There is in Eliot's writing a continuity between this notion of tradition and his notion of community.[23] Because time divides the subject, and citationality divides the text, deconstruction must aim for a relationship to tradition which exceeds the oppositions of traditional to original, of text to commentary. It demands a submission to the other, to language, and to tradition. The ethics which have lately become more prominent in Derrida's work are related to precisely this notion of otherness, and they define ethical duty as a duty to the other as absolutely other. The relationship which Derrida advocates towards the other is thus also the relationship of deconstruction to the texts it reads:

> When I take responsibility in my name for me, and since I am not identical with myself . . . , then taking a responsibility for myself means that *I act under the law of someone else in me* [my emphasis]. . . . So the strange thing is that we have to respond in the sense of having responsibility for another, which means also that we are not active in doing so, we are passive. . . . We take responsibility in a situation of heteronomy; that is, in obeying actively-passively, in what I would call a passion, the law of the other . . . I would claim that there is no such thing as an active personal decision, and that the enigma of responsibility lies in this *aporia*: that a decision is something passive in a certain sense of passivity, something to which you are applied. ('"As if I were Dead"', pp. 222–3)

Deconstruction's exceeding of the subject in the act of relating to tradition allows it to exceed the subject around which ethics can function as a delimiting of the rights and duties of particular subjects. In so doing, it points towards an ethics which is only thinkable beyond the subject and within community.[24] The concept of time which makes deconstruction post-postmodern allows it to think a relationship to the other of tradition and community which exceeds the superficial epistemological and ethical relativism which we call 'postmodern'. This analysis can only end within tradition, by citing tradition *en abîme*. Having suggested that Eliot in some way prefigures Derrida, I will cite Eliot citing Dante as his precursor, at that moment where he sees Dante going beyond Virgil:

But he [Virgil] was denied the vision of the man who could say:

'Within its depths I saw ingathered, bound by love in one volume, the scattered leaves of all the universe.'

Legato con amor in un volume.[25]

NOTES

1. Nick Royle, 'Nor is Deconstruction: Christopher Norris, *Deconstruction: Theory and Practice*', *Oxford Literary Review*, 5:1–2 (1982), 170–7 (p. 173).
2. Jürgen Habermas, 'Modernity – an Incomplete Project' (1981), in Peter Brooker (ed.), *Modernism/Postmodernism* (London: Longman), pp. 125–38 (p. 127).
3. Anthony Giddens, 'Modernism and Postmodernism' (1981), in Thomas Docherty (ed.), *Postmodernism: A Reader* (Brighton: Harvester, 1990), pp. 11–13 (p. 11).
4. Aristotle, *Physics* 219a, trans. R. P. Hardie and R. K. Gaye, in Jonathan Barnes (ed.), *The Complete Works of Aristotle*, 2 vols (Princeton and Guildford, Surrey: Princeton University Press, 1984), vol. 1, pp. 314–446; quoted in Karl Simms, 'The Time of Deconstruction and the Deconstruction of Time', *Imprimatur*, 1:2–3 (Spring 1996), 194–9 (p. 194).
5. G. W. F. Hegel, *Philosophy of Nature*, trans. A. V. Miller (Oxford: Oxford University Press, 1970), p. 39; quoted in Simms, 'The Time of Deconstruction', p. 197.
6. Such an interpretation of postmodernity is in fact envisaged by Lyotard in his discussion of 'postmodernism' in what he calls its 'mechanistic meaning': 'In an amazing acceleration, the generations precipitate themselves. A work can become modern only if it is first postmodern. Postmodernism thus understood is not modernism at its end but in the nascent state, and this state is constant' (Jean-François Lyotard, 'Answering the Question: What is Postmodernism?' (1982), *Modernism/Postmodernism*, pp. 139–50 (p. 148).
7. 'Tympan' (1972), *Marges – de la philosophie* (Paris: Minuit, 1972), pp. i–xxv (p. i)/*Margins – of Philosophy*, trans. Alan Bass (Brighton: Harvester, 1982), pp. ix–xxix (p. x).
8. *Aufhebung* is of course the key concept of Hegelian dialectics, and describes the opposition between the spirit and that which is its negation, and in which the negation of the spirit is 'raised up' into a new term in which that opposition is resolved. *Aufhebung* is usually but inadequately rendered as 'sublation' in English.
9. Quoted in Derrida, *Given Time: I, Counterfeit Money* (1991), trans. Peggy Kamuf (Chicago: University of Chicago Press, 1992), p. 1.
10. *Marges – de la philosophie*, pp. 31–78/'*Ousia and Gramme*: Note on a Note from *Being and Time*', *Margins – of Philosophy*, pp. 29–67.

11. Trans. Thomas Dutoit (Stanford: Stanford University Press, 1993).

12. Cf. 'Différance' (1968), *Marges – de la philosophie*, pp. 1–29/*Margins – of Philosophy*, pp. 1–27.

13. Cf. inter alia Derrida, 'Limited Inc. a b c . . .' (1977), trans. Samuel Weber (1977), in Gerald Graff (ed.), *Limited Inc* (Evanston: Northwestern University Press, 1990), pp. 29–110 (p. 49).

14. Cf. Philippe Lacoue-Labarthe, 'Le paradoxe et la mimésis' (1979), *L'imitation des Modernes* (Paris: Galilée, 1986), pp. 15–36 (pp. 28–9), and James Joyce, *Ulysses* (1922) (New York: Random House, 1934), ch. 6, p. 187.

15. Mikhail Mikhailovitch Bakhtin, 'Epic and Novel: Toward a Methodology for the Study of the Novel' (1941), in *The Dialogic Imagination*, trans. Caryl Emerson and Michael Holquist, ed. Michael Holquist (Austin and London: University of Texas Press, 1981), pp. 3–40 (p. 11).

16. 'From the Prehistory of Novelistic Discourse' (1940) [hereafter 'Prehistory'], *The Dialogic Imagination*, pp. 41–83 (p. 44).

17. By this I mean that Bakhtin seems to regard (at least in the essays discussed here) formal developments in literature as following the development of material events in history. These events follow a logical path in which society moves away from authoritarianism toward democracy.

18. Derrida, 'Signature événement contexte' (1971)/'Signature Event Context', trans. Samuel Weber and Jeffrey Mehlman (1977), *Limited Inc*, pp. 1–23 (p. 12).

19. *De la grammatologie* (Paris: Minuit, 1967), part 2, ch. 1, p. 227/*Of Grammatology*, trans. Gayatri Chakravorty Spivak (Baltimore: Johns Hopkins University Press, 1974), p. 158; trans. modified.

20. 'The exteriority of the signifier is the exteriority of writing in general, and I shall try to show below that there is no linguistic sign before writing. Without that very exteriority, the very idea of the sign goes to ruin [tombe en ruine]. Since our entire world and language would collapse with it, and since its evidence and value keep, to a certain point of derivation, an indestructible solidity, there would be a certain amount of silliness [niaiserie] in concluding from its belonging [appartenance] to an epoch that it is necessary to "move on to something else" . . . For a proper understanding of the gesture we are trying to sketch here, one must understand the expressions "epoch", "closure of an epoch", "historical genealogy", in a new way; and first remove them from all relativism' (*Of Grammatology*, part 1, ch. 1, p. 25/14; trans. modified).

21. Derrida, '"As if I were Dead": An Interview with Jacques Derrida', in John Brannigan, Ruth Robbins and Julian Wolfreys (eds), *Applying: To Derrida* (London: Macmillan, 1996), pp. 212–26 (pp. 220–1).

22. 'Tradition and the Individual Talent' (1919), in *The Sacred Wood* (1920) (London: Methuen, 1960), pp. 47–59/*Selected Essays* (1932), 3rd edn (London: Faber, 1951), part 1, pp. 13–22 (p. 14).

23. Cf. *Notes towards the Definition of Culture* (London: Faber, 1948), ch. 2, pp. 43–4 and Appendix 114; 'The Social Function of Poetry' (1945), in *On Poetry and Poets* (London: Faber, 1957), pp. 15–25; 'Leçon de Valéry', *The Listener*, 37 (9 January 1947), p. 72; *After Strange Gods: A Primer of Modern Heresy* (London: Faber, 1934), ch. 1, p. 29; 'A Brief Introduction to the Method of Paul Valéry', in Paul Valéry, *Le Serpent*, trans. Mark Wardle (London: R. Cobden-Sanderson,

1924), pp. 7–15 (p. 7); and 'Tradition and the Individual Talent', pp. 14–17.

24. Ralph Pite has remarked that the idea of community is unthinkable outside of a relationship to tradition, a notion which sustains parts of his excellent monograph on Dante: *The Circle of Our Vision* (Oxford: Oxford University Press, 1994).

25. 'Virgil and the Christian World' (1951), in *On Poetry and Poets*, pp. 121–31 (p. 131).

Chapter Six

PIERRE BOURDIEU AND THE CHRONOTOPES OF 'POST-THEORY'

Jeremy Lane

We will give the name *chronotope* (literally, 'time space') to the intrinsic connectedness of temporal and spatial relationships that are artistically expressed in literature. . . . We understand the chronotope as a formally constitutive category of literature; we will not deal with the chronotope in other areas of culture.[1]

Thus Mikhail Bakhtin, at the opening of his essay, 'Forms of Time and Chronotope in the Novel', defines the terms of his inquiry into 'the literary artistic chronotope', leaving hanging the tantalising prospect of the chronotope's possible application to 'other areas of culture'.

As Robert Young argues, the reception of Bakhtin's work in the English-speaking world was itself mediated through a particular chronotope, through certain specific conditions of institutional space and time. He suggests that in the early 1980s, Bakhtin's work offered 'the possibility of deliverance' from 'the beleaguered situation' in which Marxism found itself, its influence increasingly challenged by structuralism and poststructuralism:

Bakhtin was heralded as offering a 'way out' of the impasse that had cut Marxist knowledge off from the social. Bakhtin's attraction was that he seemed to offer the possibility for Marxism to return to the old certainties of the everyday world outside.

To this effect, Young quotes Terry Eagleton: 'Bakhtin recapitulates *avant la lettre* many of the leading motifs of contemporary deconstruction', putting those motifs 'scandalously, in a firmly social context'.[2] What Young does not analyse, however, is the rather bizarre chronotopicity of Eagleton's remark. For Bakhtin to have 'recapitulated' the 'motifs' of deconstruction '*avant la lettre*', before they had even been formulated as such, would seem to imply an enviable capacity to cross the conventional boundaries of space and time. The strangely recursive, not to say wholly contradictory structure of this statement might itself be read as symptomatic of Eagleton's ill-disguised desire to be rid of deconstruction the quicker to return to the 'certainties' of Marxism.

If the term 'Theory' is taken, in its most generic and imprecise sense, to encompass everything from structuralism to postmodernism, poststructuralism and postcolonialism, then Eagleton might be seen as attempting to co-opt Bakhtin to the cause of 'post-Theory'. In this case, 'post-Theory' would imply an ability to transcend or move beyond the limitations and weaknesses of 'Theory'. The desire to challenge and transcend that set of theoretical concerns which dominates the intellectual field at any one time is of course entirely laudable. Yet the mode of this transcendence seems to be somewhat paradoxical; what we might term the chronotope of post-Theory would seem typically to involve a *moving beyond* which is somehow also a *return*, as Young so tellingly put it, 'to the old certainties of the everyday world outside'. It might be argued that such a chronotope suggested less a willingness to engage critically with a set of theoretical concerns than a certain nostalgia for those certainties which 'Theory' has apparently undermined.

Over recent years, the avowedly historicist and scientific work of Pierre Bourdieu has increasingly come to be heralded as one other solution to the perceived impasses of Theory, a 'welcome relief for anyone suffering from post-Lacanian excess', to quote one recent critic.[3] In Bourdieu's case, such claims have been made not in the name of Marxism but of an empirical, 'scientific' and historicist tradition of sociology, considered to be increasingly under threat from postmodernism and poststructuralism. Bourdieu himself has been eager to encourage such an interpretation, seeking to 'dissociate' himself 'clearly' from 'the tradition of philosophical critique (be it in the form of deconstruction or archaeology) of texts, in particular scientific texts, that originated in France (in particular in the work of Derrida and Foucault) and that . . . realises itself in a nihilistic questioning of science'.[4] He describes the reflexivity on which he grounds his claim to scientificity as 'fundamentally anti-narcissistic', contrasting it to a certain 'postmodern turn' in anthropology, that 'thinly veiled nihilistic relativism . . . that stands at the polar opposite to a truly reflexive social science'.[5]

This trenchant critique of poststructuralism and postmodernism in the name of science has, perhaps unsurprisingly, earned Bourdieu the plaudits of many in the British and American sociological communities. Thus, Derek Robbins contrasts Bourdieu favourably with Derrida and Lyotard, 'Parisian postmodernists' and 'intellectual cowboys', who, it appears, are 'intellectually dishonest and have forfeited moral integrity by indulging in a shallow form of academic journalism'.[6] A rather more measured assessment of Bourdieu's work has been offered by Craig Calhoun, who suggests it might offer 'a sensible third path' between Habermasian universalism and postmodern 'relativism'.[7] For Calhoun, Bourdieu's ethnological studies of Kabylia, *Outline of a Theory of Practice* (1977) and *The Logic of Practice* (1990), constitute a 'different poststructuralism', 'better grounded', 'more scientific', but nonetheless sensitive to the ethical and political implications of representing the anthropological 'other'.[8] This finds an echo in Nicholas Thomas's study, *Colonialism's Culture* (1994), in which he plays Bourdieu's concept of 'practice', 'his interest in located subjectivities . . . which situates colonial representations and narratives in terms of agents, locations, and periods' against the 'global theorising' of postcolonial theorists like Homi Bhabha, Gayatri Spivak or Edward Said.[9]

These are major claims which suggest Bourdieu's work could contribute much to current debates concerning the strengths and limitations of 'Theory' in general, and postcolonial theory in particular. However, it might be argued that such claims reveal as much about the institutional time and space of Bourdieu's reception into the British and American sociological fields as they do about the nature of the work itself. Certainly, one can detect the same chronotope that determined Eagleton's appropriation of Bakhtin behind these claims that Bourdieu has somehow transcended the failings of 'Theory' by staging a 'return' to Science and History. Moreover, this chronotope seems itself to mobilise a series of somewhat predictable binary oppositions. On one side stands Bourdieu, guarantor of the certainties of science, objectivity and history against the 'narcissism', 'relativism', 'nihilism', perhaps even self-indulgent literariness of the assorted postmodernists and poststructuralists ranged on the other.

This rather comforting schema would seem, however, to come undone at a crucial moment in the argument of *Outline of a Theory of Practice*. For this text, whose firm scientific and historical grounding has been so favourably contrasted to the perceived 'relativism' of postmodern and postcolonial theory, seems to hinge on an apparently problematic recourse to the literary, to a nostalgic evocation of times past by that most determined defender of the value of subjective sentiment over sociological objectivity, Marcel Proust. In the passage in question, Bourdieu is attempting to communicate what he terms the subjective experience of 'originary doxa', or the 'primal state of innocence of doxa', that specific set of social, spatial and temporal relations characteristic of 'pre-literate', 'pre-capitalist' societies like Kabylia.[10] Having noted the difficulty of finding first-hand testimony to describe this state, Bourdieu first quotes an old peasant woman's account of the rituals surrounding illness and healing prior to the introduction of western medicines. To this account of a native informant, he then juxtaposes, 'in all seriousness', the following quotation from the 'Chambres' section of Proust's *Contre Sainte-Beuve* (1954):

From the position of the bed, my side recalled the place where the cru-
cifix used to be, the breadth of the recess in the bedroom in my grandparents' house, in the days when there were still bedrooms and parents,
a time for each thing, when you loved your parents not because you
found them intelligent but because they were your parents, when you
went to bed not because you wanted to but because it was time, and
when you marked the desire, the acceptance and the whole ceremony
of sleeping by going up two steps to the big bed, where you closed the
blue rep curtains with their raised velvet bands, and where, when you
were ill, the old remedies kept you for several days on end, with a night
light on the Siena marble mantelpiece, without any of the immoral
medicines that allow you to get up and imagine you can lead the life of
a healthy man when you are ill, sweating under the blankets thanks
to perfectly harmless infusions, which for two thousand years have
contained the flowers of the meadows and the wisdom of old women.
(*Outline*, pp.166–7)

On a purely thematic level, this quotation from Proust would seem well
suited to Bourdieu's needs, providing a concise evocation of the subjective
experience of doxa, what he terms 'the subjective experience of this world of
realised ought-to-be' (p. 166). The state of doxa, which characterises Kabyle
society according to Bourdieu, corresponds to a specific form of sociopolitical
organisation in which social norms and imperatives are not formalised or
codified into laws or imposed by institutions but rather are internalised
directly, 'incorporated' pre-thetically 'from body to body, i.e. on the hither
side of words or concepts' (p. 2). It is this state of doxa, Bourdieu argues,
which ensures that the cycle of social reproduction in 'pre-capitalist' societies such as Kabylia is 'simple' or unproblematic. In Kabylia, social imperatives are rarely expressed or objectified in discourse and thus are not open to
dispute or question: 'what is essential goes without saying because it comes
without saying', as Bourdieu puts it. Or, in more technical terms:

> The adherence expressed in the doxic relation to the social world is the
> absolute form of recognition of legitimacy through misrecognition of
> arbitrariness, since it is unaware of the very question of legitimacy, which
> arises from competition for legitimacy and hence from conflict between
> groups claiming to possess it. (p. 168)

As Bourdieu emphasises, the doxa also represents a spatio-temporal relationship, a form of social organisation in which there is a time and a place for
everything. Doxa implies 'circular' rather than 'linear' time (p. 162). In doxa,
the experience of time is unproblematic, self-evident, even pre-reflexive, since
the collective sense of what might constitute a reasonable or thinkable course

of future action is 'incorporated' into the dispositional structures of the 'habitus' at the pre-predicative level and hence placed beyond the reflexive grasp of the Kabyles themselves.

It is this sense of inhabiting a social universe in which things are as they are because they have always been so and hence, it can only be imagined, always will be so, that Bourdieu finds so powerfully evoked in Proust's childhood reminiscence. There is, of course, a danger that, in having recourse to this nostalgic evocation of childhood, Bourdieu risks reproducing a characteristically ethnocentric and Romantic trope according to which 'primitive' societies such as Kabylia are to the west what childhood innocence is to adulthood. In Bourdieu's defence, it should be stated that he is at pains to emphasise that the state of doxa corresponds not to an actual state of innocence but rather to the appearance of such innocence. It does not represent a state of primal unity in which there are no inequalities or social hierarchies, but rather a period in which those hierarchies are naturalised to such a degree as to be placed entirely beyond question. Furthermore, since doxa, by definition, implies a lack of consciousness as to its existence, it can only ever be articulated retrospectively, from a position outside doxa. Doxa is thus, by its very essence, not only a fictional or ideological construct, it is also an experience that can only ever be evoked nostalgically, since from the moment its truth can be spoken, it must already have passed: 'The truth of doxa is only ever fully revealed when negatively constituted by the constitution of a *field of opinion*, the locus of confrontation of competing discourses . . .' (*Outline*, p. 168).

The doxa is, then, an ideological representation of space and time. In having recourse to a literary quotation to evoke the 'subjective experience' of doxa, Bourdieu recalls Bakhtin's argument that the various temporal and spatial relationships, or chronotopes, expressed in different novelistic genres themselves reflect the different political régimes or modes of social organisation under which those genres were produced. Indeed, in a 'pre-class agricultural stage in the development of human society', Bakhtin identifies what he calls the 'folkloric chronotope' ('Forms . . .', p. 206). This folkloric sense of time, like the doxa, is essentially cyclical and repetitive. It is linked to the cycles of agricultural production and the passage of the seasons, and through its 'cyclical repetitiveness' constitutes both a time of closer communal bonds and a kind of sealed-off time in which the possibilities for change remain strictly limited: 'its cyclicity is a negative feature, one that limits the force and ideological productivity of this time. The mark of cyclicity, and consequently of cyclical repetitiveness, is imprinted on all events occurring in this time. Time's forward impulse is limited by the cycle' (pp. 209–10).

This cyclical conception of time, 'under conditions . . . that took for granted the immanent unity of time' (p. 210), is very close indeed to Bourdieu's notion of doxa which demands 'submission to the collective rhythms of agricultural production' (*Outline*, p. 163). Moreover, in common with the doxa, the folkloric chronotope precludes awareness of its specific characteristics and can thus only be constituted retrospectively:

> Such a time is *unified* in an unmediated way. However, this immanent unity becomes apparent *only in the light of later perceptions of time* in literature (and in ideology in general), when the time of personal, every-day family occasions has already been individualised and separated out from the time of the collective historical life of the social whole. (p. 208, my emphasis)

In *Outline*, Bourdieu provides an account of how this unified, cyclical conception of time comes to an end. He suggests that the end of the state of doxa involves a kind of collective *epoche*, the practical suspension of a previously unquestioned faith in the self-evidence of the doxic order. Such a collective *epoche* can be determined either by 'the political and economic crises correlative with class division' or by 'culture contact', which, in forcing the Kabyles to confront alternative models of social organisation, reveals the potentially arbitrary nature of their own customs and rituals. A 'field of opinion' or 'universe of discourse' opens up, the site of a struggle between 'heterodoxy' and 'orthodoxy', between the dominated classes, who seek to challenge the status quo, and the dominant, who seek to restore 'the primal innocence of doxa' through the imposition of 'orthodoxy' (*Outline*, pp. 168–9). Once again, this has a very close equivalent in Bakhtin's account of the competing forces of a 'centrifugal' 'polyphony' or 'dialogism' and the 'centripetal' forces of 'monologism', which 'serve to unify and centralise the verbal-ideological world'.[11]

In his account of the events of May 1968 in *Homo academicus*, Bourdieu offers a specific example of this breakdown in doxa. He contrasts an 'organic' state in French higher education, a 'cycle of simple reproduction' in which the system unproblematically reproduced France's dominant class who hence respected its values and hierarchies without question, with a 'critical' stage on the eve of the events of May. Massive expansion in the numbers of students and graduates, and the shift in French higher education from an 'elite' to a 'mass' system, had signalled an end to this 'cycle of simple reproduction' and a collective *epoche* or suspension of belief in the values of the universities. A 'field of opinion' thus opened up in which what had previously been taken for granted was subjected to radical questioning, and, in a telling phrase, Bourdieu compares those lecturers who clung to the *status quo ante* to 'old Kabyle peasants' stubbornly resisting the introduction of modern agricultural methods.[12] Combining with a series of analogous developments in parallel fields, this breakdown in the universities' cycle of reproduction took the form of a 'suspension', a 'rupture' or '*epoche*' in the conventional experience of time: 'the rupture of temporal rhythms' which produced 'free, holiday, or festive time'. In this 'festive' or 'public' sense of time, the possibilities for future action and effective social change appeared real and numerous:

> time becomes a *public time*, identical for all, measured according to the same landmarks, the same presences, which, by impinging on everyone simultaneously, makes everyone share the same present. Moreover, just as in the festival everyone has their festive dispositions reinforced by the spectacle of others' enjoyment, so here everyone is revealed to themselves, and also reinforced, or legitimated, in their malaise or their revolt . . . (*Homo*, p. 185, translation modified)

Once again, it is to Proust that Bourdieu turns in order to illustrate his conception of this rupture in spatial, temporal and social relationships. In this instance, he turns to those passages of *A la recherche du temps perdu* in which Proust describes the inversion of conventional social relationships within the world of the Parisian *salons* wrought by the Dreyfus Affair (pp. 318–19 nn. 44, 46). Once again, Bourdieu's account of the temporal experience of workers and students in May 1968 has a remarkably close equivalent in the work of Bakhtin, namely his concept of 'festival' or 'carnival' time in which all stable notions of time and space are subverted and a new world of possibilities opens up. In his book on Rabelais, Bakhtin describes 'carnival time' as follows:

> However, medieval laughter is not a subjective, individual and biological consciousness of the uninterrupted flow of time. It is the social consciousness of all the people. Man experiences this flow of time in the festive marketplace, in the carnival crowd, as he comes into contact with other bodies of varying age and social caste. He is aware of being a member of a continually growing and renewed people.[13]

These striking similarities between Bourdieu's conception of time and historical change and Bakhtin's concept of the chronotope might help clarify the role of the Proustian quotations which appear in *Outline* and *Homo academicus*. The importance of the 'state of originary doxa', which Bourdieu attempts to describe, aided by Proust, is not simply that it characterises the inherent nature of social relations in a 'pre-capitalist' society such as Kabylia. The doxa, as Bourdieu puts it, represents 'the *absolute* form of recognition of legitimacy through misrecognition of arbitrariness'. More attenuated forms of such misrecognition can also be found in capitalist societies such as France. Indeed, according to Bourdieu, prior to the 'critical' events of May 1968, French students and lecturers enjoyed a 'doxic' relationship to the institutions of higher education, 'misrecognising' the 'arbitrariness' of the values they inculcated. Kabylia, then, serves as the archetypal instance of that 'doxic relation to the world' which Bourdieu places at the heart of the process of social reproduction and the workings of the habitus in capitalist and 'pre-capitalist' societies alike. Social change, or history itself, is thus theorised by Bourdieu as the sporadic 'rupture', 'suspension', or *epoche* in this state of doxa, as the passage from the 'organic' state of doxa to the state of 'crisis'. Literature's role in this schema is to evoke and attest to the 'generality' of the subjective experience associated with living through each of these contrasting states, to demonstrate that the sporadic alternation between the 'doxic' and the 'critical' is a recurrent feature of historical change and that this alternation itself is an 'invariant', 'transhistorical' feature of any such change.[14]

The concept of 'originary doxa' thus plays a pivotal role in Bourdieu's sociology; it is both the kind of 'point zero' from which all history and social change begins and the most extreme form of that 'doxic relationship' to the world characteristic of the 'habitus'. In his ethnological studies such as *Outline*, Bourdieu seeks to hold up Kabylia as an observable, empirically verifiable, historically situated case of the 'state of doxa', thereby grounding his theories of both social reproduction and historical change 'scientifically'. However, closer scrutiny of this 'state of doxa', at both the empirical and the conceptual levels, reveals that what characterises the 'doxa' is precisely its resistance to any form of straightforward observation, empirical verification, or indeed historical location.

As we have seen, Bourdieu argues that the state of doxa is such as to deny those living under its sway consciousness of its existence. Only from a position outside doxa can its truth be articulated, and Bourdieu goes on to cite a peasant woman lamenting precisely the passing of doxa. Logically then, if he has found an informant capable of recounting the experience of doxa, the state of doxa must, by definition, have come to an end. Yet, throughout his works of Kabyle ethnology, Bourdieu employs the present tense to describe a Kabylia apparently still in the state of doxa, implicitly drawing on the authority of the ethnologist who has observed and is faithfully reporting what he saw, as he does so. It is only in a footnote to *The Logic of Practice* that Bourdieu hints that what lies behind his use of the present tense is in fact a process of *reconstructing* Kabylia as an archetype of 'originary doxa': 'The narrative present is used here systematically to describe practices that were present in the informants' memories at a given moment though *they may have more or less completely fallen into disuse for a greater or longer time*'.[15] This process of reconstruction, whose traces are systematically effaced from Bourdieu's ethnological texts, seems to rely on the inherently unreliable resources of personal reminiscence in a way which stands at odds with his much-vaunted commitment to 'scientific', 'objective' and 'historical' rigour.

Moreover, that Bourdieu should have to rely on personal reminiscences of practices which have 'more or less completely fallen into disuse for a greater or longer time', that he should have arrived in Kabylia *post festum*, as it were, after 'the state of doxa' had come to an end, is by no means coincidental. For, if his definition of the doxa is taken seriously, it is clear that, for both western anthropologist and native informant alike, the state of doxa must always already have (just) passed. A native informant cannot observe doxa since to do so would imply that he or she occupied a space outside doxa, something which can apparently only be achieved after doxa has come to an end. A western anthropologist cannot observe doxa since his or her very presence presupposes that 'cultural contact', in the case of Kabylia the French colonial occupation of Algeria, which signals the end of doxa. Further, since doxa is characteristic of 'pre-literate' societies, there can be no historical archive to attest to its past existence.

Indeed, it is sufficient for either native informant or professional anthropologist to declare that 'this society is characterised by the state of originary doxa' for that state to be over. Wherever and whenever the anthropologist thinks he or she has located doxa, it will always in fact have just passed, it will always already be somewhere else, at some elusive point as yet 'untouched' by 'cultural contact'. No sooner will the anthropologist reach that more distant point, that more isolated village or community, than their very arrival will signal the end of doxa there also. The pivotal concept of 'doxa' thus marks the site of an absence or lack in Bourdieu's theoretical discourse, that lack of evidence to attest to its existence which Bourdieu himself notes in *Outline*. This lack must now be read not as merely contingent but as in some sense originary, and Bourdieu's recourse to the wholly 'unscientific' resources of personal reminiscence and literary quotation to supplement that constitutive lack as obeying what Derrida has termed a 'logic of supplementarity'.[16] Far from representing a more 'scientific', 'better grounded', historically situated alternative to postmodern ethnologies, a work such as *Outline* might be read as recounting the vain quest or desire to locate and ground an eternally elusive concept of doxa whose originary lack or absence must be supplemented by recourse to literature and personal reminiscence, precisely those elements against which Bourdieu's 'scientific' rigour apparently defines itself.

Ironically, this structure of desire, of originary lack and supplementarity, is foreshadowed in the very quotation from Proust which Bourdieu chooses to illustrate the certainties of doxa. Read in context, this quotation can be seen to represent something rather more complex than a straightforwardly realist evocation of a lost age of more ordered temporal, spatial and social relationships. Proust's memory of the bedroom at his grandparents' house is revealed to be an illusion, a dream; what it evokes is both the struggle to secure some sense of certainty and the disturbing realisation that such a struggle will always be in vain. For it forms one of a series of mistaken impressions that strike Proust as he struggles to awake in unfamiliar surroundings. From this kaleidoscope of dream images, memories of his grandparents' house, of convalescence at Dieppe, of dozing in a cane chair in the garden at Auteuil, Proust seeks to secure some sense of temporal and spatial certainty, of precisely where and when he is.

This search for some sense of certainty in the face of a series of fleeting memories and mistaken impressions will form the opening of Proust's later novel, *A la recherche du temps perdu*. As Leo Bersani notes, 'The dizziness described at the beginning of "Combray" is the physical symptom of a general instability of being which Marcel tries to cure in various ways'. This 'dizziness', the symptom of a struggle to impose order and certainty on the external world, will be mirrored in Marcel's vain efforts to know, possess and control the various objects of his desire:

> without a reliably fixed, immobile image in the outer world, possession of others and of the self is impossible. Identities disintegrate into several unconnected pictures; attempts to project or recognise the self in visible external scenes are frustrated by the elusive metamorphoses of those scenes.[17]

It is this sense of instability and flux that endows Proust's novel with its own characteristic chronotope. As Georges Poulet remarks in his study, *Proustian Space* (1977), 'one can imagine nothing which might be further from Proustian thought' than a conventional philosophy of space and time, such as that implicit in Bourdieu's work, in which space is an orderly arrangement of places and objects against which all temporal discontinuity erupts *a posteriori*, as pure contingency:

> Instead of being a sort of general simultaneity which extends itself on every side to support, contain and secure relations between things, space [in Proust] is quite simply an incapacity which manifests itself everywhere, in every object of the world, to form together a stable order. (translation modified)[18]

For Poulet, Marcel's bedroom at Combray, the site of the refusal and ultimate concession of the mother's kiss, is marked by an anguishing sense of absence or lack. The narrative of the novel then supplements and is structured by that lack, which recurs throughout *A la recherche* . . . as the insuperable distance between desire and fulfilment:

> He, for whom his mother's kiss would have been the token of a happy *rapprochement* of a presence which Proust compares to 'real presence', must resign himself to accept the terribly real evidence to the contrary,

the evidence of an absence. Evidence which is reiterated throughout Proust's novel, as if to make of this novel an interminable demonstration of the impossibility of beings ever managing to be present one to another. (pp. 43–4, translation modified)

By an intriguing paradox, the quotation which Bourdieu wants to illustrate the certainties of doxa would seem rather to connote the confusion, even the anguish associated with both the lack of such stability and the consequent, constantly thwarted desire to impose some order or certainty onto an ever-shifting social and affective universe. This structure of a lack supplemented by a narrative which recounts 'the series of disappointments', to use Bersani's phrase, contingent on a desire to achieve grounded certainty is, of course, what characterises Bourdieu's own efforts to ground the notion of doxa 'scientifically'.

The inevitability of Bourdieu's failure to ground doxa either empirically or historically points to the conceptual weakness at the heart of the notion itself. For the state of 'originary doxa', the starting point or 'point zero' for Bourdieu's theories of historical change and social reproduction is inherently ahistorical; it is the point outside history which, paradoxically, grounds Bourdieu's notion of history, the point beyond empirical verification which underpins a sociological theory whose empirical groundings are so frequently contrasted with the 'empty theorising' of postmodern or poststructuralist philosophers.

It might therefore be argued that those critics who have seen Bourdieu's work as a panacea for the malaise engendered by 'Theory', in all its multifarious forms, have embarked on a quest for the lost certainties of History and Science destined to prove as vain as Bourdieu's quest for the certainties of the state of doxa or Marcel's search to regain time past. Indeed, such was surely already implicit in the chronotopicity both of Bourdieu's reception into the English-speaking world and of those claims that he had somehow transcended the impasses of 'Theory' by staging a return to those certainties that 'Theory' had placed in question.

NOTES

1. M. M. Bakhtin, 'Forms of Time and Chronotope in the Novel', in *The Dialogic Imagination*, trans. C. Emerson and M. Holquist (Austin: University of Texas Press, 1981), pp. 84–258, (p. 84). Further references to 'Forms . . .' are given after quotations in the text.
2. R. J. C. Young, 'Back to Bakhtin', in idem, *Torn Halves: Political Conflict in Literary and Cultural Theory* (Manchester: Manchester University Press, 1996), pp. 33–66.
3. B. Fowler, *Pierre Bourdieu and Cultural Theory: Critical Investigations* (London: Sage, 1997), p. 1.

4. P. Bourdieu, 'On the Possibility of a Field of World Sociology', trans. L. J. D. Wacquant, in C. Calhoun (ed.), *Social Theory for a Changing Society* (Oxford: Westview Press, 1991), pp. 373–87 (p. 385).

5. P. Bourdieu and L. J. D. Wacquant, *An Invitation to Reflexive Sociology* (Cambridge: Polity Press, 1992), p. 72.

6. D. Robbins, *The Work of Pierre Bourdieu: Recognising Society* (Milton Keynes: Open University Press, 1991), p. 173.

7. C. Calhoun, 'Habitus, Field, and Capital: The Question of Historical Specificity', in C. Calhoun, E. LiPuma and M. Postone (eds), *Bourdieu: Critical Perspectives* (Cambridge: Polity Press, 1993), pp. 61–82 (p. 62).

8. C. Calhoun, 'A Different Poststructuralism', review of *Outline of a Theory of Practice, Contemporary Sociology*, 25:3 (1996), 302–5.

9. N. Thomas, *Colonialism's Culture: Anthropology, Travel, and Government* (Cambridge: Polity Press, 1994), pp. 8–9, 58–60.

10. P. Bourdieu, *Outline of a Theory of Practice*, trans. R. Nice (Cambridge: Cambridge University Press, 1977), p. 169. Further references to *Outline* are given after quotations in the text.

11. *The Dialogic Imagination*, op. cit., pp. 270–2.

12. P. Bourdieu, *Homo academicus*, trans. P. Collier (Cambridge: Polity Press, 1988), p. 183. Further references to *Homo* are given after quotations in the text.

13. M. M. Bakhtin, *Rabelais and his World*, trans. H. Islowsky (Cambridge, MA: MIT Press, 1965), p. 92.

14. In *Homo academicus*, Bourdieu argues that his use of Proust is intended to give his analyses 'their general validity' (p. 318 n. 44). For his assertions regarding the 'transhistorical', 'invariant' validity of his analysis, see chapter 1, 'A Book for Burning'.

15. P. Bourdieu, *The Logic of Practice*, trans. R. Nice (Cambridge: Polity Press, 1990), p. 311 n. 2 (my emphasis).

16. See J. Derrida, *De la grammatologie* (Paris: Minuit, 1967).

17. L. Bersani, *Marcel Proust: The Fictions of Life and Art* (New York: Oxford University Press, 1965), p. 75.

18. G. Poulet, *Proustian Space*, trans. E. Coleman (Baltimore and London: Johns Hopkins University Press, 1977), pp. 41–2.

Part II

Inter

Chapter Seven

INTER

Geoffrey Bennington

Let's bury our differences. We can all agree now, or soon enough. Consensus is nigh. Theory is finished. They think it's all over. Dead and buried. Interred. Sound the last post. Post-theory; post post. Theory, and the terror Lyotard associated with it in the 1970s, is over because we have no differences: and if we have no differences, it's because we *all* love difference so much. Post-theory, we all do very different things, but they're all the same, because they all proclaim difference.

That, or such is my hypothesis here, is the call more or less concealed and more or less encouraged by recent, post-theoretical appeals to difference as a *value*. All our carefully won interest in difference in its difference from opposition or contradiction, and the ethical consequences we have sought to draw from difference, has (and this is 'post-theory') become a quick way of forgetting the very difference we set out to think and respect. Difference is dead and buried in the prevailing consensus about difference that we might appear to have reached. Interdisciplinarity has become a watchword for a soft historicist cultural idealism; internationalism for a rather feeble liberal good conscience and self-righteousness.

Inter. As a prefix, this term displays an uncanny obedience to the difference of its own meanings, one in which we can imagine Hegel finding something of the speculative pleasure he famously finds in the word *Aufheben*, in the *Greater Logic. On the one hand*, inter- separates, places between two or more entities, keeps them apart, puts up a frontier, prevents them meeting, joining, mingling and maybe identifying. Inter-val is perhaps the clearest case of this sense. Inter-calating, inter-posing, inter-polating, inter-mitting all obey this logic. But *on the other hand*, inter- joins, provides a means of communication and exchange. This can go from inter-view to inter-action to inter-course to inter-penetration, and implies just the opposite of the first sense of inter-: here the gap or difference is not being established or reinforced, but diminished, overcome or denied. 'Inter' in this second sense inters 'inter' in the first sense, or, if you like, 'inter' in the second sense comes after, is *post* with respect to 'inter' in the first sense.

In this way, the semantics of the word 'inter' tell us a dialectical story about our subject here today. First, it seems to say, there is the sense of 'inter-' as implying separation and difference: then the contradictory sense of 'inter-' as joining and overcoming difference; but that contradictory sense of joining and overcoming must *also* join and overcome the initial separation or contradiction between the two senses of the word, negating the negation, so that 'inter' finds its own truth in the sublation of its two contradictory senses. The joining after the separation joins the joining and the separation. And as soon as we start telling stories like the one I have told about meanings, it seems we are committed to this type of dialectical set-up, and that however hard we attempt to hold on to difference as our value, we are condemned to lose it in the identity that our second sense of 'inter' promises to deliver. This seems to confirm the analysis of difference given by Hegel in the *Greater Logic*: difference, says Hegel, if taken to an absolute (as it must be if it is to be properly conceptualised), must be absolute difference. Absolute difference must be absolutely different. If it is to be *absolutely* different, it must differ from absolutely everything, including itself. So absolute difference must be absolutely different from absolute difference. What's absolutely different from absolute difference? Identity. So absolute difference is absolutely identical with absolute identity. And although this analysis has its *specific* place in the architecture of the *Greater Logic*, and therefore in the Hegelian system more generally, it has (as indeed does every moment in that system) a certain generalisable virtue with respect to the system as a whole.

This Hegelian demonstration seems to me to be the truth of a certain fate of difference in recent 'post-theory'. We began – this was poststructuralism or postmodernism – by celebrating or proclaiming difference as the undoing of theory, only to find ourselves seeing it overcome in the very consensus about difference we were also arguing towards. We have no differences about difference any more. We all agree about difference now. This is what 'postmodernism' has come to signify in its softer sense: agreement about difference, consensus about discrepancy, anything goes, it's all culture, innit?

Let's not be too cynical about this situation. In certain forms, postmodernism promotes a sort of decent liberalism there's no need to be ashamed of, even if there are good reasons not to be satisfied with it. The main reason for not being satisfied with it, which I am tempted to call a theoretical reason, except that 'post-theory' sounds a quite proper note of caution about that term, is that it is impossible (not just undesirable, but impossible) to agree about difference. Difference cannot be the object of our agreement, just because difference is not an object. This apparent truism, or so it seems to me, is one of the hardest things to think that there are, and just this that I think is concentrated in the 'inter-', in the interdisciplinarity or internationality which give this section its title, that are here our concerns.

One symptom of this situation is the tendency to discuss what we would

once have called theoretical issues as *cultural* phenomena. So, for example,
to take an instance near home for me, deconstruction is now often invoked as
a movement which is no longer fashionable, which has had its moment,
which is on the wane, which is finished. Sociologically or culturally speaking, this may be true (though I suspect it isn't: as Derrida said at the Luton
conference, nothing seems so clearly to indicate the vitality of deconstruction
as announcements of its imminent demise), but even if it is, this says nothing
whatsoever about the *'theoretical'* or philosophical issues raised by deconstruction.[1] Deconstruction (or any other 'theoretical' movement) does not
depend on the number of people who believe in it or practise it or profess it.
'Post-theory' can easily become an excuse not to think very hard, a sidestep
from thinking into a simple, slightly phantasmatic cultural monitoring or
reporting service, 'Late-Show' journalism, legacy perhaps of Raymond
Williams and Stuart Hall (or even Pierre Bourdieu for the sociologistic version) which proudly steps back, observes and analyses trends in cultural
and intellectual life, as though this were the main or determining issue. Post-
theory has often become a thinly made-up return to pre-theoretical habits
and a sort of intellectual journalism (preoccupied by the question of *news*).

The driving impulse behind this tendency appears, unfortunately for
politics, to be political (the confusion of the cultural and the political is – or
such is my hypothesis – a basic feature of post-theory). 'Theory', from this
perspective, is (was) not political, or at any rate not political *enough*, never
political enough, so it must be politicised. Politicising it means culturalising
it (probably under the name of 'materialism'), culturalising it means historicising it, historicising it means interring it. The logic of this position stems
from an influential argument put most clearly in 1981 in Tony Bennett's 'New
Accents' book on *Formalism and Marxism*[2] (but slightly different versions
can be found in, say, Eagleton or Jameson, and any number of other discussions of reading), going something like this: theory shows us that texts have
no intrinsic identity in themselves independent of the readings they are
given; reading is therefore essentially *free* with respect to the text being read;
so the readings we in fact come up with must have motivations that are not
prescribed by the text being read; those motivations are, like it or not, essentially political; so it is incumbent upon us, on the Left, to read for socialism,
towards socialism. All *other* readings and reading methods are also therefore
accountable in political terms, and most importantly, readings or reading
methods that do not recognise this intrinsic politics of reading are *ipso facto*
reactionary.

The ('theoretical') problem with this argument, which is admirably well-
meaning (meaning well is one of the distinguishing marks of post-theory), is
that it is caught in a contradiction between the sense that meaning is indeterminate (i.e. texts do not determine their meanings), and a sense that it is
determinable (i.e. we know what it means to read for socialism, or indeed to

be on the Left). Knowing what we want (socialism) means being confident that we know what we mean – but this means that we believe *we* can write texts – our readings – which are determinate with respect to their meanings, whereas our basic premise is that texts are radically indeterminate with respect to their meanings. The short version of this is that we surreptitiously believe we are in a transcendental position in a situation where we are supposed to have denied transcendentality altogether. Hidden under the associated talk about politics and struggles for meaning is a calm certainty that is nowhere justified or justifiable, namely that we already know our meaning and what it should be: this depends on a teleological faith in History which is itself not at all historical.

This set-up, which is repeated across a whole range of Left criticism, is essentially historicist (not to say idealist) in character, and indeed the problem with the persuasive argument I have taken from Bennett just is a version of the problem with historicism more generally. Historicism is based on the premise that the final appeal for analysis is History; that History provides the ultimate determination of all phenomena of meaning. The problem with this is that it places History 'itself' in a position which is transcendental with respect to the phenomena being investigated, whereas the basic premise of Historicism is that there *are* no transcendental positions (in Bennett's version, that there is no Meaning). The problem, then, with post-Theory in its dominant historicist form, is that it performs an operation I've described elsewhere with the Derridean term 'transcendental contraband':[3] claiming to operate a radical detranscendentalisation, historicism puts up a transcendental term (History), which its own premises prevent it ever from understanding. The last thing historicism can understand is History (and this is true more generally of all '-isms': -isms smuggle into a transcendental position the term that gives them their name, and it's the one thing that in principle they cannot understand, while it is the one thing they suggest it is crucially important to understand, because it is the principle according to which all the rest can be understood). But historicism is the worst-ism of all, perhaps, because it is involved in all-isms: historicism is-ismism, the movement of transcendental contraband itself, *transcendental* transcendental contraband, and, to that extent, a concealed theoreticism. If this is post-theory, then what it has lost is enough theoretical sophistication to understand its own predicament: what is left is an interminable self-confident and self-righteous political-cum-cultural-studies-speak. What goes by the name of 'Political Correctness' is an inevitable corollary of this position. If post-theory thinks it has interred theory and can dance on its grave, it does so in a sort of constitutive blindness as to what's actually inscribed on the headstone.

It seems to me that the root of the more or less complacent historicism which I am suggesting characterises post-theory is, as in the dialectical story I told about the word or concept 'inter-', Hegelian. I want to suggest that the 'inter-', which seems to lend itself so readily to the Hegelian operation, and thereby to history, in fact, in Hegel himself, exceeds the dialectic as its undialectisable reserve or resource, as its historicity: and that this historicity cannot itself be thought of as historical, and cannot to that extent answer to any historicism whatsoever. This might allow for a retrieval of 'post-theory' as anything but something that comes *after* theory. I'll be doing this by pursuing in greater detail an argument I've already put up more briefly elsewhere.

History is obviously enough to do with an at least apparent violence and contingency, and violence and contingency show up in political philosophy most saliently in the form of frontiers between states. This argument is put forcefully by Kant (who is even, in *Religion Within the Bounds of Reason Alone* (I, 3), prepared to see in the persistence of frontiers the clearest proof of the existence in man of a principle of radical evil) and accepted by Hegel, who is prepared to push the thought of contingency much further than Kant (or almost anyone else) because of a paradox (that just is dialectics) whereby the more negativity there is, the better and more triumphantly it can be overcome in sublation. I'll be returning to this paradox, which concentrates a number of issues. Kant attempted to overcome the problem of the persistence of national frontiers (the place of nature, contingency and violence) by the projection, first of a cosmopolitan world-state in which frontiers would disappear, subsequently of an internationalist confederation of states established with a view to preserving peace as perpetual peace (for Kant, peace is worth its name only if it is perpetual: anything less is mere cessation of hostilities). In the *Philosophy of Right*, Hegel complains that Kant's solution remains 'infected with contingency' (Hegel's phrase) insofar as such a confederation remains subject to the whims of any one member of it – a single state can easily disrupt the supposedly perpetual peace at any point (§333). Hegel's solution to the undeniable problem posed by the contingency of frontiers (it being the task of philosophy in general to sublate contingency into necessity) is going to have to be quite different, and we shall see that it engages the whole of what Hegel famously calls the cunning of reason (but reason in Hegel is nothing other than its own cunning).

Hegel concedes in the *Philosophy of Right* that the situation of national differentiation (and there must be such differentation, that is, a plurality of states, if there is to be a state at all: the tension in Hegel's political philosophy comes from the claim that on the one hand 'the' state is 'the' ethical totality, but on the other that there is never 'the' state, but always a plurality of states, because the state is only the state to the extent that its identity as a spiritual (ethical) totality is gained by the fact of fighting other states along its frontiers, exposing the nullity of the mere material concerns of civil society, and even of life, by exposing them to destruction in frontier warfare), and therefore the persistence of frontiers, is indeed one of contingency to the highest degree, before beginning the sublation of that contingency into necessity via the operator of the *Weltgeist*.

> In their relations among themselves, because they are determined as *particular*, there is to be found [*fällt*: there befalls, precipitates out, linked of course to the case (*Fall*), but also to *Zufälligkeit*, contingency] the most mobile play of the inner particularity of passions, interests, aims, talents and virtues, violence, injustice and vice, of external contingency *in the greatest dimensions of its appearance* [my emphasis] – a play in which the ethical totality itself, the independence of the state, is exposed to contingency. (§340)

The argument I am interested in following suggests that Hegel deals with the apparently contingent dispersion we have been describing by in a sense serialising it historically in what appears to be a violent and dogmatic resingularisation of that violent plurality: from a situation where there appears to be no right which can dominate or regulate the relations between states along their frontiers (this being the situation of contingency itself), Hegel conjures up a sort of right by arguing that at a given historical moment *one* state in this plurality is dominant, that each state is only dominant *once*, and that the currently dominant state has in fact an *absolute* right over all the others at that time, that right being justified before the tribunal of world history. This does not mean that it acts *consciously* in a different way from other states (all states, insofar as they are states, must defend their own interests by being actually prepared to fight on their frontiers, and there is no higher right for them: even a state which claims to embody the absolute right of Spirit is only doing so dishonestly as a way of furthering its own interests), but that in quite rightly defending its own interests it is in fact *unconsciously* furthering the progress of reason in history. Hegel says:

> States, peoples and individuals in this march of world-spirit rise each in its *particular defined principle*, which has its expression and actuality in its *constitution* and the whole *breadth* of its *situation*: they are conscious of this principle and absorbed in its interest, but are at the same time unconscious instruments and moments of that inner activity in which these shapes disappear, and Spirit in and for itself prepares and works for the transition to its next higher level. (§344)

This means that what looks like contingency at the level at which we have been taking things (i.e. the level of the state becoming conscious of itself as ethical totality only in its violent frontier-confrontations with other states) can be claimed as necessity at that higher level. Hegel makes this very clear by a verbal echo from the next paragraph to the one which ended the

'International Right' section and insisted on the highest degree of contingency. That paragraph said that in their mutual relationships, states behave as individuals (Kant says the same thing, and indeed this is what defines inter-nationalism as a state of nature), and that therefore this involves the highly agitated 'play of the inner particularity of passions, interests, aims, talents and virtues, violence, injustice and vice' (§340), which is precisely that highest degree of external contingency we have noted, and which, via the notion of passion that is important here, will take us into the *Philosophy of History* in a moment: in §345 of the *Philosophy of Right*, clearly picking up on this list, he writes:

Justice and virtue, fault, violence and vice, talents and their actions, small and great passions, guilt and innocence, sovereignty of individual and collective life, independence, happiness and unhappiness of states and individuals have their determinate meaning and value in the sphere of conscious actuality and find therein their judgement and their justice, albeit incomplete. World history falls outside these points of view; in it that necessary moment of the idea of World-Spirit, which at present is *its* level, receives its *absolute* right, and the people living within it and their acts receive their realisation, happiness and glory. (§345)

It seems important to stress this value of unconsciousness here. One of its consequences is that Hegel is not suggesting that a given state could ever reasonably *claim* to be the current embodiment of the world-spirit (even though in fact it might *be* that embodiment) and try to justify its actions accordingly: at the level of their conscious decisions and activities, *all* states, even the one that happens at that moment to embody the world-spirit, are defending their own interests in a way which could not justifiably *invoke* the world-spirit for support. This is confirmed a little later at the level of the individual, in a way which explicitly refers back to the paragraph on the monarch (as the tip of the pyramid that is the state):

At the point [*An der Spitze*, at the peak, the summit] of all actions, even world-historical actions, are *individuals* as substance-actualising subjectivities (§279 [i.e. the paragraph on the monarch]). For these living forms of substantial action of universal spirit which are immediately identical with this action, it remains hidden, and is neither their object nor their aim (§344 [i.e. the paragraph we have just read on consciousness and unconsciousness on the level of states]). Thus they receive *honour* and thanks for this neither from their contemporaries nor in the public opinion of posterity, but as formal subjectivities have their share of this opinion only as *immortal glory*. (§348)

This argument about world-historical individuals and the famous 'cunning of reason' is probably best known from Hegel's *Philosophy of History*, and more especially the 'Introduction' to that text. This introduction is precious to us for its confirmation that, precisely insofar as it claims to sublate the contingency of frontier situations, world history *depends* nonetheless on those situations, without which there would quite simply *be* no world history. To that extent, there is history only to the extent that there is not History, or, put another way, history cannot be understood, and therefore cannot be used as a principle of explanation either, as historicism requires.

The sphere of the state proper in its ethical life begins with the rupture of the sphere of civil society and its essentially conservative concerns by war on the frontier: this is at one and the same time a more 'primitive' and 'passionate' form of behaviour, yet one which is the means of the increased spiritualisation of the state. This constitutively involves opening up the 'ethical totality' thus produced to violent frontier-contingencies which are therefore the proper domain of world history. This final stage of spiritualisation seems necessarily to dip back into what is least spiritual and least free, namely passion and violence.

The structure I have just outlined just is that of the 'cunning of reason', and suggests that reason *just is* its own cunning. The argument here in the Introduction to the *Philosophy of History*[4] tries to generalise this structure, just as it is generalised further in the 'Teleology' chapter of the *Greater Logic*. Hegel tries to show that activity *in general* generates opposition in the form of unconsciousness, that any activity, in pursuing its goal, also gives rise to something hidden from that goal and in opposition to it. In the case of universal history, Hegel says, actions not only reveal the finite goals to which they tend, but also sketch the outline of general determinations, of right, good, duty and so on. These general determinations of actions which in themselves are *always* particular and passionate pose no real problems within the confines of a *given* state (as ethical totality, remember), insofar as within those frontiers what is good, just and so on is clearly enough indicated by the objective morality embodied in the laws of the state. To that extent, there is no real history here as yet (and this is why, a little earlier, Hegel has been able to say that periods of happiness are the 'blank pages' of universal history (p. 26) – this is an idea one also finds in Rousseau, and seems in fact to be an analytical component of the concept of history). This simplicity and calm, however, does not hold in what Hegel calls 'great historical situations', which are defined as those in which there is *conflict* between different systems of laws, rights and duties – and it seems reasonable to assume that border conflict between states, which is a defining feature *of* 'the' state, is essentially an instance of this type of properly historical moment. Hegel says that in such situations

are presented those momentous collisions between existing, acknowledged duties, laws and rights, and those contingencies which are adverse
to this fixed system; which assail and even destroy its foundations and
existence; whose tenor may nevertheless seem good – on the large scale
advantageous – yes, even indispensable and necessary. These contingencies realise themselves in History: they involve a general principle of
a different order from that on which depends the *permanence* of a
people or a State. This principle is an essential phase in the development
of the *creating* Idea, of Truth striving and urging towards [conscious-
ness of] itself. Historical men – *World-Historical Individuals* – are those
in whose aims such a general principle lies. (p. 27)

Hegel's main example is Julius Caesar, but the general point remains the
same: such individuals bring out the unconscious spirit of their time, which
is why they attract followers, but also why they suffer (insofar as they necessarily break with established canons of conduct, and so on); they are to be
judged not psychologically but historically. 'Such are all great historical
men – whose own particular aims [in Caesar's case, ambition for himself
and Rome] involve those large issues which are the will of the World-Spirit'
(p. 30). Of course such individuals act out of passion (and all the contingent
subjective motivations we have seen listed in the *Philosophy of Right*), but
this is precisely the cunning of reason which holds back from the violent
contingency of actual historical events and allows these passions to act in
its place. And, according to the odd non-linearity of this structure, world-
historical individuals act with *more* passion, and therefore more violence,
than others, and are less susceptible to judgement by normal 'moral' standards:
'What schoolmaster has not shown that Alexander the Great, that Julius
Caesar were animated by such passions and that therefore they were immoral
men: whence it follows immediately that the schoolmaster is more worthy
than these people, for he has no such passions and gives as proof of this the
fact that he has not conquered Asia' (pp. 31–2). Again this produces what
can seem like a sinister passage which might appear to fit with one common
image of Hegel:

A world-historical individual does not have the necessary calm to want
merely this or that, to have much time to care, but belongs to his one
end without considering anything else. So it happens that he treats
lightly other interests which are great and even sacred, a conduct which
is assuredly subject to moral blame. Such a great figure necessarily
crushes many an innocent flower, and ruins many a thing on his path.
(p. 32)

The cunning of reason, which is just reason, is precisely to do with this ruin and destruction of particularities: the claim is that its cunning is precisely that it gets other things destroyed in its place, by proxy (this is a rather nasty operation, but reason is nasty):

> It is the particular that is worn down in combat and a part of which is destroyed. It is not the general idea which is exposed to constraints and to struggle, to dangers; it holds back out of the way of any attack and any damage. This is what must be called the *cunning of reason* when it allows passions to act in its stead, in such a way that the thing through which it comes to existence suffers losses and experiences damage. For it is the phenomenon one of whose parts is worthless and one of which is affirmative. In general the particular is too small faced with the general: individuals are sacrificed and abandoned. The idea pays the tribute of existence and decrepitude not in itself, but through the passions of individuals. (p. 33)

That this is a general point can be made clear from the 'Teleology' chapter of the *Greater Logic*.[5] Hegel says:

> That the end relates itself immediately to an object and makes it a means, as also that through this means it determines another object, may be regarded as *violence* [*Gewalt*] in so far as the end appears to be of quite another nature than the object, and the two objects similarly are mutually independent totalities. But that the end posits itself in a *mediate* relation with the object and *interposes* another object *between* itself and it, may be regarded as the *cunning* of reason. The finitude of rationality has, as remarked, this side, that the end enters into relationship with the presupposition, that is, with the externality of the object. In the *immediate relation* to the object, it would itself enter into the sphere of mechanism or chemism and thereby be subject to contingency and the loss of its determination as the Notion that is in and for itself. But as it is, it puts forward an object as means, allows itself to wear itself out in its stead, exposes it to attrition and shields itself behind it from mechanical violence. (pp. 746–7)

This is the structure we have just been explicating in the specific context of the *Philosophy of History*, where the 'violence' involved is very literally that of warfare and upheaval. In the context of our violent plurality of states, we can say that this violence always involves frontiers (either 'literally', or in the sense which comes out more strongly in the *Philosophy of History* of 'frontier' confrontations between old systems or totalities and new): the operator of the cunning of reason is an integral part of the sublation of the apparent contingency of that situation into the supposed necessity of world history, for the violence can be split off and located in the phenomenon, which can therefore be destroyed without destroying the end which is nonetheless in some sense embodied in it. The passage from the *Greater Logic* confirms that in Hegel's system this situation is generalisable to all situations in which it makes sense to talk of ends (which for Hegel means all situations in general, insofar as reason just is its cunning movement towards its self-knowing end): the object which the end elects as its means is disposable, and sacrifices itself for the end, gaining the glory that remains to it in its violent destruction from the fact that it was an object fitting for the end that chose to use it.

This apparent generalisability of the cunning of reason and what we might call teleological violence (and this is what would justify us in suspecting that the value of reassurance and even redemption we normally associate with teleology is a violent value in itself) has a number of consequences. *On the one hand*, if it makes sense to talk about violence in this way in any teleological situation whatsoever, then that might be taken to de-dramatise up to a point the *type* of teleological situation I have chosen to concentrate on, namely the literally violent situation of warfare and frontier-confrontation. This would in fact be simply a rather vivid figure of a general situation which need not therefore involve 'violence' in a way we would necessarily want to cringe away from. On this view, we could talk about the relationships between concepts as 'violent', but would perhaps not be very upset about that. *On the other hand*, though, this apparent continuity between situations of extreme literal violence and more general conceptual structures might be the more disquieting in that it could seem to give a sort of conceptual or even ontological legitimacy whereby 'real' and 'literal' violence becomes a sort of necessary emanation of conceptual structures. This complication of any opposition between violence and non-violence (which is at least implied, if not thought, in Kant's insistence on the non-symmetrical nature of the concepts of war and peace), explicitly operated by Hegel, is nonetheless 'violently' determined by him (but we're now at something of a loss to know what sense to make of this type of meta-violence) through the very teleological set-up we are still grappling with, and which eventually reposes in the restlessness of spirit itself. Our problem is that of knowing how to think this situation if we do not accept that particular meta-violence in thought.

You will remember that cunning consists in Reason's putting forward, in its place, objects which are doomed to destruction: I attempted to distinguish in this movement a complicated sort of double violence: reason, in its cunning, operates violently *on* objects as a means of withdrawing from the violence *of* objects as mechanically determined. Kant envisaged but rejected as irrational the possibility that perpetual peace (or at least a stable equilibrium) might be brought about by an Epicurean process of random collisions, whereby frontier violence would just fortuitously give rise to stability: where Kant rejects this in favour of the notion of a teleological natural providence which in itself remains unknowable, Hegel's attempt, via the operator of 'cunning', is to make the teleology immanent to the process, allowing reason its odd status of re-marking withdrawal with respect to the sphere of object reality, including that of state warfare. This re-mark or re-trait – re-trac(t)ing – of violence (in the double sense Derrida exploits: reason retreats from violence but leaves a supplementary mark of its withdrawal which just is the vanishing mark of reason (in history, for example – what allows the retrospective reconstruction of history as having been rational, namely history, *will have been rational* and that rationality is legible through the marks of reason's retrac(t)ing)) – this retrac(t)ing is just how reason works, insofar as reason is nothing outside its own cunning involvement and withdrawal in the contingency it supposedly sublates. The violence of reason in history is that it exploits world-historical individuals who are habitually destructive and themselves destroyed in the field of passion and violence it abandons them to, or, in the *Philosophy of Right*, the violence of reason is that it abandons states to their violence on the frontier as a means of furthering world history. World history is nothing outside of or elsewhere than this contingent violence (there would be no history without the complicated structure whereby spirituality advances by dipping back into the undecidable reserve of passion and nature via the persons of the world-historical individuals), but is *as* the retrac(t)ing of that violence.

We can now re-apply this situation to Hegel's own philosophy of history, which will leave it in the uncomfortable position of apparently getting stuck in the first of the four great historical empires (Oriental, Greek, Roman, Germanic) that form the broad sweep of history as Hegel tells it, leave it stuck in what he calls 'the childhood of history' (p. 83), which in a certain sense is not yet history at all. Hegel says in the Introduction to the *Philosophy of History*:

> In the life of the State we find here realized rational freedom which develops without reaching subjective freedom. This is the childhood of history. Substantial formations constitute the magnificent edifices of oriental empires, in which all rational conditions are to be found, but such that the subjects remain contingent. They move around a centre, i.e. the Sovereign who is at the head as a patriarch . . . All the factors of the State, including that of subjectivity, are indeed to be found here, but without yet being reconciled with substance. For outside the one substance before which nothing can be constituted in full independence, nothing exists, except a terrifying arbitrariness which wanders perniciously outside that substance. So we see swarms of barbarians rushing down from the high ground, invading and devastating regions, or, once

established on the inside, giving up barbarity, but in general being reduced to dust in substance, with no other result. This condition of substantiality, in a general way, is immediately divided into two moments precisely because it has not admitted into itself and reduced the opposing factor. We see on the one hand durations and stability – *as it were spatial empires – a history which is not a history* [my emphasis] . . . a prosaic empire in which the antithesis of form, infinity and ideality has not yet appeared. On the other hand, the form of time is opposed to this spatial duration [remember how the precise point of our problem in the transition to world history was the sublation of the geographical dispersion of states by their temporal ordering – there would be the general question here of Hegel's attempted sublation of space by time]. The states, without being modified in themselves or in their principle, are with respect to one another in a perpetual transformation, in a conflict that cannot be stopped and which promises those states a speedy end . . . *Even this history is still essentially without history* [my emphasis], for it is merely the repetition of the same majestic ruin. The new factor which replaces the old splendour with courage, force and generosity follows the same path of decomposition and ruin, which is therefore not effective, for all these incessant changes do not produce any progress. History then moves, and certainly in an entirely external way – *i.e. with no link with what precedes it* [my emphasis] – in general in central Asia. If we wish to pursue the comparison with the ages of man, this would correspond to the age of adolescence which no longer has the tranquillity and confidence of the small child, but knows only how to grab and fight. (pp. 105–6)

This moment too, as presented here in the *Philosophy of History*, passes into that of the Greeks with no apparent internal transition. In the full presentation of the text, however, Hegel does attempt to explain the passage from the Oriental (in which we seem to have got stuck with our plural, swarming and barbaric dispersion of contingent frontier clashes) to the Greek. This is achieved in part by differentiating to a much greater extent the 'Oriental', so that the passage from Oriental to Greek is made, not directly from Central Asia, but from Egypt, which is the last moment of the Oriental world.

Egypt is seen as essentially part of the Persian empire by Hegel. As opposed to China and India, which subsist in a sort of ahistory, stable in their very instability, Persia, though still part of the 'childhood of history' we have mentioned, is already no longer quite in that position (this coinciding of 'still' and 'already no longer' defines how identity works in Hegel):

The Persian empire brings us back into the course of history. The Persians are the first historical people, and Persia is the first empire to have disappeared. Whereas China and India remain in a static state, leading up to the present day a natural, vegetative life, Persia is subject to the evolutions and revolutions which alone betray a historical condition. (p. 173)

This means that only here does universal history really begin: as we have seen, contingency and constant dissolution are not yet history in Hegel's strong sense:

> The principle of evolution begins in Persia and this is why it forms in reality the beginning of universal history; for in history, the general interest of spirit consists in coming to the infinite interiority of subjectivity, to conciliation, via absolute antithesis. (p. 174)

At the extreme end of the Persian empire, Egypt is almost already Greece. This is figured by Hegel in the figure of the Sphinx, which, here as in the *Aesthetics*, will provide the transitional moment:

> Among the representations we find in Egyptian antiquity, we must stress especially one image, i.e. the *sphinx*, in itself an enigma, a figuration with a double meaning, half animal, half human. We can consider the sphinx as a symbol of the Egyptian spirit; the human head coming out of the body of the animal represents spirit beginning to rise out of the natural element, to tear itself free, to look around itself more freely without however freeing itself entirely from its bonds. (p. 199)

And a vital emblem of the passage from Egypt to Greece is this same sphinx as it appears in the Oedipus legend: Oedipus, by answering the riddle of the sphinx with the word 'man', announcing the liberation of spirit from animality as human consciousness.

This is how Hegel gets out of the state of contingent and essentially non-historical existence that characterises the Far East: but in the section which moves from Persia to Greece, he is still worried about the persistence of China and India, and feels the need to summarise the rather awkward transitions we have briefly rehearsed. China and India have survived; Persia, including Egypt, has vanished – but precisely that is the mark of its historicity:

> The internal passage to Greece or the concept thus starts out from the Egyptian spirit; but Egypt became a province of the great Persian empire and the historical passage is produced at the contact of the Persian world and the Greek world. We are here for the first time in the presence of an historical passage, i.e. of an empire which has disappeared. China and India, as we have already said, have remained, but

not Persia; the passage to Greece is indeed internal, but on this occasion it becomes external too, as a transmission of sovereignty, a fact which will henceforth always be the case. For the Greeks pass to the Romans the sceptre of civilisation [this is of course equivalent to the argument that world spirit resides with only one nation at a time: from this passage from Egypt to Greece, Hegel wants to argue, this movement of spirit coincides with historical events of conquest and so on – whereas the earlier transitions, up to this point, are purely internal or conceptual and do not match external historical realities, which is why China and India have not disappeared as civilisations], and the Romans are subjected by the Germans. If we consider this passage more closely, we must immediately ask ourselves, for example in the case of Persia, the reason for its ruin and the reason for the persistence of China and India. We must immediately resist the prejudice that duration is by its value superior to disappearance: the imperishable mountains do not have more value than the rose, so soon faded, in its life exhaled as perfume. In Persia, the principle of the freedom of spirit begins to oppose itself to nature and this natural existence, as a consequence, fades and dies; it is in the Persian empire that there resides the principle of separation from nature; this empire is thus above those societies sunk in nature. (p. 221)

If there is a sense in which the whole logic of the cunning of reason as exemplified in world-historical individuals and more generally in frontier clashes depends on the non-linear structure of retrac(t)ing that I have outlined – if, in other words, any advance in spirituality is achieved only by drawing on the reserve of nature or animality revealed in passion and contingency – then it should probably come as no surprise to us that Hegel should see frontier clashes, which we have stressed as constitutive of anything like a state, therefore of anything like politics and anything like history, as in themselves non- or pre-historical. To that extent, it seems reasonable enough to have them essentially characterising an essentially pre-historical people.

But this can also mean trouble for Hegel. For if the essential feature of spirit in its negativity and restlessness is the moment of contingency we have linked to the frontier, and if this moment is necessarily ahistorical as such, then we are left with the curious conclusion that what is essentially historical in Hegel is essentially ahistorical in Hegel's terms. Frontier clashes in their contingency are the paradigm of the movement of history, but are in themselves non-spiritual, contingent and therefore non-historical. What in the context of the Orient Hegel can call a non-historical history, a 'repetition of the same majestic ruin', looks in the light of our reading like the very historicity of history or, to parody Derrida, the non-historical opening of the possibility of history, which simultaneously renders impossible the sort of philosophical

history Hegel wants, because of the tenacity of its contingency. Maybe universal history has in fact gone the way Hegel describes it, but Hegel is only
interested in that to the extent that it was always going to turn out like that,
and this is what now seems doubtful in view of the persistence of this non-
historical reserve. This is of a piece with our earlier suspicion of what in the
Philosophy of Right looked like a violent temporal serialisation of the spatiality of relations exemplified in frontier clashes, and suggests a certain stupid
resistance of space, and what is irreducibly spatial about frontiers, to temporal
sublation. To the extent that sublation is always an interiorisation, let's say
that frontiers mark a point of absolute exteriority. In the *Philosophy of
History*, it seems plausible to take as a figure of that absolute exteriority, what
we might call the deterritorialised violence of the hordes of nomadic Tartar
barbarians descending repeatedly from the mountains, the 'terrifying arbitrariness wandering perniciously' outside of the unique substance. This
terrifying, repetitive nomadic violence just is the necessary contingency and
violence of frontiers without which there would be no history at all, but
which Hegelian history, at any rate, cannot in fact contain and sublate. The
operator of the cunning of reason fails to rationalise out this violence insofar
as this terrifying arbitrariness is not yet even cunning, but on the side of
the barbarity that Hegel had previously excluded, non-dialectically, as
pre-dialectical.

History then becomes not the process of spiritualisation described by
Hegel, but the repetitive rhythm of the Great Wall of China's failure to be
completed, its perpetual breaching by the nomads, which makes history both
possible and impossible. The not yet historical, not yet result-producing
(therefore not yet dialectical) reduction to dust of wall and nomads repeats
in principle at every moment there is a frontier as violence and contingency,
and any world tribunal sits and judges in the non-totalisable dispersion of
that dust.

So there is no tribunal of world history, and therefore no world history, if
history always means the overcoming of contingency by necessity: and therefore no dialectic either. This argument also asks uncomfortable questions
about the rationality of reason. This is not a vindication of Kantian cos-
mopolitanism or internationalism against Hegel's criticism, nor a condem-
nation of it, but another version of an argument which locates conditions of
possibility in difference ('inter-'), and then affirms that such conditions are
also always conditions of impossibility, the thing that shows up in Hegel as
the non-historical historicity of history, both making history possible and
making History impossible. This is not itself a historicist argument, because
it suggests something anterior to, and more powerful than, the concept of
History which historicism takes as a principle. Nor is it simply a theoretical
argument (at any rate not a theoreticist argument), because it cannot be brought
into the realm of clear vision that theory demands. If it is post-theoretical, it

is (rather like Lyotard's second attempt at defining the postmodern) a post- that seems to precede everything. This is, let's say, an *intolerable, unacceptable* argument it is impossible to *agree* with. But it suggests why the post- has always already been at work in theory, and why we will never reach a post-theoretical state. This leaves us radically 'in' the inter-, always already in the post. So what's new?

NOTES

1. See Jacques Derrida, 'As if I Were Dead', in J. Brannigan, R. Robbins and J. Wolfreys (eds), *Applying: to Derrida* (London: Macmillan, 1997).
2. Tony Bennett, *Formalism and Marxism* (London: Methuen, 1981).
3. Cf. 'Derridabase', in G. Bennington and J. Derrida, *Jacques Derrida* (Paris: Editions du Seuil, 1991), pp. 259ff. (translation: University of Chicago Press, 1993, pp. 280ff.).
4. G. W. F. Hegel, *The Philosophy of History*, trans. J. Sibree (New York: Dover Publications, 1956), p. 26. I have modified the translation in most of the passages I quote.
5. G. W. F. Hegel, *The Science of Logic*, trans. A. V. Miller (Atlantic Highlands, NJ: Humanities Press, 1989).

PART III

The Post-Theory Condition

Chapter Eight

ENGLISH STUDIES IN THE
POSTMODERN CONDITION
Towards a Place for the Signifier

Catherine Belsey

I

We are witnessing the end of literary criticism. I recognised this remarkable fact in the course of rereading a book on Shakespeare. The argument, very broadly, concerned the dramatisation of stories that were already well known, *Troilus and Cressida*, *Antony and Cleopatra*, for example, and the struggle of Shakespeare's characters to inhabit identities that were culturally pre-scripted for them. The book, which was published by Harvard University Press, was not at that time more than two years old. It was stylish, witty and persuasive; the argument unfolded logically and intelligibly; it drew on the insights of recent theoretical developments; and it made me aware of aspects of the plays that I had never seen before. Given all this, I could not account for a mounting feeling of dissatisfaction as I read. What more did I want, after all? It is unusual enough to get that particular combination of pleasures from a single volume. In fact, simple literacy is increasingly rare in these days of economics on copy-editors' fees, and this book was both literate and intelligent. 'But it's still', I heard myself say, as I put it down to reflect on my own ungracious response to a good book, 'only literary criticism'.

I felt like St Paul on the road to Damascus. What I suddenly knew, in a blinding flash, was that literary criticism is a thing of the past, and that we have entered, irreversibly, a new epoch. What a relief! Much as I welcome the change, however, which can only be for the better, I now find that I want to intervene in its direction. My concern here is to propose a place in the new English Studies for a closer attention to the signifier.

Literary criticism was officially the desire to illuminate the text, and only that, to give an account of it, explain its power. It was reading for the sake of reading. But thoughtful critics knew they could not stop there. In the first place, the text had to be worth it: to *exercise* a power that needed to be accounted for. And in the second place, since language was understood to be a medium, an instrument, the explanation of its power had to be located elsewhere, beyond the text itself, in a realm of ideas which was, paradoxically, more substantial than words. In its heyday, therefore, literary criticism had two main preoccupations: aesthetic value as justification for the study of the text, and the Author as explanation of its character. Traces of the Author remain, not just in critical biographies, but in examination papers which divide the syllabus under author's names, and in the resulting discussions students conduct about their revision plans. 'I'm not doing Dickens: I thought I'd concentrate on George Eliot.' The implications of this division of the available material were that the natural way to make sense of a text was to locate it in relations of continuity and discontinuity with other works by the same author. And the implications of that assumption in turn were usually that texts were intelligible primarily as expressions of something that preceded them, a subjectivity, a world view, a moral sensibility, a rhetorical skill. Literary criticism of this kind was neither, it turned out, criticism nor particularly literary: on the contrary, it was a quest for an origin which was also an aetiology, an identification of an explanatory source prior to the text: insight, creativity, genius.

This last category was the one that linked the Author with aesthetic value. How deep an insight? How much creativity? What degree of genius? To us, in these days of quality control, the notion of grading literary works begins to seem as vulgar as assessing commodities, or indeed departments of literature. The British government and its quangos seem preoccupied with reductive classifications. They, or our colleagues on their behalf, rate our teaching as excellent, satisfactory or unsatisfactory (and since almost no department is unsatisfactory – even those who are willing to do the assessing seem to have *some* residual capacity for professional loyalty – satisfactory has come, by an interesting semantic shift, to mean unsatisfactory). Our research, meanwhile, is graded by a national committee on a scale from 1 to 5. If this kind of evaluation seems gross as applied to academic departments, how much more offensive to do it to Authors, some of whom are, after all, alleged to be geniuses, in possession of insight and creativity.

It was the practice of making aesthetic judgements on Authors which vindicated the construction of the canon, and literary criticism has been brought into disrepute by the process of unmasking the ideological element inscribed in the ostensibly disinterested list of canonical texts. The Western Canon, we now know, is the location of political as well as aesthetic values. Only the purest formalism has been able to escape the recognition of its own investment in the works selected for approval, and the blindness to misogyny, imperialism and heterosexism which has characterised not so much the texts themselves, since they are often more ambiguous than their admirers allow, as the criticism which endorses them.

In my own case, it was feminism, alongside Marxism, that played the largest part in the process of unmasking. In 1970 Kate Millett's witty and devastating accounts of Henry Miller, Norman Mailer and, above all, D. H. Lawrence began to ensure that my reading life would never be the same again. What was at stake was injustice. This was not primarily injustice on the part of the authors themselves. What, after all, was to be gained by blaming them? Some of the most culpable ones were dead, and the others probably beyond reconstruction. The point was that they themselves were products of their culture. Exit, therefore, the Author, and enter a mode of reading which was closer to cultural history. The next move was that texts, like history itself, began to be perceived in consequence as the location of conflicts of meaning. Unity was no longer a virtue – where, after all, was the special merit in a monologic misogyny? – and coherence ceased to be grounds for praise. The text, we discovered, might display symptoms of resistance to its own propositions, might be open, in its undecidability, to more than one interpretation. Moreover, what *perpetuated* injustice was not so much *Lawrence's* anti-feminism (say) as the way *criticism* reaffirmed the misogyny readers were already in danger of taking for granted, by praising his work without drawing attention to its implications for sexual politics. Exit, therefore, the idea of criticism itself as a transparent practice in the service of literature, and enter a new attention to the institution of literary studies and the power relations confirmed by the knowledges it produced.

Since then we have learned to identify injustices of other kinds. Homoerotic and postcolonial criticism are currently leading the field. The universal wisdom attributed to canonical texts was, we now know, white, Western and homophobic, as well as bourgeois and relentlessly patriarchal. The voices silenced for so long by the grand narrative of a humane and humanising literary tradition are now insisting on being heard, offering new readings of the canonical texts, and drawing attention to works the canon marginalised. Suddenly we can't get enough of incitements to acknowledge injustices, past and present. As we repudiate the illusion of impartiality, the goal of objective interpretation and the quest for the final, identifiable meaning of the text, English studies has found itself entering the postmodern condition.

Restored by my recognition of the terminal state of literary criticism, I returned to the elegant book on Shakespeare, and found that I had radically misjudged it. The conclusion made clear that this was a book about identity on the eve of the Cartesian moment; it was about subjectivity as always and inevitably pre-scripted, and about the longing for total individuality and self-determination which in those circumstances can never be realised. Mercifully, it was not literary criticism at all. Instead, it was an extremely skilled and sophisticated reading of some very complex and sophisticated texts, locating them in the cultural history of the emergence of what was in due course to become the American dream – and the political implications of that for all of us can hardly be overstated.[1]

II

The backlash, of course, was inevitable, and it is by no means over. The inappropriately named humanism of literary criticism has been singularly reluctant simply to lie down and die, though it is beginning to look very long in the tooth. Some of the outcry against the new developments is journalistic and trivial, knockabout stuff, based on a radical failure or, worse, refusal to understand the issues or the theoretical positions that define them. Some of it represents no more than a cry of anguish from white heterosexual men who have reached a point on the salary scale when they ought, in the normal course of things, to have expected a certain deferential attention, only to find that they have been upstaged by lesbian critics half their age, or poststructuralists doing unspeakable things which render familiar texts suddenly impenetrable.[2]

Most of it depends on a reaffirmation of the autonomy of the aesthetic. Wily conservatives do not make their politico-literary agenda explicit, any more than they ever did. What is at stake for them is officially the submergence of great art in a welter of the second-rate. Politics, it is argued, has supplanted purely aesthetic values; sympathy with injustice has taken over from imaginative experience; the quest for novelty has replaced true appreciation of literature. Students are therefore being encouraged, the conservatives argue, to waste their time reading bad books – bad aesthetically, that is. When it comes to defining the aesthetic, the assertions become rather more mysterious: what has been lost, apparently, is 'response', 'feeling', 'inwardness with the work'. I have to confess that I am not sure what these things are and, as far as I can tell, the wielders of the backlash are not willing to tell me. If you can't recognise them when you see them, you might as well forget it, apparently. We have not advanced much, it seems, beyond the 'plainly' or 'clearly' which tended to preface the murkiest and most polemical pronouncements of F. R. Leavis.

The temptation with most of this backlash material is to leave it unread and uncontested: there is, after all, a great deal of serious analysis still to be done. But I wonder whether here, too, some of the reactionary texts might be shown to say more than their authors appear to know. I hope it goes without saying that I welcome the new developments, the plurality of voices now audible in the institution, and the challenges to the narrowness of what used to constitute the body of texts worth reading. Indeed, I take it so much for granted that the entry of English studies into the postmodern condition marks a much-needed improvement on the bad old days, that I want to risk pausing to consider the unlikely possibility that we have something to learn from the cries of pain we hear so regularly and repeatedly. I want, in other words, to take the backlash seriously.

Because of its centrality, its relative intelligence and its widespread exposure, I take as an instance Harold Bloom's *The Western Canon*, published in 1994 in America and the following year in the UK. My impression of the British reviews in the newspapers and weeklies was that they just about broke even between rapture and ridicule. James Wood in *The Guardian* loved it; Peter Conrad in *The Observer* thought it was the silliest thing he'd ever read. A lot depends on your point of view. The book is in part an elegy for the dear, dead days beyond recall, when you could put a Shakespeare play on the high-school syllabus, and still have enough energy left over to get the children to think about the merits of *Paradise Lost*. And in part it's also an elegy for the 1970s, when Bloom's own book, *The Anxiety of Influence*, first formulated the challenging hypothesis that made Bloom himself a star. This was the idea that strong writers are those who have been impelled to overthrow the influence of a powerful precursor, and that their work is intelligible as a struggle against this literary father. The Western Canon, Bloom now argues, consists of these great writers, all of them survivors of the Oedipal struggle, all of them in turn identifiable as powerful precursors for the next generation. There are twenty-six of them, none of the names very surprising, with Shakespeare, who is nearly everyone's precursor, at the centre. Bloom concludes with a canon of world books, beginning with *Gilgamesh* and *The Egyptian Book of the Dead*, and ending with a list of American works, some of which are not widely known outside the United States. Among those that are, Toni Morrison is there for *Song of Solomon* and Ursula Le Guin for *The Left Hand of Darkness*, but not *The Dispossessed*. I was impressed to see that Jeanette Winterson is included for *The Passion*. At the level of personal taste, I'm with Bloom to a high degree. I couldn't help thinking that it would make a good party game to give people marks for guessing which authors are listed, and for which of their works. Then they could make their own lists . . .

The principles of selection, Bloom insists, are resolutely aesthetic. What makes a work great, which is to say strong and deep, is not ideology or metaphysics. He entirely acknowledges what the last twenty-five years has brought to our attention, that most canonical works are politically incorrect:

> The silliest way to defend the Western Canon is to insist that it incarnates all of the seven deadly moral virtues that make up our supposed range of normative values and democratic principles. This is palpably untrue. The *Iliad* teaches the surpassing glory of armed victory, while Dante rejoices in the eternal torments he visits upon his very personal

enemies. Tolstoy's private version of Christianity throws aside nearly everything that anyone among us retains, and Dostoevsky preaches anti-Semitism, obscurantism, and the necessity of human bondage. Shakespeare's politics, insofar as we can pin them down, do not appear to be very different from those of his Coriolanus, and Milton's ideas of free speech and free press do not preclude the imposition of all manner of societal restraints. Spenser rejoices in the massacre of Irish rebels, while the egomania of Wordsworth exalts his own poetic mind over any other source of splendor.

If we read the Western Canon in order to form our social, political, or personal moral values, I firmly believe that we will become monsters of selfishness and exploitation.

The final injustice of historical injustice is that it does not necessarily endow its victims with anything except a sense of their victimization. Whatever the Western Canon is, it is not a program for social salvation.[3]

I have quoted Bloom at some length in the hope of demonstrating that it is possible to discern in the rhythms of his prose how much he owes to a powerful precursor whose influence is not, perhaps, adequately overthrown. Matthew Arnold also believed that literature had no obligation to put right specific injustices, and that critical judgement was not a matter of agreeing with the propositions of the text.

The rule may be summed up in one word – *disinterestedness*. And how is criticism to show disinterestedness? By keeping aloof from what is called 'the practical view of things'; by resolutely following the law of its own nature, which is to be a free play of the mind on all subjects which it touches. By steadily refusing to lend itself to any of those ulterior, political, practical considerations about ideas, which plenty of people will be sure to attach to them, which perhaps ought often to be attached to them, which in this country at any rate are certain to be attached to them quite sufficiently, but which criticism has really nothing to do with. Its business is, as I have said, simply to know the best that is known and thought in the world . . .[4]

What Bloom takes from Arnold is an 'authority' derived from the illusion of a personal speaking voice. The mode of address is direct, casual at times, allusive, and then almost colloquial. Bloom also borrows Arnold's habit of repeating words and sentences, the reiterated sructures often leading to a summarising parataxis or an epigrammatic closure. These are the rhythms of oral rhetoric, the imitation of speech in written prose simulating for a phonocentric culture authenticity, integrity, resounding conviction.

Here is Arnold again, arguing that criticism is failing in its crucial task:

It is because criticism has so little kept in the pure intellectual sphere, has so little detached itself from practice, has been so directly polemical and controversial, that it has so ill accomplished, in this country, its best spiritual work.[5]

Bloom's case, meanwhile, is that what he calls the School of Resentment, broadly, Marxists, feminists and multiculturalists, has vulgarised literary studies by distracting criticism from its proper object, which is to enhance 'the mind's dialogue with itself'. 'The true use', he says, 'of Shakespeare or of Cervantes, of Homer or of Dante, of Chaucer or of Rabelais, is to augment one's own growing inner self',[6] 'to enlarge a solitary existence'.[7]

The problem here for both Arnold and Bloom is that what takes the place of the despised polemic and controversy in their scheme of values, what rises above the merely contingent, is an individualist self-cultivation, which is itself deeply political. Arnold, optimistic about the possibilities for the future, manages, as liberals often do, to evade specificity by reference to a not very clearly defined 'criticism of life'. Bloom, however, who sees it all slipping away, is correspondingly more impassioned and more revealing. The literature he admires is, he tells us, not only 'strong' and 'deep', but also 'dark', individual ('solitary'), 'competitive' and 'free' – which brings us right back again to the heart of the American dream for the second time, but now uncritically. (Bloom also indicates that his favourite characters from Shakespeare are Falstaff and Lear: passionate, patriarchal, imperious, solitary and ultimately desperate old men.)

III

What then is there to take seriously here? The personal and political investments are barely disguised; the prose, however vigorous, is also derivative; the definition of criticism has been familiar for at least 130 years. The logic of Bloom's position requires, however, that if what makes literature strong, deep and dark is not a matter of content, morality and ideology, then the value that elicits his passionate defence, literature's aesthetic autonomy, must reside at least in part elsewhere. What is aesthetically exciting, his book reiterates, is not only meaning but form, language, the signifier itself. As a self-proclaimed Romantic,[8] Bloom repudiates any theory that would enable him to account for the power of the signifier, or to identify its materiality, so the textuality of the text is necessarily collapsed back into a property of the Author, recuperated as a psychological propensity, a 'will to figuration',[9] and barely differentiated from the signified, the meaning as insight or under-standing. But the signifier is named, nonetheless, and repeatedly, as a con-stituent of 'aesthetic strength', which is said to reside in 'mastery of figurative language . . . exuberance of diction',[10] 'linguistic energy'.[11] Shakespeare demonstrates 'a verbal art larger and more definitive than any other'.[12] And again, 'Rhetorically, Shakespeare has no equal; no more awesome panoply of metaphor exists'.[13]

Bloom's vocabulary is impressionistic, not analytical: as he sees it, the language of literature is masterful, exuberant, energetic, large, awesome. And yet there is a consistency here which takes the place of precision: Bloom's own signifying practice invests literature with the kinds of qualities we might attribute to an epic hero or to one of the gods: an exceptional vigour, power, grandeur. The relation of the critic to creative writing is devout, fervent and perhaps inspired. The text, or rather, in Bloom's terms, the Author, is an object of veneration for a secular world.

Arnold also saw literature as a secular replacement for a discredited religion, and was so pleased with this insight that he opened 'The Study of Poetry' by reiterating his own earlier formulation:

> The future of poetry is immense, because in poetry, where it is worthy of its high destinies, our race, as time goes on, will find an ever surer and surer stay. There is not a creed which is not shaken, not an accredited dogma which is not shown to be questionable, not a received tradition which does not threaten to dissolve. Our religion has materialised itself in the fact, in the supposed fact; it has attached its emotion to the fact, and now the fact is failing it. But for poetry the idea is everything; the rest is a world of illusion, of divine illusion.[14]

Arnold too affirmed the importance of the signifier. His vocabulary here is more limited than Bloom's, but his accounts of literature display the same emphasis on what he calls 'style and manner'. These qualities are not to be defined, he insists: on the contrary, they are better 'felt' and 'recognised' than analysed. And they are not to be seen as independent of meaning: 'Both of these, the substance and matter on the one hand, the style and manner on the other, have a mark, an accent, of high beauty, worth, and power'. The signifier precisely signifies, and what it signifies is power. Power, indeed, is the distinguishing quality of the truly poetic: familiarity with the famous touchstones, those instances which in Arnold's account permit us to recognise genuine poetry, will enable us to be thoroughly 'penetrated' by it – like Adam, perhaps, animated by the breath of God.[15]

IV

If I have an anxiety about English studies in the postmodern condition, it is that we may have neglected the signifier. There is, perhaps, a tendency for current readings to go straight to the signified, to uncover the thematic content of the text, whether conscious or unconscious, and ignore the mode of address. How ironic if postmodernity, so conscious of surfaces that it is often accused of taking style for substance, should generate a criticism which, though often eminently stylish in itself (I think here particularly of American New Historicism, for example), takes little or no account of the signifying practices of the texts it interprets. This is a loss. I am not, of course, asking for an empty formalism, a descriptive account of register or structure. But conventions, and breaches of convention, do signify; genres, and generic surprises, constitute something of the meaning of the text. How ironic if poststructuralism, which draws attention to the opacity of language, should be invoked in support of a new assumption of its transparency.

The mode of address offers the reader a specific subject position in relation to the text's explicit propositions. It might be important to recognise, for instance, that Arnold's prose owes part of its authority to the illusion of expressiveness, the use of the first-person pronoun, and the casual, direct phrase invading the regularities of the rhythm, so that the text appears to mimic the process of reflection itself. And its persuasiveness owes something, too, to the repetition of specific words and phrases: 'the fact' four times in one sentence, or a single term woven through a whole essay ('disinterestedness', 'high seriousness', 'the criticism of life') to the point where the words seem to invoke an already familiar, already taken for granted, 'obvious' value. And it might be useful to acknowledge that the section of the British press which greeted Bloom's book with such rapture was responding, at least in part, to a genuine familiarity which was not named, a recognition, conscious or not, of the diction of Arnold with a difference, which is also the diction of our 'best' journalists.

To put a case for attending to the rhetorical strategies of the text is not, of course, to defend the canon. On the contrary, if the signifier has such persuasive power, the most useful thing we can do for our students is alert them to the modes of address that characterise the artefacts they encounter daily: news bulletins, Mills and Boon romances, Hollywood movies and advertisements. This is not, contrary to popular belief, to affirm that cornflakes packets are as good as *King Lear*, but simply to take into account the possibility that cornflakes packets may have designs on us. If people in democratic societies subscribe to the most extraordinary values, and after nearly two decades of right-wing government in the UK it is clear to me that they do, it might be because something in their culture coaxes and cajoles them into beliefs that would be unaccountable in a world where language was a neutral instrument of communication. Right-wing political rhetoric doesn't just peddle policies: it elicits deference to an authority which will do our political thinking for us. Advertisements don't just sell shampoo or cars: they identify happiness with consumption. If English departments do not attend to the seductions of the signifier across a range of practices, who will?

But rhetorical strategies are not all that is at stake in attending to the signifier.

Arnold and Bloom treat the language of literature with an awe that is commonly reserved for the heroic or the supernatural. Postmodernity is inclined to a greater scepticism, but is not, I want to propose, indifferent to the issue they identify. Bloom is more loquacious about it than Arnold, but also more diffuse. One emphasis, however, running through his book, is that literature promotes an encounter with the unexpected, the alien, an effect he calls 'weirdness'.[16] This seems to be more than what the Russian formalists meant by defamiliarisation, though it shares some of the same ground. What is the common quality, Bloom asks, that makes his twenty-six writers great?

> The answer, more often than not, has turned out to be strangeness, a mode of originality that either cannot be assimilated, or that so assimilates us that we cease to see it as strange. Walter Pater defined Romanticism as adding strangeness to beauty, but I think he characterized all canonical writing rather than the Romantics as such. The cycle of achievement goes from *The Divine Comedy* to *Endgame*, from strangeness to strangeness. When you read a canonical work for a first time you encounter a stranger, an uncanny startlement rather than a fulfilment of expectations. Read freshly, all that *The Divine Comedy*, *Paradise Lost*, *Faust Part Two*, *Hadji Murad*, *Peer Gynt*, *Ulysses*, and *Canto general* have in common is their uncanniness, their ability to make you feel strange at home.[17]

(The recurrence of 'strangeness' here closely resembles Arnold's affirmative repetitions.) The uncanny is a sensation beyond pleasure, resembling, no doubt, the frisson that delayed A. E. Housman if he thought of a line of poetry when he was shaving, because it made his skin bristle.[18] Conversely, Shakespeare, Bloom says, renders the unfamiliar familiar, 'making us at home out of doors'.[19] In Shakespeare, what is most outlandish becomes obvious; Shakespeare, Bloom proposes, 'largely invented us'.[20]

Paradoxically, this confrontation with otherness, with what is irreducibly deep and dark, is said to bring its own kind of comfort. Like Arnold, who found in poetry a 'consolation and stay', a capacity to 'interpret life for us, to console us, to sustain us',[21] Bloom argues that the canon reconciles us to the nature of things. In this sense, great books have a lesson to teach, though the lesson is neither moral nor political:

> The study of literature, however it is conducted, will not save any individual, any more than it will improve any society. Shakespeare will not make us better, and he will not make us worse, but he may teach us how to overhear ourselves when we talk to ourselves. Subsequently, he may teach us how to accept change, in ourselves as in others, and perhaps even the final form of change. Hamlet is death's ambassador to us . . .[22]

What is the connection between the uncanny power of literature and its capacity to sustain? Death, it appears, plays a part.

Bloom's purchase on current theory is distinctly shaky. He seems to believe that Michel Foucault wrote 'The Death of the Author',[23] that Roland Barthes argues in favour of the pleasure of an easy read[24] and that Jacques Lacan sees the unconscious as a structure of phonemes.[25] But Bloom *has* read Freud, and especially Freud on the uncanny. In Freud's account, the uncanny is what ought to have remained hidden but has come to light. The *Unheimliche* is the unhomely but familiar secret, which has become unsecret and is experienced as unfamiliar: it is, in other words, the return of the repressed. Literature, in Bloom's account, offers us a sense of the strangeness of the familiar, or of familiarity with what is strange. It invites us to confront what might or should have remained hidden, to encounter a secret which is otherwise repressed. And this deep, dark secret is constitutive for the reader: Shakespeare 'largely invented us'. Bloom then backs away from the possibilities of his own recognition: the weirdness must, he decides, be accountable in some other way, at the level of the signified. In Shakespeare it is attributable to character, it turns out, and the banality of that proposition surely indicates that something serious is being kept at bay. 'No other writer has ever had anything like Shakespeare's resources of language, which are so florabundant in *Love's Labour's Lost* that we feel many of the limits of language have been reached, once and for all. Shakespeare's greatest originality is in representation of character, however.'[26]

But there is nothing particularly uncanny in Bloom's account of Shakespeare's characters, and the gap between what he says about the limits of language and his character sketches might be read psychoanalytically as itself a mark of repression. Suppose, then, we follow the path opened by Bloom's attention to the signifier and its power to disturb? According to the poststructuralist theory that Bloom so vehemently rejects, and particularly according to Lacan's rereading of Freud in the light of Saussure, the subject is what speaks, or rather signifies, and it signifies always and only from the place of the Other. The imperatives of the organism that we also are return to us alienated, from outside, from the language that precedes us and makes us subjects. Subjectivity, identity, is learnt; it is an effect and not an origin; it depends on the signifier.

In daily life it is possible to repress this recognition to the degree that we seem to master the language that constitutes us. Inasmuch as language appears transparent, an instrument that we use, the subject is able to imagine itself given in nature, an essence, the origin of its own desires, and in possession of the objects of its knowledge, repudiating, which is to say disavowing, the precariousness which results from its linguistic composition. But to encounter language at the limits of mastery, to confront the signifier as difficult, errant or opaque, is to risk coming face to face with the Other, the material of our own identity, confronting in the process the insubstantial character of subjectivity itself. The Other is the non-full, non-present, non-existent source of meaning and truth, the ungrounded guarantee of the knowledges we seem to possess, and it is constitutive for the subjects we are. No wonder the encounter is experienced as disturbing, awe-inspiring, beyond pleasure; no wonder Bloom finds it deep, dark and uncanny.

To reach the limits of language is to stand at the edge of what we know, on the threshold of the undefined and unknowable, though we can name it: Lacan's real, Jean-François Lyotard's event. In one sense, we do this every day. I encounter the unknown every time I listen to the football results or the shipping forecast, both of which I find utterly impenetrable. But the uncanny moment is not there. These are discourses that I could learn – with whatever difficulty. The Freudian uncanny, at least in fiction, is also a moment of undecidability, when it is impossible to be sure of the genre of the text. Supernatural beings are disturbing when they invade an apparently mimetic text: *The Turn of the Screw* is uncanny; *Julius Caesar* is not. Similarly, the poetic frisson results from the unexpected, not the unintelligible. Like the anamorphic skull in *The Ambassadors*, an uncanny phrase or figure disrupts our seamless mastery of the text, takes it in an unpredicted direction, or leaves us undecided between possible interpretations. It invites us suddenly to read from another position, and thus draws attention to the subject as precisely *positioned*, making sense from a specific and limited place. This place is at once located – in history, in culture, in this moment as opposed to that – and dis-located, other than it is, beside itself, outside the comfortable, confident command of the text, and of the objects of knowledge, the mastery that was always imaginary.

The place is above all subject to mortality. 'Hamlet is death's ambassador to us . . .', Bloom says, and again, 'The Canon, far from being the servant of the dominant social class, is the minister of death'.[27] (Is Bloom, I wonder, who includes non-fictional prose in his canon, making a bid, with this resounding phrase, for canonical status for his own book?) It is surprising how many of Arnold's touchstones in 'The Study of Poetry' allude in one way or another to mortality. Death is the supreme example of what can be named but not known. As Freud points out, it is a well-known fact that all human beings are mortal, but although we perfectly understand the premise of the syllogism, there is a sense in which we do not really grasp its application to ourselves at the level of experience.[28] Elsewhere he puts it differently: 'It is indeed impossible to imagine our own death; and whenever we attempt to do so we can perceive that we are in fact still present as spectators'.[29] Derrida makes a similar point in *Aporias*.[30] In Lacanian terms, death is the moment when the organism finally rejoins the unknowable but inextricable real. There is therefore a sense in which the subject knows nothing of death because it is not the subject that dies. On the contrary, what dies is precisely the organism, which is something other than the subject.[31] At the same time, the (living) subject is always destined for death, since its existence depends on difference. Subjectivity ceases to be when the organism dies, and that cessation is both inevitable and impossible, nameable and unintelligible. Death is thus one kind of instance of the signifier at its most opaque.[32]

But death is in my view an example of the uncanny, not its origin. Indeed, it is not death itself which disturbs in fiction, but ghosts and revenants, figures who contradict the meaning of the term. Contradiction, paradox, oxymoron: these are all cases where we might feel that 'the limits of language have been reached', as Bloom puts it. They are also recurrent features of Arnold's touchstones: 'In cradle of the rude imperious surge' is one of the Shakespearean cases he cites; 'Darken'd so, yet shone/Above them all the archangel' from *Paradise Lost*; and 'Absent thee from felicity awhile', where it is death that is defined as felicity, and life is identified as an absence.[33]

In *Paradise Lost*, to invoke a single instance of my own, Milton's Satan asserts:

> my self am hell;
> And in the lowest deep a lower deep
> Still threatening to devour me opens wide. (IV, 75–7)

In the lowest a lower still: Satan's acknowledgement of a subjectivity encountering an infinite regress of loss demonstrates that representation, not experience, not imagination, is the location of meaning. His agonised affirmation of a lower deep within the lowest makes sense, even while it defies visualisation, logic, grammar itself: everyone knows that it is not possible to exceed the superlative, 'the lowest'. There is no referent here, and no imaginable concept. But meaning is neither referential nor psychological: on the contrary, it is an effect of language. Language is not transparent to an imaginable reality on the other side of signification; it is not, precisely, a medium. Satan's unimaginable horror, his affirmation of a subjectivity which is forever ungrounded, makes sense by enlisting the non-transparency of language, which is in turn the subject's only (insubstantial and dis-located) ground.

From a religious point of view, it might well be that the proper response to the opacity of the signifier, or to signifying practice that brings us face to face with the Other that made us, is awe, a sense of the ultimate mystery of things. Both Arnold and Bloom inhabit, it seems to me, a profoundly supernatural world, though for them formal religion is secularised as art. We do not need to share their metaphysics in order to recognise the possibility that there are instances of language which invite us to confront our own uncanny double, the Other which is the condition of our existence as subjects, and in the process to acknowledge the experience as frightening. I don't want to attribute these cases to genius, or invoke them in defence of the canon. On the contrary, it seems to me that they are likely to be culturally relative, and to be found in quite unexpected places. The project is not to reintroduce principles of selection, or to smuggle aesthetic value back onto the agenda. But I think we could usefully acknowledge the opacity of the signifier when we consider the role of English studies in the postmodern condition. No other discipline confronts the strangeness of language in a way which enables us to glimpse the corresponding strangeness of the subject to itself.

It remains to account for the fact that people choose these uncanny encounters, that they enjoy the frisson. Arnold finds poetry consoling; Bloom believes literature reconciles us to death. It is possible that the signifier protects us from a relation to death, from a *direct* relation, to the degree that to name is always to misrecognise or, in Derridean terms, to defer the signified.[34] Derrida's differance (with an a) ensures that meaning is always relegated, supplanted, distanced and postponed by the signifier, which takes the place of the imagined absence or presence. (As is so often the case, Shakespeare also invented this point: 'the worst is not/So long as we can say, "This is the worst"'.[35]) The signifier, which in its opacity brings the subject to the edge of a confrontation with its own relativity, paradoxically also permits it to back away again, reaffirms the distance between the subject and the unthinkable condition of its existence.[36]

Arnold had no vocabulary for the analysis of the experience he identified; Bloom refuses to engage with the theory that would enable him to go beyond a Romantic relation to textuality. But then both Arnold and Bloom are confined within the discipline of literary criticism. English studies in the postmodern condition, however, has no excuse for evading the implications of the uncanny power of the signifier that both Arnold and Bloom, as well as others, have brought to our attention. The frisson engendered by certain signifying instances is not best understood either as a Romantic self-indulgence, or as an encounter with a mystery that can be named and relegated as genius. On the contrary, it can more usefully be read as a reminder of our own linguistic constitution as subjects, and our consequent vulnerability to the meanings and values in circulation in our culture. Whether our motive in reading is solitary self-cultivation or a struggle against social injustice, we should, in my view, do well to remember what we are, and the relativity of the place we speak from.

NOTES

1. Linda Charnes, *Notorious Identity: Materializing the Subject in Shakespeare* (Cambridge, MA: Harvard University Press, 1993).
2. See, for example, Hilton Kramer and Roger Kimball, 'Farewell to the MLA', *The New Criterion* (February 1995), pp. 5–16.

3. Harold Bloom, *The Western Canon: The Books and School of the Ages* (London: Macmillan, 1995), p. 29.

4. Matthew Arnold, 'The Function of Criticism at the Present Time', *Poetry and Prose* ed. John Bryson (London: Rupert Hart-Davis, 1967), pp. 351–74 (pp. 360–1).

5. Ibid., p. 362.

6. Bloom, *The Western Canon*, p. 30.

7. Ibid., p. 518.

8. Ibid.

9. Ibid., p. 12.

10. Ibid., p. 29.

11. Ibid., p. 46.

12. Ibid., p. 49.

13. Ibid., p. 60.

14. Arnold, 'The Study of Poetry', *Poetry and Prose*, pp. 663–85 (p. 663).

15. Ibid., pp. 670–1.

16. Bloom, *The Western Canon*, p. 26.

17. Ibid., p. 3.

18. A. E. Housman, *The Name and Nature of Poetry* (Cambridge: Cambridge University Press, 1933), p. 47. Housman also insisted that poetry was not a matter of meaning, but of language, and that its effects were unaccountable. True poetry appealed to 'something in man which is obscure and latent, something older than the present organisation of his nature, like the patches of fen which still linger here and there in the drained lands of Cambridgeshire' (p. 46).

19. Bloom, *The Western Canon*, p. 3.

20. Ibid., p. 40.

21. Arnold, 'The Study of Poetry', pp. 664, 663.

22. Bloom, *The Western Canon*, p. 31.

23. Ibid., p. 60.

24. Ibid., p. 30.

25. Ibid., p. 371.

26. Ibid., p. 47.

27. Ibid., p. 32.

28. Sigmund Freud, 'The "Uncanny"', *Art and Literature*, ed. Albert Dickson, Penguin Freud Library vol. 14 (London: Penguin Books, 1985), pp. 335–81.

29. Sigmund Freud, 'Thoughts for the Times on War and Death', *Civilization, Society and Religion: Group Psychology, Civilization and its Discontents and Other Works*, ed. Albert Dickson, Penguin Freud Library vol. 12 (London: Penguin Books, 1985), pp. 57–89 (p. 77).

30. Jacques Derrida, *Aporias*, trans. Thomas Dutoit (Stanford, CA: Stanford University Press, 1993), p. 22.

31. Cf. ibid., p. 76.

32. Like the real, death can be named but not conceived. It is thus in one sense parallel to the Kantian sublime, which can be conceived but not exemplified. Unlike the sublime, however, which for Kant vindicates the subject-as-origin, the existence of the named but unknowable (postmodern) event places meaning beyond the command of the 'knowing' subject.

33. Arnold, 'The Study of Poetry', p. 670.
34. Cf. Derrida, *Aporias*, p. 76.
35. *King Lear*, Act 4, Scene 1, lines 27–8.
36. Cf. Lyotard's account of the Burkean sublime: the sublime in Burke is kindled by terror of privation, death, the fear of 'nothing happening'; art, meanwhile, suspends this menace by making something happen. Strange combinations in art are shocking, and the shock is the evidence of 'something happening' (Jean-François Lyotard, *The Inhuman: Reflections on Time*, trans. Geoffrey Bennington and Rachel Bowlby (Cambridge: Polity Press, 1991), pp. 99–101).

Chapter Nine

ETHOPOEIA, SOURCE-STUDY AND LEGAL HISTORY

A Post-Theoretical Approach to the Question of 'Character' in Shakespearean Drama

Lorna Hutson

'CHARACTER' – AN INAPPROPRIATE CATEGORY?

Theory – more precisely, poststructuralist theory – 'threatens', in Alan Sinfield's words, 'to make character an altogether inappropriate category of analysis' in Shakespeare criticism.[1] What a relief, one might well think, after reading all those neo-Bradleyian student essays condemning the inadequacies of Desdemona's personality or the failure of an Olivia or an Isabella to 'know' herself sexually. But Sinfield's word is 'threatens'. His essay is less a defensive anticipation of the consequences of such a threat than an open-eyed, some-what regretful acknowledgement of the inability of poststructuralism to carry it out. He quotes from two theoretical assaults on the category of character, both, as it happens, published in 1985: Jonathan Goldberg's 'Shakespearean Inscriptions: The Voicing of Power', in *Shakespeare and the Question of Theory*, and Catherine Belsey's 'Disrupting Sexual Difference: Meaning and Gender in the Comedies', in *Alternative Shakespeares*.[2] Both Goldberg and Belsey, here and elsewhere, borrow from Roland Barthes the question 'Who is speaking?' in order to trouble a liberal humanist readiness to construct, in relation to any Shakespearean speech prefix, an 'imaginary fulness', such as that of 'the feeling, self-conscious, "poetic" Macbeth, a full subject, a character'.[3] As Sinfield points out, it is hard to disagree with Goldberg's and Belsey's conclusions that 'what is recognised in our culture as "character" must be the effect of "the entire culture" and "a point of intersection of a range of discourses,"'[4] but the fact remains that the plays of Shakespeare are distinguishable from those of contemporary vernacular dramatists in Renaissance Europe to the extent that 'they are written so as to

139

produce . . . what are interpreted (by those possessing the appropriate decoding knowledges) as character effects'.[5] It's a paradox of the current critical situation that while poststructuralists busy themselves identifying the discontinuities and slippages that mark the difference of the Shakespearean subject from itself, Shakespeare's playwriting contemporaries are still considered inferior to the extent that they *fail* to realise dramatic voice as anything more coherent or individualised than a 'point of intersection of a range of discourses'. No one would dream of praising Elizabeth Cary's *Tragedy of Mariam* for being replete with 'slippages and multiplications which determine and fix only to unmoor again, making all places provisional, all sites relational, all identity a matter of differences scarcely perceivable because forever changing', yet these phrases of Goldberg's, applied in celebration of Shakespeare, might be apter thus transferred.[6]

The poststructuralist rejection of a liberal humanist notion of 'character as self-same, owned, capable of autonomy and change'[7] fails to acknowledge the extent to which the notion of character is itself the historical legacy of Shakespearean drama. Consequently, it has helped to produce the new and powerfully tacit assumption that Shakespeare's cross-cultural intelligibility (once attributed to his superior affective powers, particularly his powers of characterisation) is an index of the relevance of his drama for a 'cultural poetics' of early modern society. Such an equation is, for example, made by Stephen Greenblatt's *Shakespearean Negotiations*, which announces the author's desire to engage with the whole of early modern culture – a 'desire to speak with the dead' – as the justification for a book of essays confined to the analysis of Shakespearean theatre. The justification is made on the grounds that, although it is 'paradoxical to seek the living will of the dead in fictions', yet fictions are 'simulations undertaken in full awareness of the absence of life they contrive to represent' and so are legitimately identified with the voices of that 'dead' or vanished culture with which the literary critic wishes to converse.[8]

Work yet remains to be done on the pre-history of the late seventeenth-century emergence of the concept of dramatic 'character' ('the ordinary word for a person in a drama', as Peter Womack defines it[9]), but one important strand of that pre-history, locatable in the pedagogy of sixteenth-century Northern European humanism, might be relevantly invoked here. Greenblatt's description of his engagement with fictions of the past as 'simulations undertaken in full awareness of the absence of life they contrive to represent' may recall to us Paul de Man's identification of Romantic autobiography's deployment of the figure of *prosopopoeia* ('the fiction of an apostrophe to an absent, deceased or voiceless entity, which posits the possibility of the latter's reply, and confers upon it the power of speech').[10] To a sixteenth- or seventeenth-century schoolboy, however, both the figures of 'prosopopoeia' (personifying a lifeless thing) and 'idolopoeia' (making up a spirit, or speaking for the dead) were ordinarily subsumed under the more general figure of 'ethopoeia' (from ηθοσ ποιεν, to make up character), which was the name of one of the 'progymnastic' exercises composed by the fourth- century scholar Aphthonius. The book known to sixteenth-century grammar schoolboys as the *Progymnasmata* of Aphthonius consisted of fourteen elementary exercises in original composition. Performing these exercises marked the boy's transition from being able to parse and translate to being able to write and deliver declamations.[11]

In sixteenth-century discussions of *ethopoeia*, as distinct from *prosopopoeia* and *idolopoeia*, the emphasis falls upon the apt invention of voice or discourse, rather than upon the act of personification itself. Thus Agricola's translation of Aphthonius calls *idolopoeia* a 'figure of speech' (*conformatio*), but equates *ethopoeia* with *sermoncinatio*, or discussion.[12] Elsewhere, sixteenth-century commentaries on Aphthonius cite Quintilian, who defines *ethopoeia* as 'the imitation of another person's characteristics (*mores*)' ('Imitatur morum alienorum, quae ηθοπιια... dicitur').[13] In the classic definition, Aphthonius explains *ethopoeia* as having for its subject a known person, so that the invention concerns the character only ('Est autem ethopoeia, quae notam habens personam, mores solum effingit').[14] Or, as Richard Rainolde's English translation puts it: 'That parte, which is called *Ethopoeia* is that, whiche hath the persone knowne: but only it doth faigne the maners of the same, and imitate in an Oracion of the same . . . *Ethopoeia* is called of Priscianus . . . an imitacion of the talke referred to the maners, aptly of any certaine knowen person'.[15]

The point of invoking a sixteenth- and seventeenth-century familiarity with the concept of characterisation under the name of '*ethopoeia*' is not, however, to embark upon the history of a rhetorical exercise, nor is it to argue that such a history could in any way account for the capacity of Shakespeare's plays to give rise to 'character criticism'. It is, rather, to point out that, at the most fundamental educational level of sixteenth-century literary culture, an awareness was being fostered of the complex dependence of strategies for the maximisation of pathos or affect on the exploitation of representations of shared social codes and customs (*mores*). Reading his Aphthonius, the schoolboy would learn that there are three sorts of *ethopoeia*: affective, moral and a mixture of the two ('Dividitur autem ethopoeia: nanque alia affectum exprimit, alia mores, alia utrunq*ue*').[16] *Ethopoeia* is simultaneously referred, then, to 'ηθοσ', ethos or *mores*, and to 'παθυσ' or affect; indeed, it is sometimes known as '*pathopoeia*'.[17] So where New Historicist and poststructuralist approaches to Renaissance drama have rejected literary formalism, reading dramatic discourse as one among many sorts of cultural artefact from which we can glean a fuller knowledge of the conditions of subjectivity in the past, a post-theoretical approach might be one in which it was possible to acknowledge, and take account of, the

Renaissance dramatist's own strategic engagement, as a technician of *ethopoeia*, with the relationship between what translations of Aphthonius render as 'affection' and 'maners'; that is, the relationship between a person's feelings, and the *mores*, or codes of behaviour through which the 'affections' have social meaning.

NARRATIVE AND DRAMATIC SOURCES: OUR NATURALISATION OF SHAKESPEAREAN 'CHARACTER'

The question of source-study, and its wholesale rejection by poststructuralist and New Historicist criticism of Shakespeare, is also relevant here. For source-study, as traditionally carried out, is naively confessional of the cultural *mores* – which it offers as criteria of psychological plausibility, and so of literary merit – of its own historical moment and community. The rejection of source-study, however, does not so much critique the cultural and historical specificity of these moral codes as render them, and the implications of Shakespeare's capacity to satisfy them, inscrutable. In refuting the naive character realism of some early feminist work on Shakespeare, Goldberg invoked Derrida's 'The Law of Genre', arguing, in relation to Shakespeare's *Measure for Measure*, that all characters act under 'the compulsion of genre', in a play in which 'generation by substitution is the representational law'.[18] However, if the law of genre represents 'an arbitrary limit on the generativity of language',[19] and if 'representation by substitution' is the name of that limit in *Measure for Measure*, then, one might ask, what is it about Shakespeare's development of this particular organisational device that has guaranteed the historical survival of *his* version of the play over its innovative and self-conscious dramatic precursors? For it is well established that Shakespeare was, in writing *Measure for Measure*, heavily indebted to two or three earlier versions: a novella in the collection called *Gli Hecatommithi* by Gianbattista Giraldi Cinthio, a ten-act comedy by George Whetstone called *Promos and Cassandra*, and (probably) Cinthio's revision of his novella as the tragicomedy, *Epitia*.[20] The last two texts make much of the use of representation by substitution in the interests of achieving tragicomic effect. So when Goldberg singles out Shakespeare's Barnadine as the essence of that 'resistance to representation' which he finds ubiquitous in the play, it is worthwhile noticing, as the source-studies tell us, that the figure of Barnadine – that is, the figure of a substitute for the heroine's condemned brother – is an innovation already introduced by Cinthio in his revision of his novella as the play *Epitia*, and by Whetstone, apparently independently, in *Promos and Cassandra*.[21] It is tempting to pursue the observation that Shakespeare's is the only play which develops this substitute in an *ethopoetic* fashion (that is, his is the only play that gives 'a lively expression of the manner and affection' of the brother's substitute). More revealing on the subject of 'character', however, is the single instance in which Shakespeare's play uses the device of substitution in a way which departs radically from his sources.

In Cinthio's and Whetstone's plays, the heroine agrees to have sex with the magistrate who has condemned her brother; it is only in Shakespeare's version that the notion of substitution extends from the substitution of the ruling magistrate, and that of the condemned brother, to the substitution of the heroine herself, thereby changing the meaning and consequences of the terrible sacrifice she is asked to make. In the earlier versions of the play, the laws of genre (tragicomedy) and of cultural *mores* can only be satisfied at the expense of what we think of as the heroine's psychological reality. For a happy ending requires not only that the heroine be married to the magistrate before the latter is condemned to die for his crime, but that she switch abruptly, still in ignorance of her brother's having been saved from death, to plead for clemency towards her brother's killer, now her husband. Source-study of the traditional kind, exemplified by Geoffrey Bullough's magisterial *Narrative and Dramatic Sources of Shakespeare*, finds the rationale for Shakespeare's departure from his sources in such instances in the increased psychological realism, the superior effect of 'character' achieved by Shakespeare. Both Cinthio's tragicomedy and Whetstone's ten-act dramatic experiment are pronounced inadequate by comparison with Shakespeare primarily because in each the heroine fails to persuade us of her inner continuity as a 'character'. Of Whetstone's heroine, Cassandra, Bullough writes: 'Once married to Promos, her desire for revenge changes conventionally'.[22] And he concludes that Whetstone's play suffers from 'the psychological improbability' of the heroine in this respect. Shakespeare's transformation of the heroine into the novice Isabella, whose vocation explains her refusal to entertain Angelo's proposal, then becomes intelligible to Bullough as a reaction against the pyschological improbability (the aesthetic inferiority) of the heroine in the earlier plays:

> Isabella, unlike her predecessors, is a 'novice'. This daring change was probably made for several reasons. First, the quite obvious difficulty Shakespeare saw in having the heroine agree to Angelo's proposal. If she agreed the play must be a tragedy, for Shakespeare was the author of *Lucrece*, and Whetstone's play revealed the psychological improbability inherent in making her suddenly turn after the forced marriage to a dutiful angel of mercy.[23]

Bullough implicitly acknowledges, while seeming to deny, the pressures that his codes of morality exert on his standards of psychological verisimilitude. The only solution to the inevitable tragedy of the heroine's having had extra-marital sex is the tragicomic solution of marriage to her seducer, and this, as Bullough maintains Shakespeare perceived, was psychologically unsatisfactory, because we cannot believe in Cassandra's *affective* consent to the marriage that her culture's *mores* demand for the saving of her 'crased Honor'.[24] The psychological improbability of a chaste heroine who pleads disinterestedly for mercy for her brother's murderer was, Bullough seems to have felt, much less of a problem:

> Can she [Isabella] bring herself to forgive her enemy (not her husband as in the sources) while still believing that he murdered Claudio? . . . Isabella responds to Mariana's desperate prayer, but the terms she uses are rational and earthly. She pardons; she admits that Claudio was justly condemned; she distinguishes between the act and the intention, but . . . she does not love her enemy; nor should we wish it. That made the end of Cinthio's novella monstrous.

If Bullough's reasoning seems to appeal to the idea of universal and purely formal standards of dramatic craftsmanship, while denying the specific cultural investments (the *mores*) that underlie these standards, then surely our own refusal to consider the historical conditions that have rendered a chaste Isabella more 'psychologically probable' than her unchaste dramatic antecedents is itself a kind of complicity with Bullough's formalist myth. Such complicity is evident at a fairly casual level in a great deal of Shakespeare criticism, and even, at times, in accounts of that criticism's history. Jonathan Bate's enthusiasm for the modernity of Hazlitt in *Shakespearean Constitutions* is a case in point. Hazlitt was, according to Bate, the first critic to sketch the 'outlines of a "modern" reading of *Measure for Measure*'. Hazlitt, according to Bate, turned 'the comfortable reading of the play upside down: the "original sin in the nature of the subject" is not sex, as a pedantic moralist would have it, but "want of passion"'.[25] But in contriving a Hazlitt modern enough to disagree with the prevailing moralistic view of the play, Bate suppresses Hazlitt's own acknowledgement of a moral and emotional investment in the chastity of the heroine. In Bate's words, 'Hazlitt also questioned the strict moral code of Isabella, saying that he "was not greatly enamoured" of her "rigid chastity"'.[26] What Hazlitt actually said, however, was slightly different: 'Neither are we greatly enamoured of Isabella's rigid chastity', he admitted, '*though she could not act otherwise than she did*' (my italics).[27] It is Bate, then, not Hazlitt, who reads Isabella's chastity as *characteristic* of her, as the expression of her own neurotic self-discipline, rather than as Shakespeare's conformity to a code of manners that agreed with Hazlitt's own. The nineteenth and twentieth centuries would not have tolerated the retrospective chastity of an Epitia or a Cassandra, both on grounds of affective implausibility, and, importantly, on moral grounds: 'she *could not* act otherwise than she did' are Hazlitt's words, or, as Bullough puts it, 'she must not agree'.

How, then, might we find an approach to the fictions of women in

Shakespeare that would acknowledge and historicise our almost inevitable preference for Shakespeare's version of such fictions over the others that were available in the sixteenth and seventeenth centuries? How can we avoid mistaking a critical apostrophe to our own reflection in our preferred, Shakespearean version of the past, for an authentic conversation with the voices of a culture that is now strange to us, the voices of the dead, who could imagine what Hazlitt could not, an unchaste Isabella? Shakespeare appears to achieve the affective continuity that the earlier heroines lacked by ensuring Isabella's refusal of Angelo; the question of her 'character' therefore begins to turn on the conjecture about the motive for this refusal, which we seek in the figure of Isabella herself, not respecting, as Jacqueline Rose pointed out, 'the limits of characterization'.[28] More than that, as Rose's account shows, the question of Isabella's character becomes, in the wake of Hazlitt's anticipation of a 'modern' distaste for her 'rigid chastity', the focal point of modernist criticisms of *Measure for Measure*:

> Isabella has been described as a 'hussy' (Charlton, *cit.* R. M. Smith 1950, p. 213), 'hysterical' (Lever, Introduction to Arden edition, Shakespeare 1965, p. lxxx), as suffering 'inhibition' (Knight, 1930, p. 102) or 'obsession' (Jardine, 1983, p. 192) about sex . . . Given that *Measure for Measure* is one of Shakespeare's plays where it is generally recognized that his method of characterization cannot fully be grasped psychologically, . . . then the extent to which Isabella has been discussed in terms of consistency, credibility and ethics is striking. In the critical debates about Isabella, it is as if we can see anxiety about aesthetic or representational cohesion turning into sexual reproach.[29]

Typical of post-Bradleyan and modernist approaches to Shakespeare, of which Bullough's source-study remains a recognisable type, is the pretence that there can be purely aesthetic criteria of psychological verisimilitude;[30] so, as Rose says, we find, in the modernist criticism of more than one play, 'anxiety about aesthetic or representational cohesion turning into sexual reproach'. The poststructuralist reaction to all this – the observation that subjectivity itself is 'the point of intersection of a range of discourses' and that, therefore, the subject in Shakespeare, as elsewhere, is not a 'unified presence' but 'occupies a series of places in the signifying system'[31] – is undeniable, but offers no way of distinguishing the forms of fictional characterisation which have been judged weak or obsolete from those which have provoked, over a remarkably long period of time, and through a number of different critical movements, the passionate reactions Rose describes. A post-theoretical approach to the concept of 'character', then, would concede the historical legacy of Shakespeare's ethopoetic dramatic tradition in the formation of psychoanalysis itself, and would look, in the moment of that drama's first production, for signs of change in the allocation of value to certain kinds of 'manners' or '*mores*', in order to try and understand the conditions under which Shakespeare so successfully reshaped and reorganised the affective power of given dramatic material. The final section will therefore be given over to a consideration of Isabella's 'rigid chastity' in relation to sixteenth-century developments in legal history; specifically, in relation to the development of a common-law action for defamatory words, and its implications for conceptions of the comparable value, in material and measurable terms, of male and female sexual honour.

Present-day authorities in legal history, such as J. H. Baker and R. H. Helmholz, are at a loss to explain why a common-law action for slander ballooned from non-existence at the beginning of the sixteenth century into a form of litigation so common that by 1647 a 'directory' of defamatory words – John March's *Actions for Slander* – could appear on the market.[32] Until the beginning of the sixteenth century, cases of defamation had been tried by the spiritual courts under the constitution known as *Auctoritate dei Patris* (1222), supplemented by the Roman law of *iniuria*.[33] Towards the end of the fifteenth century, however, a distinction began to be observed between 'spiritual' and 'temporal' slander, the latter being defined by the involvement of the accusation of secular crimes and the consequence of material loss. Thus, a commission of 1535 reported that the common-law courts should take over jurisdiction over defamation cases 'whereby the party defamed or reproved hathe any worldly lost, as lost of goodes or service or frendshipp'.[34] Now, it is obvious that sexual slander caused the women so accused, and anyone in their household, both 'lost of . . . frendshipp' and the economic losses therewith associated. Indeed, Laura Gowing's study of women's litigation in the ecclesiastical courts in sixteenth- and seventeenth-century London has gone so far as to argue that the economically damaging effects of sexual slander on the household could only be understood to have been incurred through the sexual conduct of its women:

> The honour of the household is invested in a monogamous sexual bond, a joint marital honour which gives words like 'cuckold' and 'whore' implications for both parties. But the responsibility for that honour rests in practice upon women: *only women's sexual misconduct damages the household honour* (my italics).

Nevertheless, the sixteenth-century emergence of a conceptual division between common-law slander and spiritual slander (part of a more general Reformation project to wrest away from the church all jurisdiction over things economic) theoretically redefined the sexual slander of women, and its consequences for their kinsmen, as being, in a sense, *immaterial*. Thus, at the end of the seventeenth century, John Godolphin could argue that 'where the Prosecution is merely for the Punishment of Sin and Money not demanded, there the Spiritual Court shall have the Cognizance: But where Money is demanded for the satisfaction of the Wrong, there the Temporal'.[35] Money could not, by definition, be demanded for damage to sexual reputation, unless a specific marriage negotiation could be proved to have been ruined by an allegation of sexual misconduct, so a man who sought financial damages for the losses incurred by having his wife called a whore would be disappointed.

The last decade of the sixteenth and the first of the seventeenth were, according to John March's *Actions for Slander*, years of unprecedented increase in common-law slander litigation. There was not one such action in all of Henry VII's reign, March noted, but they 'began to multiply in the *Queenes* time, as we find in my Lord Cokes 4.book, where there is no less than 17 adjudged cases. And you may easily judge, they did not abate in *King James* his time.'[36] Edward Coke himself apparently attested to the same phenomenon in the Star Chamber on 9 June, 1602: 'There are more infamous libels [now] within a few days then ever there were in the ages last past', he is reported to have said.[37] The first performance of *Measure for Measure* anticipates by a year one of the great Star Chamber trials for slander against the government, in the course of which the Lord Chief Justice, Sir John Popham, reminded the court that

> A libelle is a breach of ye peace, & is not to be suffered, but punished: yf a man kill one with a sworde or poison, there is defence & iustice for it, & this is a poison in ye Common wealthe: & th'offence to the state dyes not.[38]

In almost every case of a slander action in the Star Chamber in the 1590s and 1600s, some remark was passed about the unprecedented rise of the problem of slander and about the need to introduce harsher laws to punish it. The Lord Keeper remembered, in one such slander trial in 1596, that 'The lawes of Edgar and Ethelbert, kings of this land before the Conquest, were that the slanderer should lose his tongue', while in another it was observed that, in Roman law, 'this offence was Capitall till Augustus'.[39] Nor were such outbursts of indignation against the ineffectuality of modern penalties confined to cases of slander against the state. A case in November 1607 concerned a Dr Wotton who had written to a Dr Edwards as 'Mr Docturdo & Fartado', continuing in this vein for a further two sides of paper full of 'vile matter, ribaldrie and defamacyon'.[40] It was considered by the court that, although it was only a private letter,

> forasmuch as the same doth provoke malice & breache of the peace and revenge, yet it shall be punished in this Courte and nippe it *dum seges*

in herba, for being a letter only kept cloase yt giveth no cause of action because he hathe no dammages & this being an offence that dothe provoke revenge, bring danger to the state and common weale *et interest reipublicae*, & therefore in this courte to be severely punished.[41]

Textual critics and historians have begun to take an interest in the sudden eruption into prominence of slander in these years as a perceived 'danger to the community'[42] even when not explicitly anti-government. This scholarly interest is part of a wider concern to construct a more discriminating picture of the various media – oral, printed, scribal – through which, in this period, information might have been spread, and communities of political opinion formed across the country. In this context, the circulation of libellous material so troubling to the court of Star Chamber can be understood, in David Colclough's words, as 'part of an attempt in Jacobean England to find an effective means of exchanging news and expressing grievances'.[43] M. Lindsay Kaplan's Foucauldian reading of *Measure for Measure* situates it in this context, and sees the play as tracing the growth of a kind of state monopoly over the theatrical power of defamation: Lucio is threatening to the Duke because he challenges that monopoly; 'in naming and condemning an incompetent deputy', she writes,

> the duke opens his government up to the slanders he himself articulates in act 5. His subsequent condemnation of Lucio for 'slandering a prince' (5.1.521) calls into question his own defamatory practice . . . Lucio's slanders of the duke are dangerous precisely because they ultimately expose the danger of the duke's slanders.[44]

Kaplan's analysis, of course, is not concerned with the question of sexual slander. Yet something like sexual slander is, in the last few lines of the play, held to be comparable to the penalties of 'pressing to death, whipping and hanging' by a Lucio who begs that he should not be made a cuckold by marrying the woman he has made a 'whore' ('I beseech your Highness, do not marry me to a whore . . . good my lord, do not recompense me in making me a cuckold'). Though the Duke's remission of the death penalty, with the words 'Thy slanders I forgive', at first suggests the envisaged capital punishment of slander, his subsequent response to Lucio's definition of 'marrying a whore' concedes the equation of Lucio's defamatory punishment and his crime: 'Slandering a prince deserves it'.[45]

Measure for Measure throughout exhibits awareness of the latest legal rulings on questions of defamation in the common law. In the opening exchange between Lucio and the first and second gentleman, there occurs a curiously evasive skirmish over the charge of syphilis, or the 'French pox'. A textbook case, recorded in Coke's *Reports* as having taken place in 1599, turned on the actionability of the words 'Hang him, hang him he is full of the pox; I marvel you will eat or drink with him. I will prove that he is full of the pox' (innuendo of the French pox).[46] Lucio adroitly turns aside the first gentleman's 'I had as lief be a list of an English kersey, as be piled, as thou art pilled, for a French velvet. Do I speak feelingly now?', with a reply which recalls this case: 'I think thou dost: and indeed, with a most painful feeling of thy speech. I will, out of thine own confession, learn to begin thy health; but whilst I live, forget to drink after thee' (Act 1, Scene 2, lines 31–7). The gentleman's insinuation that Lucio suffers from the French pox is transformed into self-slander as Lucio pounces on the possible implications of 'speaking feelingly'. Lawyers turned to Coke's report of the 'Hang him, he is full of the pox' case to learn that for a slander to be actionable 'the person scandalised must be certain'.[47] Lucio's riposte seems to joke on this famous judgement; so uncertain were the first gentleman's words that 'the person scandalised' by his innuendo about the French pox turned out to be himself.

Nevertheless, it's a moot point whether this exchange can be linked with anything that could be described as the 'sexual slander' of men. To accuse a man of having the French pox was defined as an actionable slander in the common law not because it implies anything about a man's sexual behaviour, but because words 'which charge a man to have an infectious disease by reason of which he ought to separate himselfe, or to be separated by the law from the society of men' are actionable in causing men loss of goods and trade.[48] Indeed, it seems that, according to the common law of slander, words which imply anything about a man's sexual behaviour are in themselves irrelevant, unless they involve crime, such as sodomy. As William Sheppard wrote in 1662,

> It is held that to call one *Bastard, Whore, Whoremaster, Adulterer, Fornicator*, and the like, these slanders . . . are meerly spiritual, and are properly examinable and determinable in the Ecclesiastical court. And therefore the Common Law doth not intermeddle with them, but in cases where they are intermingled with some temporal damage occasioned by them to any man.[49]

Sexual slander is defined, in the common law, as being essentially *immaterial* to men – it brings 'spiritual' damage, but not 'temporal damage' or material loss. And, what is more, the textbook example of an exception to this rule – the sexual slander which brings about temporal loss – is always the point, in legal treatises, in which the exemplary slandered 'man' turns into a woman. So Sheppard defines slanderous words as

> all scandalous words which touch or concern a man in his life . . . or which slander a man in his calling or trade . . . or which tend to the

losse of a mans preferment . . . as to say of a woman like to have a
husband, that shee is a whore . . . or which charge a men to have any
dangerous disease.[50]

And yet, in *Measure for Measure*, not only is Lucio's dangerous slander
against the duke explicitly sexual ('He's now past it; yet, and I say to thee, he
would mouth a beggar, though she smelt brown bread and garlic': Act 3,
Scene 2, lines 176–7), it is also punished, as we have seen, by the imperative
to live out the life of a cuckold, which was the most common kind of 'sexual
slander' men were subject to. For, as Laura Gowing points out, although
common-law treatises on slander never mention sexual slander as damaging
to men, it is nevertheless evident from cases both in the King's Bench and in
the Star Chamber that 'very many defamations of men turned out to concern
their wives', for the insult of cuckoldry 'regularly proved the most effective
way of defaming men'.[51] In his *Treatise of the Court of Star Chamber*, William
Hudson included 'setting up horns at a man's gate' as a punishable slander,
and recalled

> The great libel at *Wells*, there being a fame against a townsman that he
> lived incontinently with the wife of the plaintiff *Hole*, in a May-game
> used yearly in the town they brought a man riding with a board before
> him on which was a pair of nine-holes, one riding at the side, saying,
> *He holes for a groat.*[52]

Whether acknowledged by the common law or not, then, it would appear
that in practice a man's honour was materially vulnerable to the sexual slander
of a kinswoman, sister or wife. A cuckold can't be a 'real man', because he can't
face others or fend off the slanders against his wife.[53] Hence it is, presumably,
that Lucio's punishment of 'marrying a whore' is considered a suitable
penalty for the crime of slandering a prince, for it subjects the offender to a
lifetime of humiliating defamation, worse than 'pressing to death, whipping
and hanging'.

But *Measure for Measure* is unusual for going out of its way to deny the
discourse of cuckoldry, which is part of the usual early modern construction
of manhood as protective of, and invested in, the sexual reputation of
kinswomen. Take, for example, the scene which intervenes between the
order for Claudio's execution and Angelo's first interview with Isabella (a
scene which we might reasonably suppose has some function in preparing
the audience emotionally for the Angelo–Isabella encounter). Having learned
that Claudio is to die, we are left, with Escalus, to hear at some length the
incoherent case against Pompey and Froth, who appear to have done something unspeakable to the wife of the linguistically chaotic Elbow. Elbow
attempts to 'protest' (though he uses the word 'detest'), on his wife's evidence,

that Mistress Overdone's house is a brothel, which he knows 'by my wife, who, if she had been a woman cardinally given, might have been accused in fornication, adultery and all uncleanliness there'. Elbow is, therefore, charging the two men with some kind of sexual offence against his wife, but he expresses it as if trying to fend off any accusation that she herself participated in the sexual act: she merely 'might have been accused' if 'she had been a woman cardinally [carnally] given'. Thus he is less concerned to insist on the perpetration of an offence than to insist that the reputation of his wife is undamaged. As Pompey and Froth get into their stride with the hilarious routine of their defence, however, the reputation of poor Mrs Elbow hasn't a chance against the build-up of sexual innuendo – the longing for stewed prunes, the china dishes, 'the thing you wot of' – which, compounded by Pompey's excruciating prolongation of the circumstantial detail of Froth's exact whereabouts and activities on the night in question, produce a kind of hysteria in the audience. The climax of this hysteria comes at the height of equivocation:

> *Pompey*   Why very well: I hope here be truths. He, sir, sitting, as I say,
> in a lower chair, sir – 'twas in the Bunch of Grapes, where
> indeed you have a delight to sit, have you not?
> *Froth*   I have so, because it is an open room, and good for winter.
> *Pompey*   Why very well, then: I hope here be truths.
> *Angelo*   This will outlast a night in Russia
> When nights are longest there. I'll take my leave,
> And leave you to the hearing of the cause.
> I hope you'll find good cause to whip them all.
> (Act 2, Scene 1, lines 124–36)

Angelo's abrupt departure forces Escalus to try and dispense with further equivocation and get to the point – 'Now, sir, come on. What was done to Elbow's wife, once more?' But the effect of this, of course, is an explosion of suppressed hysteria, as Pompey replies, 'Once, sir? There was nothing done to her *once*' (my italics).

This use of comic innuendo touches upon an area of dispute in common-law actions for slander. In order to stem the tide of actions for words, which were (as I said earlier) considered to be increasing beyond all control, it had been established in the second half of the sixteenth century that '*Words that are of double or indifferent meaning, the Law will take in the best sence for the Speaker*'.[54] Obviously, this ruled out a lot of actions that plaintiffs might take against words that enigmatically, yet arguably, charged them with some scandal (the first gentleman's 'French kersey', for example). However, there was a decisive slander case in 1606 which exposed the inadequacy of this rule in the face of sexual innuendo. A woman brought an action in the King's Bench against a man for reporting of her that another man had 'had the use of her body at his pleasure'. Hobart, the Attorney General, argued against the plaintiff that, 'because that the wordes the use of her Body were incertain and of a double intendment, and therefore should be taken in the best sense, to have the use of her body as a Tailor in measuring, or a Phisitian in giving Physick or the like, and not in any worse sence'.[55] However, Popham, Chief Justice, objected that

> the words are actionable, when words are spoken that may have a double intent or meaning, they shall be expounded according to common intent for otherwise he which intends to slander another, may speak slanderous words which by common intendment shall be expounded a slander, and yet no Action lie. And here the words hath had the use of her body at his pleasure shall not be intended in any lawful manner, but licentiously and dishonestly for this is the common intent.[56]

The woman was awarded £200 damages for the loss of marriage prospects these words had occasioned. Obviously, in the case of Pompey's 'Once, sir? There was nothing done to her once', it's less clear what the 'common intendment' of the syntax would be, as audience laughter proves that the addition of 'once' qualifies Pompey's denial in such a way as to bestow a pair of horns on Elbow.

But the point, of course, about such innuendo – as the common law struggles to recognise, in its attempt to make innuendo actionable at all – is that the more skilfully it conceals its appeal to a 'common intent to slander' the more decisively it achieves its effect. What takes place in the hearing of Elbow's cause, in other words, is an audience collusion with the slanderous implication of Pompey's words. The scene's purpose, I would suggest, is, in effect, to alienate, through our laughter, any sympathetic imagination of the effects of sexual slander on a woman. Thus, the scene ends with a mistaking on Elbow's part that ostentatiously both invokes and erases the possibility of legal redress which is society's recognition of the material damage done by sexual slander against women. Elbow confuses the word 'respected' with the word 'suspected' and is incensed at the compliment paid to his wife by Pompey: 'By this hand, sir, his wife is a more respected person than any of us all'. Elbow's outraged crescendo is worth quoting:

> Elbow   O thou caitiff! O thou varlet! O thou wicked Hannibal! I
>   respected with her, before I was married? If ever I was
>   respected with her, or she with me, let not your worship think
>   me the poor Duke's officer. Prove this, thou wicked Hannibal,
>   or I'll have mine action of battery against thee.

Esc.   If he took you a box o' th' ear, you might have your action of
         slander too. (Act 2, Scene 1, lines 171–8)

The scene, I suggest, pushes the question of female sexual activity and its
implications for masculine sexual honour into the realm of the unspeakable.

What could be the motive for suppressing audience consciousness of the
material consequences of sexual slander? It is surely no coincidence that the
Elbow trial scene prepares us for the central, sexually charged scenes of
Isabella's encounter with the corrupt magistrate, Angelo. Jacqueline Rose's
analysis of modern reaction to the play, which I cited earlier, has demonstrated how these scenes have proved pivotal to a reading which makes
Isabella's refusal to yield to Angelo determinant of the play's categorisation
as a 'problem play'. Critics have, as Rose explains,

> alternatively revered and accused [Isabella] in such a way that her
> sexual identity has become the site on which dissatisfaction with the
> play, and disagreement about the play, have turned . . . the accusations
> against Isabella . . . suggest . . . that it is the desire provoked by the
> woman which is above all the offence, and that the woman who refuses
> to meet that desire is as unsettling as the one who does so with excessive
> haste . . . G. Wilson Knight's essay . . . gives the strongest illustration of
> the proximity between Isabella's evil and her sainthood . . . Her rejec-
> tion of Angelo's sexual demand and her refusal to sacrifice herself for
> the life of her brother make that same sanctity, 'self-centred', 'ice-cold',
> lacking 'humanity', 'feeling' or 'warmth' . . . Isabella's sex-inhibitions'
> show her 'horribly as they are, naked'.[57]

Thus, the dominant way of making sense of the play since Hazlitt – that is,
one which understands Isabella's refusal to sacrifice her chastity for the life
of her brother purely in terms of her 'character' – is also a reading which
ignores the masculine investment in female sexual honour that makes terms
like 'whore' and 'cuckold' equivalently defamatory (as Lucio's final statement
proves). In other words, it is a reading made possible by our collusion in
refusing constable Elbow his action for slander.

In Whetstone's *Promos and Cassandra*, the drama of Cassandra's eventual
yielding to the corrupt magistrate is entirely played out on the stage of
honour and reputation; or, if you like, on the stage of slander. Whetstone
permits Cassandra to be persuaded to yield to Promos, but he makes it
clear that her capitulation is not related to her brother's persuasion that she
will not be condemned for her sexual offence in so doing. '*Justice*', her
brother speciously argues, 'will say thou dost no crime commit: / For in forst
faultes is no intent of yll'.[58] She, however, makes it absolutely clear that the

mitigation of her circumstances will not be taken into consideration by the power of slander, against which she will have no defence:

> *Andrugio* so my fame shall vallewed bee,
> *Dispight* will blase my crime, but not the cause:
> And thus although I fayne would set thee free,
> Poore wench, I feare the grype of slaunders pawes.[59]

Whetstone's Cassandra, then, voices an argument which occupies the very conceptual space which, in *Measure for Measure*, has been occluded through the travesty of Elbow's mismanaged attempts to fasten an action of slander on Pompey and Froth for defaming his wife. Of course, one effect of this is to make Cassandra a less dramatically interesting character than Isabella. As Linda Hardy puts it,

> Cassandra is a much more consistent (more rational) speaker than Shakespeare's Isabella, since her arguments all proceed with reference to codes which she thoroughly understands, or rather, of which she is the efficient medium. Her relation to Promos is not 'sexual' in any way... since the sexual act has no affect for her, only meaning. It is one thing if it occurs under the legitimating sign of marriage, another if not. One can recognise such explicitly coded sexual acts or relations everywhere in Renaissance writing without being able to respond to them with any sort of frisson, as one might to what we call 'sexuality'.[60]

Hardy here distinguishes between the figure of 'Cassandra' and that of 'Isabella' on the ground that the former speaks of the sexual act only in conformity to the vocabulary of honour and dishonour, which is codified and recognised as materially affecting men and women in the records of spiritual and common-law actions of slander. This would seem to suggest that the effect of character that Shakespeare has achieved with 'Isabella' – that is, the sense that we have of Isabella possessing passionate feelings about sex that are independent of its 'honourable' or 'dishonourable' designations – is actually made possible by the play's suppression of the materiality of sexual slander as it affects women.

The point at which readers have traditionally recognised the signs of Isabella's 'sexuality' is in Act 2, Scene 4, the scene in which Isabella slowly comes to understand what Angelo is proposing to her. This scene is marked by Angelo's reluctance to name the thing he desires, his longing that Isabella should understand him by implication. It is, then, a serious counterpart to the comic innuendo that preceded it; a similar sort of tension around the weight of unspoken sexual meaning, of *double entendre*, is aroused in the audience. Thus, as Angelo (whose feelings we know) labours to make

Isabella complicit in his desires at the level of understanding them, the audience is wound up by the passionate insistence of her incomprehension. Finally, Angelo puts to her a hypothesis:

> *Angelo* Admit no other way to save his life –
> . . . that you, his sister,
> Finding yourself desir'd of such a person
> Whose credit with the judge, or own great place,
> Could fetch your brother from the manacles
> Of the all-binding law; and that there were
> No earthly mean to save him, but that either
> You must lay down the treasures of your body
> To this suppos'd, or else to let him suffer:
> What would you do? (Act 2, Scene 4, lines 89–98)

Isabella's answer, emphatically 'innocent' as it is, demands to be read as the serious equivalent of innuendo – that is, as an unwitting revelation of sexual feeling, or desire:

> *Isabella* As much for my poor brother as myself;
> That is, were I under the terms of death,
> Th'impression of keen whips I'd wear as rubies,
> And strip myself to death as to a bed
> That longing have been sick for, ere I'd yield
> My body up to shame. (Act 2, Scene 4, lines 99–104)

Though Angelo understands this as a refusal, for most critics and editors it is a clue to Isabella's true feelings; Brian Gibbons, editor of the New Cambridge *Measure for Measure* writes: 'Unconsciously Isabella provokes Angelo's sadistic lust with the talk of whips . . . rubies . . . strips . . . longing', while J. W. Lever in the Arden edition, writes: 'Death and sexuality are similarly associated in Antony, . . . *Ant.* IV.xii.99–101 cf. Claudio, III.i.82–4. The image is more obviously suited to an Antony or Claudio than a chaste Isabella: but its occurrence here is psychologically revealing.'[61]

In a curious way, then, what we in the last decade of the twentieth century value in the depiction of the past – the 'frisson' which transforms a coded sexual act into a representation of 'sexuality' – comes close to being identical with the rhetorical figure of innuendo or 'enigma' that dominates the scene of Elbow's accusation against Pompey; the half-disclosed meaning, which, in the words of the rhetorician and lawyer George Puttenham, 'may be drawn to a reprobate sence'.[62] This figure, like Pompey's syntax, allows the 'reprobate sence' to be acknowledged and not acknowledged at the same time, and in this it resembles what Hardy, quoting Judith Butler, refers to as the 'constitutive opacity' of sexuality. Judith Butler, indeed, contends that 'sexuality' ceases to be the point at which enigma becomes transparency:

> Can sexuality even remain sexuality once it submits to a criterion of transparency and disclosure, or does it perhaps cease to be sexuality precisely when the semblance of full explicitness is achieved? Is sexuality of any kind even possible without the opacity designated by the unconscious, which means simply that the conscious 'I' who would reveal its sexuality is perhaps the last to know the meaning of what it says?[63]

According to Butler's analysis here, the 'unconscious' is coextensive with, or generated by, the temporal lapse, the delay, between the availability of sexual meaning and the speaking subject's awareness of having produced this availability. Thus Shakespeare's Isabella seems to have an 'unconscious' where Whetstone's Cassandra does not, because Shakespeare ensures that Isabella's response to Angelo's enigmatic meaning is characterised by precisely this sort of temporal lapse. Nineteenth-century critics, whether expressing distaste or praise for Isabella's chastity, were nevertheless as responsive as we are to Shakespeare's effective personification and feminisation of sexual innuendo in her 'unconscious passion'. Thus, Anna Jameson, in *Characteristics of Women Moral, Poetical and Historical*, speaks of Isabella's 'exclamation, when she first *allows herself to perceive* Angelo's vile design'[64] (my italics), a phrase which nicely captures the sense of liability which tends to be present in representations of the revelation of so-called 'unconscious' sexual feeling.

What I have tried to show here is that it is possible, through the comparative work on sources once used to study 'influence', to isolate differences in the ethical and affective organisation of dramatic material which correspond, with some degree of credibility, to historically identifiable changes in the mechanisms for recognising and acknowledging the material value of reputation and honour. The same late sixteenth-century upsurge in common-law actions for words that makes *Measure for Measure*, according to recent critics, a play which is intelligible within the terms of an increased anxiety about the political effects of slander, also makes it a play which, unlike Whetstone's of twenty-six years before, is inclined to downplay the explicitness of men's investment in the sexual honour of women. This, in turn, has enabled an ethopoetic development of the play's heroine which has proved congenial to nineteenth-century codes of proper feminine behaviour, and to twentieth-century psychoanalytic readings of those codes. Shakespeare, as the Arden editor, J. W. Lever, notes, makes a decisive lexical change to his sources when he makes Isabella speak the famous couplet:

> Then Isobel, live chaste, and brother, die:
> More than our brother is our chastity. (Act 2, Scene 4, lines 183–4)

The affirmation derives from Cinthio, 'la vita di mio fratello è molto cara, ma più caro mi è l'honor mio',[65] and from Whetstone's Cassandra, who says 'Honor Farre dearer is then life'. To change 'honour' to 'chastity' is to reinforce the process begun in the Elbow's wife scene, the process of downplaying the general societal investment in female honour, as codified in the spiritual action for slander. And it is a process which leads directly to a modern interpretation of *Measure for Measure* which centres, as Jacqueline Rose has shown, on the sexual identity of Isabella as 'the site on which dissatisfaction with the play, and disagreement about the play, have turned'. Only this year, I read a finals paper on *Measure for Measure* which spoke of 'the near-frigid Isabella' as one who was 'running away from her sexuality and participation in worldly love': it seems that even in these days of a theoretical recognition of the differences within subjectivity, we may still need to find a way of speaking about the rhetorical persuasiveness of Shakespeare's *ethopoeia*.

NOTES

1. Alan Sinfield, 'When is a Character not a Character? Desdemona, Olivia, Lady Macbeth and Subjectivity', in idem, *Faultlines: Cultural Materialism and the Politics of Dissident Reading* (Oxford University Press, 1992), p. 58. I bear sole responsibility for the argument which follows, but I'd like to thank Terence Cave for helping me find out more about 'ethopocia', Linda Hardy for making me think about *Measure for Measure*, and Jacqueline Rose and Neil Rhodes for reading earlier versions.
2. For Goldberg's essay, see Patricia Parker and Geoffrey Hartman (eds), *Shakespeare and the Question of Theory* (London and New York: Methuen, 1985), pp. 116–37; for Belsey's, see John Drakakis (ed.), *Alternative Shakespeares* (London and New York: Methuen, 1985), pp. 166–90.
3. Catherine Belsey, *The Subject of Tragedy: Identity and Difference in Renaissance Drama* (London and New York: Methuen, 1985), p. 51.
4. Sinfield, *Faultlines*, p. 58.
5. Ibid.
6. See, for example, the introductory passages on 'structure and characterization' in Elizabeth Cary, *The Tragedy of Mariam*, ed. Barry Weller and Margaret W. Ferguson (Berkeley: University of California Press, 1994), pp. 38–41, and Margaret Ferguson's remarks on the character of 'Graphina' in 'Running On with Almost Public Voice: The Case of "E. C."', in Florence Howe (ed.), *Traditions and the Talents of Women* (Urbana and Chicago: University of Illinois Press, 1991), pp. 47–8.
7. Goldberg, 'Shakespearean Inscriptions', p. 118.
8. Stephen Greenblatt, *Shakespearean Negotiations* (Oxford: Clarendon Press, 1988), pp. 1–2.
9. See Womack's illuminating remarks in *Rereading Ben Jonson* (Oxford: Basil Blackwell, 1986), p. 35.
10. Paul de Man, 'Autobiography as De-Facement', in *The Rhetoric of Romanticism* (New York: Columbia University Press, 1984), pp. 67–81, 75–6.

11. See 'Ethopoeia' in *Aphthonii Sophistae Progymnasmata Rudolpho Agricola Phrisio interprete* (1540), sig. C1v. For a translation of Aphthonius, *Progymnasmata*, see Ray Nadeau, *Speech Monographs* (1952), vol. 19, pp. 264–85; Nadeau translates 'ethopoeia' as 'characterisation', p. 278. On Aphthonius in classical rhetoric, see George Kennedy, *A New History of Classical Rhetoric* (Princeton, NJ: Princeton University Press, 1990), pp. 202–8; on the enormous influence of Aphthonius in the Renaissance, and on his place in the curriculum, see Walter G. Crane, *Wit and Rhetoric in the Renaissance* (New York: Columbia University Press, 1937), pp. 60–5; T. W. Baldwin, William Shakespere's *Small Latine and Lesse Greeke*, 2 vols (Urbana, Ill.: University of Illinois Press, 1944), vol. 1, pp. 82, 88–90, 93, 101, 121–2, 158, 221–4, 231–3, 272, 300, 343–4; Anthony Grafton and Lisa Jardine, *From Humanism to the Humanities* (London: Duckworth & Co 1986), pp. 129–35; Quentin Skinner, *Reason and Rhetoric in the Philosophy of Hobbes* (Cambridge: Cambridge University Press, 1996), pp. 29–30. Aphthonius is recommended in Charles Hoole, *A New Discovery of the Old Arte of Teaching Schoole* (London, 1660), p. 184; John Brinsley, *Ludus Literarius: or the Grammar Schoole* (London, 1612), pp. 172–5, and translated by Richard Rainolde, *The Foundacion of Rhetorike* (London, 1563).
12. *Aphthonii Sophistae Progymnasmata*, sig. C1v, 'Ethopoeia (id est, ita diximus, imitatio) est expressio morum personae propositae. sunt autem tres ipsius species: idolopoeia, id est, conformatio: prosopopoeia, id est efficitio: & eo quo diximus nomine ethopoeia, id est sermoncinatio'.
13. See *APHTHONII SOPHISTAE PROGYMNASMATA, partim a Rudolpho Agricola, partim a Janne Maria Cataneo Latinate donata, cum . . . scholiis* (London: Thomas Marsh, 1580), fol. 1784v. See also Quintilian, *Institutio Oratoria*, trans. H. E. Butler (London: Heineman, 1936), vol. 3, IX.2.58.
14. *Aphthonii . . . Progymnasmata*, sig. C1v.
15. Richard Rainolde, *The Foundacion of Rhetorike* (1563) (Amsterdam and New York: Da Capo Press, 1969), sig. N1r.
16. *Aphthonii . . . Progymnasmata*, sig. C1v.
17. See Heinrich Lausberg, *Handbuch der Literarischen Rhetorik*, 2 vols (Munich: Max Hueber Verlag, 1960), vol. 2, p. 408, §821.
18. Goldberg, 'Shakespearean Inscriptions', p. 125.
19. Ibid.
20. See Geoffrey Bullough, *Narrative and Dramatic Sources of Shakespeare*, vol. 2, *The Comedies 1597–1603* (London: Routledge, 1958), pp. 401–6. Bullough is of the opinion that Shakespeare knew of Cinthio's revision of his novella as a tragicomedy.
21. Ibid., p. 409.
22. Ibid., p. 404.
23. Ibid., p. 408.
24. George Whetstone, *Promos and Cassandra* (1578), in Bullough, *The Comedies*, p. 445.
25. Jonathan Bate, *Shakespearean Constitutions* (Oxford: Clarendon Press, 1989), p. 158.
26. Ibid.
27. William Hazlitt, *Characters of Shakespears Plays* (London: R. Hunter, 1817), p. 320.

28. Jacqueline Rose, 'Sexuality in the Reading of Shakespeare', in John Drakakis (ed.), *Alternative Shakespeares*, p. 105.
29. Ibid., pp. 104–5.
30. On this subject, see Hugh Grady, *The Modernist Shakespeare* (Oxford: Clarendon Press, 1991), pp. 104–5.
31. Belsey, 'Disrupting Sexual Difference', in John Drakakis (ed.), *Alternative Shakespeares*, p. 188.
32. See J. H. Baker, *The Reports of Sir John Spelman*, 2 vols (London: Selden Society, 1978), pp. 238–9; R. H. Helmholz, *Select Cases for Defamation to 1600* (London: Selden Society, 1985), p. xliii. See also John March, *Actions for Slander, or a Methodicall Collection under Certain Grounds and Heads of what words are actionable in the LAW, and what not?* (London, 1647).
33. On the *Auctoritate de Patris*, see R. H. Helmholz, *Select Cases on Defamation to 1600*.
34. 'Certen consideracions why the spirituell jurisdiccion wold be abrogatt', BL Cotton MS Cleopatra, FII, fos 250, 253, quoted by J. H. Baker, *The Reports of Sir John Spelman*, p. 240.
35. John Godolphin, *Repertorium Canonicum or an Abridgement of the Ecclesiastical Laws of this Realm consistent with the Temporal* (London, 1680), p. 514.
36. John March, *Actions for Slander*, p. 8. March's title page also points out that actions for slander 'do much more abound than in times past: And when the malice of men so much increases, well may their tongue want a directory.'
37. *Les Reportes del Cases in Camera Stellata 1593 to 1609 from the original MS of John Hawarde*, ed. William Paley Baildon (London, 1894), p. 143.
38. Hawarde, *Les Reportes*, p. 226. On this case, see Alistair Bellamy, 'A Poem on the Archbishop's Hearse: Puritanism, Libel and Sedition after the Hampton Court Conference', *Journal of British Studies*, 34 (1995), 137–64.
39. Ibid., p. 45.
40. Ibid., p. 344.
41. Ibid.
42. Hawarde, *Les Reportes*, p. 152: 'This libelling was much disliked by the community, and [is] a danger to it', *Roper v. Martin*, 16 June 1602.
43. David Colclough, 'Of the Alleadging of Authors': The Construction and Reception of Textual Authority in English Prose, c. 1600–1630*, D.Phil. thesis (University of Oxford, 1996), p. 105. For work of this kind, see note 5 above, and Richard Cust, 'News and Politics in Early Seventeenth Century England', *Past and Present*, 112 (1986), 60–90; Alistair Bellamy, ' "Rayling Rhymes and Vaunting Verse": Libellous Politics in Early Stuart England 1603–1628', in Kevin Sharpe and Peter Lake (eds), *Culture and Politics in Early Stuart England* (London: Macmillan, 1994); Pauline Croft, 'The Reputation of Robert Cecil: Libels, Political Opinion and Popular Awareness in the Early Seventeenth Century', *Transactions of the Royal Historical Society* (1991), 43–69.
44. M. Lindsay Kaplan, 'Slander for Slander in *Measure for Measure*', *Renaissance Drama*, n.s. 21 (1990), 23–54, 46–7.
45. *Measure for Measure*, ed. J. W. Lever (London and New York: Methuen, 1965), Act 5, Scene 1, lines 510–22, 148–9. Further references to this edition will appear in the text.

46. *The Reports of Sir Edward Coke, Knt*, ed. John Henry Thomas and John Farquhar Fraser, 6 vols (London: Butterworth, 1826), vol. 2, p. 305.

47. Ibid., p. 305.

48. John March, *Actions for Slander*, p. 11.

49. William Sheppard, *Action upon the Case for SLANDER or a Methodicall Collection under certain Heads, of Thousands of CASES Dispersed in the Many Great Volumes of the LAW, of What Words are Actionable, and What Not* (London, 1662), p. 74.

50. Ibid.

51. Ibid., p. 109.

52. William Hudson, *A Treatise of the Court of Star Chamber*, in *Collectanea Juridica, consisting of tracts relative to the Law and Constitution of England*, ed. Francis Hargrave, 2 vols (London, 1791–2), vol. 2, p. 101.

53. See David Gilmore, *Manhood in the Making: Cultural Concepts of Masculinity* (New Haven and London: Yale University Press, 1990), p. 47, and Gowing, *Domestic Dangers*, p. 94: 'Defamers presented cuckoldry as a loss of men's marital authority'.

54. John March, *Actions for Slander*, p. 27.

55. Ibid., p. 31.

56. Ibid. See also 'Dame Morrson *versus* Cade', in *The First Part of the Reports of Sir George Croke, Kt*, trans. Sir Harebottle Grimston (London, 1669), pp. 162–3.

57. Jacqueline Rose, 'Sexuality in the Reading of Shakespeare', in John Drakakis (ed.), *Alternative Shakespeares*, p. 104.

58. Whetstone, *Promos and Cassandra*, p. 460.

59. Ibid., p. 462.

60. Linda Hardy, 'Banality in Early Modern Studies', unpublished paper delivered to the Shakespeare Association of America, Chicago, March 1995.

61. Shakespeare, *Measure for Measure*, ed. Lever, p. 60n.

62. George Puttenham, *The Arte of English Poesie*, ed. G. D. Wilcox and A. Walker (Cambridge: Cambridge University Press, 1936), p. 188.

63. Judith Butler, 'Imitation and Gender Insubordination', in Henry Ablove et al. (eds), *The Lesbian and Gay Reader* (London: Routledge, 1993), p. 309.

64. Anna Jameson, *Characteristics of Women Moral, Poetical and Historical*, 2 vols (London: Saunder and Otley, 1858), vol. 2, p. 121.

65. *De Gli Hecatommithi di M.Giovanni Battista Giraldi Cinthio*, 2 vols (Venice: 1566), vol. 2, p. 259.

Chapter Ten

THE DEATH DRIVE DOES NOT THINK

Robert Smith

In the theory of psychoanalysis we have no hesitation in assuming that the course taken by mental events is automatically regulated by the pleasure principle. We believe, that is to say, that the course of those events is invariably set in motion by an unpleasurable tension, and that it takes a direction such that its final outcome coincides with a lowering of that tension – that is, with an avoidance of unpleasure or a production of pleasure. In taking that course into account in our consideration of the mental processes which are the subject of our study, we are introducing an 'economic' point of view into our work . . . (Opening of *Beyond the Pleasure Principle*)

Setting prices, determining values, contriving equivalences, exchanging – these preoccupied the earliest thinking of man to so great an extent that in a certain sense they constitute thinking as such . . . (*On the Genealogy of Morals*, 2nd essay, §8)

My title alludes to an essay by Jean-François Lyotard, 'The Dream-work Does Not Think',[1] which in turn alludes to Freud's *Interpretation of Dreams*. The issue is whether 'the' Freudian theory of psychoanalysis construes the individual psyche as having any capacity to *think* whatsoever. It might be problematised thus: if the psychic mechanism is compelled to repeat, can any of its intellections be considered as thought or cogitation, as opposed to Pavlovian reaction? The compulsion to repeat is one – perhaps the arch – element making the psychic mechanism mechanical, hence the structural role it plays, and consequently its tolerance of being notated and theorised. Theoretically it calls for a concept of the death drive whose presence it betrays: we repeat patterns of mental and social behaviour so as to keep psychic expenditure to a minimum, not risking any authentically new investments, preferring old wine in new bottles no matter how sour in reality it

161

always was. This profoundly conservative attitude is tantamount to a death drive insofar as a state of minimum exertion, or maximum inertia, is its *telos* – its end, purpose and nature. Thought, were that activity to contain any requirement of intellectual effort, would be anathema to it and could be countenanced only in circumstances where it represented the sole remaining route back to the state of rest, repetition having become for whatever reason unviable. We are practically describing, in Nietzsche's words, 'the attempt to win for man an approximation to what in certain animals is *hibernation*, in many tropical plants *estivation*, the minimum metabolism at which life will still subsist without really entering consciousness'.[2] We can disclose an intimate negative connection between thinking and death as *vis inertiae*, a connection which orients the present discussion.

That connection itself connects with a third element, time – with public time and therefore with history, for 'history is public time', to quote from a source I shall return to. How so?

In the aspect of Freudian theory which concerns us, concentrated in the paper *Beyond the Pleasure Principle*, the psyche shirks anything but the least exertion possible. For reduction of excitation equals pleasure: an equation that is legitimate because congruent with the Freudian premiss which is not 'I am' so much as 'I wish'. For the Freudian psyche, establishing ontological identity is secondary to fulfilling wishes (Lacan would seem to re-philosophise this position by restoring the former to equal prominence). I wish, therefore I am, and pleasure furnishes the constant object of my actions. Freud lends this axiom genetic cladding which I re-describe as follows.

The Oedipal phase occurs when the infant understands the father to be a check to its own access to the mother, imposing the stricture of delay upon the child for whom, in effect, a sense of time is created. To adapt the language of Kant, time arises subjectively as the form of the intuition that there now exists a block to what was previously porous, that I now have to pay for what before was free, that satisfaction has turned out to be a privilege and not a right; time impinges upon me as limit and frustration and the necessity of supererogation. Time implies 'the other' and vice versa: if now I have a sense of time it is because the other, whose type is the father, inhabits the same wish-dimension and thus creates the competition which means that in principle I will not always be the first to get what I want and that I will have to bestir myself to make sure of getting it at all. An economy is born.

The genetic schema allows for the psychologistic interpretation that preoccupies psychoanalysis as a therapeutic institution. For example, if the father impedes my wish-fulfilment, the formative attitude I hold towards him is that of vengeful rival, while in this moment of Oedipal pathos – in a sense the first moment of pathos of any kind in the infant's young life – I realise I love the mother, though it is only in the context of hating the father that loving the mother has any meaning or value. I am now conscious of my wishes even though, cruelly enough, this coincides with the consciousness that they may well remain unfulfilled. Such is the condition of consciousness, in truth. In its circularity, the argument resembles that concerning the Big Bang and the origin of time. For I now have wishes only because some obstacle to them has new-fangled them as wishes, whereas in the prelapsarian phase I had neither wish nor no-wish, I merely prosecuted my animal functions without either consciousness or unconsciousness. A wish is inherently retrospective: 'I want' has no psychoanalytic currency; only 'I have always wanted' can claim that. It resembles the Big Bang paradox in that the prelapsarian world lacked all temporal attributes so could not have been a state of 'pre-' at all. The nature of time having been established as medium of wish-fulfilment, the prevailing object of wishing can be apprehended as occupying a mythic and impossible 'absolute past'. The psyche is consigned to seeking out shadows of that object in the Platonic after-time that is real time, trusting that the anamnesic affect of such shadows will retain enough aura from the original to afford a modicum of fulfilment, or, more naively, taking the shadow for the real thing. Whence the compulsion to repeat and save time, to hearken back to the origin that is like a hologram.

Among the less naive, of course, Freud's contemporary Walter Benjamin will have said in another context that aura only fades with each (mechanical, but the psyche is also mechanical) reproduction.[3] He is speaking about the reproduction of works of art, but his co-religionist Theodor Adorno held opinions about repetition directed more specifically at psychoanalysis. The latter was one of a number of *bêtes noires* for Adorno, and precisely because he felt or feared psychoanalysis to be inimical to *thought* (and thus also to himself). In psychoanalysis, '*ratio* is degraded to rationalisation', writes Adorno in the course of some astonishingly dyspeptic paragraphs in *Minima moralia*.[4] Compared with the relatively magnanimous Aristotelian 'moralia' to which the title of his book cuttingly alludes, ethical life in the psychoanalytic domain is reduced to economic rationalisations that are part and parcel of 'bourgeois self-alienation'. Exactly so: the paradigm of all social relations for the Freudian psyche is the infantile relation with the father. Any social life that gathers thereafter can at best dissimulate the filial competition that provides its deep structure and motive. It is just this dissimulating competitiveness and goal-seeking that lends social life its bourgeois and alienated character, Adorno rather maladroitly dismissing any notion of 'sublimation' which might make of such dissimulation a redeeming feature. If Freud says that the sublimation of Oedipal pressure produces society, Adorno retorts that it is not worth having the bourgeois society that is produced, and against it he opposes the civilised society of 'tact' and good manners.[5]

But if we apply an Adornian filter to our view of Freud, that bourgeois world is just what people want, and the economically driven state can only be the winner by it, for the psyche of its subjects is predisposed to economic competition and complicity in mass production as a form of repetition. Not only that but a state that assumes, as it can all too easily, the iconic power of the father will be practically unassailable. A state driven by social-political ideals such as Adorno's, on the other hand, will find the administration of such subjects far more problematic, since the generation of political interest and will goes against their post-Enlightenment natures and, since only education could be an effective means, it will be costly – a price presumably worth paying, even if Adorno wants to keep money and civilised culture quite separate. While thought implies society for Adorno, on account of its dialectical structure, it is to be differentiated sharply from the commerce implied in society.

This paradox constitutes something of a *topos*, the preservation of culture and thought from filthy lucre, though it may be possible to date it by looking at the Enlightenment from the other end, and from a quite different point of view. The Cambridge historian J. G. A. Pocock traces that *topos*, in Britain at any rate, to a Romantic reaction at the beginning of the nineteenth century against the explosion of commercialisation in the century or so after 1688. And it is really on this last date that his gaze settles, seeing the Whig revolution as a profound transitionary period that ushered in the Enlightenment. Our interest in this period is that Pocock argues, *contra* Adorno, for the strong bind yoking *together* commerce, speculation, 'thought' and the bourgeoisie. The Enlightenment is inconceivable apart from bourgeois eminence, so much so that the latter actually functions as 'condition of possibility' for the former. At the same time, however, those texts which Pocock fastens upon, Hume, Gibbon, Smith *inter alia*, classics of the Enlightenment, are written largely in reaction to this condition. That ambiguity typifies the age, and I shall first say something about it.

Pocock analyses the transition period in 'Britain' from the seventeenth to the eighteenth century (I refer especially to his 1985 collection *Virtue, Commerce and History*).[6] 'Transition' is the operative word: in the post-Restoration world, what fascinates Pocock is the transition from landed to mobile property which brings with it broadly a transition from, in terms Pocock grafts from Machiavelli, a 'virtuous' to a 'commercial' and even 'corrupt' social atmosphere – but 'social atmosphere' is also the result of the general transition, from the political to the same social. On one side of this transition then are landed property, virtue and politics; on the other side mobile property, commerce, society and also the cultivation of 'manners'. But the shift is not simple, and the interest of reading Pocock derives from his attention to the ambivalence as two sides of a transition continue to act upon one another, particularly as invoked in the texts of reaction which are already deploring the forked genesis of what would become known as the Enlightenment. In the figure of this ambivalence, we as readers are observing a phenomenon that is at once radically and exclusively conceptual but dressed up in historical clothes; or perhaps psychological-political, but again dressed up in historical clothes; and thoroughly historical since the very concept of 'manners', for example, could have received its gestation nowhere else than in that very particular historical soil. The notion of a *persistence of transition* in other words is a very rich paradox. It could be said, but I shall not elaborate on it, that Pocock's own repetition compulsion is at play, in that the same ambivalence is targeted by him in diverse writings throughout the eighteenth century, thus calling into question what is meant by history in this fecund body of work. The transition is obviously so profound that it becomes the very form of political history, its terms as well as its object, in the British eighteenth century. If the two sides of the transition do continue to act upon one another, then their more hospitable locus will be not history, which will tend to separate them across time, but the mental configuration of history that we call thought, permitting them to oscillate together. Pocock addresses works of political theory themselves from Locke to Burke – leading to an emphasis on 'language'. As the introduction leaves little room for doubting, 'language' is the element of political history, but of course is also the medium where it is represented. Pocock's method too is intrinsically confused with his object – an observation, not a criticism.

It was from Pocock's book that the epigram 'history is public time' was taken, from an essay entitled 'Modes of Political and Historical Time in Early Eighteenth-century England'. As Pocock would no doubt be surprised to learn (given the aspersions he casts towards it), the epigram agrees well with a psychoanalysis according to which the minimal predicate of time is the public exposure that attends upon the relation to the father in the Oedipal phase. That is when the child enters history, or rather when history begins for the child – that is, 'public time' is a tautology. Pocock goes on to distinguish public from social time, the former being institutional and the latter more generally discursive, though this need not detain us. In conformity with the methodological imbrication just noted, the essay, the most speculative in the volume, takes speculation itself as one of its themes. It detects an emergence of 'speculation' in the period originating in the establishing of the Bank of England in 1696 and more particularly in the institution of the National Debt.[7] Pocock's reference to probability in this book is interesting not least because one could add it to the dossier of debate surrounding Ian Hacking's *The Taming of Chance*.[8] Hacking traces to the same period the emergence of probability theory, wondering *why* it emerged only then, given that the mathematical resources to generate it had long been available. Pocock's brilliant speculation gives the germ of an answer, arguing for the near-simultaneous nativity of psychological and economic imagination, though the economic fact (the National Debt) just has the edge and so subdues the passion that would make Pocock himself an old-fashioned Spirit of the Age historian. And in the next but one paragraph, Pocock cites Defoe, the conjunction of whose economic and literary interests as one of the new breed of men of letters incites us to extend the speculation further still: to the novel which, along with other novelties, newsbooks and newspapers, is 'rising' at the time. A novel borrows from the future in the sense of the realm experienced in the imagining of contingencies: fiction never pays but is rather, at least in principle, the pure expenditure of imagination, structurally has to be *credited*, believed, extended a kind of imaginistic overdraft. Robert Newsom has written a book called *A Likely Story* which takes up some of the implications. The speculative spirit spreads through the National Debt, capitalist imagination, probability theory, novelistic fiction – and the arbitrariness of making the one the cause of all the others becomes disconcertingly pressing. The rampancy of this network might be called 'hysterical' by Pocock: the early eighteenth century (which by projective identification now includes himself) must devote energy to keeping the 'hysteria' of speculation balanced by the cultivation of Opinion, 'what Montesquieu was later to describe as the conversion of *crédit* into *confiance*'.[9] This constitutes a second ambivalence then, the dialectic of enlightenment tilting between opinion and hysteria, reason and imagination, empirical and transcendental.

Time is public time (public because credit is so by definition), and again its chief quality is delay. The delay by which payment of debt is deferred, time is the 'never-never', literally, to use the colloquial phrase for buying on credit. It is conducive to imagination and speculation, though thought proper – works of intellectual bearing, the texts Pocock rereads – is the dialectical capacity to consider imagination and reason in dialectical combination, and is therefore at one with polity as the tempering of bourgeois hysteria or credit-inflation; after all, it shortens the speculatory delay, contracts it, bringing thought closer to 'real' action. Time is the suspension of real time, of the real as what comes home to roost, as the calling-in of a debt; the suspension gives buoyancy across the board culturally, as prospecting for capital is secured by the future archive that is credit. It is worth noting how at odds with a Weberian notion of capital generation this schema is, and not just on the grounds that Pocock appears to allow all religious feeling simply to evaporate after the Civil War. Capital accumulation is the result for Weber of a precisely counter-speculative ethos, that of the Protestant whose wealth is merely the by-product, and yet the commendable evidence, of industry and abstemiousness united. Speculation arises as a temptation glinting back at you from the hard-won pile, and Weber will aptly quote John Wesley on that dangerous supplement.[10] He would have found Pocock's 'capitalist imagination' quite contradictory.

From what we have seen of him, Adorno would be bound to concur, but then his political sympathies are manifestly remote from Pocock's: he is interested more in the fate than the origin of the Enlightenment, and in any case what they each denote by that term is divergent to say the least. Yet, for both men, thought is an enlightened, social and dialectical activity, fostered by 'transitions', even if Pocock attributes what would have been too much of its phenomenon, for Adorno's liking, to bourgeois venture. Without such venture, Enlightenment thought would not have been the ambivalent thing so choice for intellectual perusal, for Pocock; for Adorno the Enlightenment could have been so much more enlightened without it – look at psycho-analysis, for instance, that unconscionable hybrid of regressive bourgeois thinking and promising quasi-Marxist insight – though one wonders how much of its dialectical quality would have been removed in the removal of the ambivalence.

I would like to run this excursus a little further before coming back to more recognisably psychoanalytic questions. Economic attention, the enjoinder to expediency or contingency-as-necessity, sets the environment of the psychoanalytic subject, and to that degree it is right to 'speculate' in an economic vein about it. It is not certain that thought – that consciousness as sceptical apprehension in a perhaps Cartesian mode – is not supplementary to such a subject's economy, though we should concede the bad logic of this: economy is already supplementary, being the structure that develops around the Oedipal fact that to go back one must first go forward, that the psycho-social 'sphere' must be a circle. Consciousness is the consciousness only of this supplementarity, indeed of this speculation, while the unconscious keeps the wishes in reserve until that supplementarity which sublimates them is gone through – except during patches of thinner vigilance, like slips of the tongue, when the wish in the form of a symptom momentarily darkens con-scious time, or more generally when that vigilance is actively encouraged to decontract in the course of a session. (That suggests conversely that in the unconscious, like in a black hole, time has no dimension, and this might explain why narrative time in dreams appears instantaneous and why somatic stimuli can trigger an extended dream sequence in the twinkling of an eye.) What is interesting about Adorno and Pocock, miles apart though they be in other respects, is that both posit two types of thought measurable in relation to the economy of supplements. There is bourgeois thought and there is dialectical thought. Bourgeois thought, for Pocock, thrives under conditions of credit-boom, as speculation. To take up Pocock's 'language' thesis rather more absurdly than he may condone: it thrives under the semantic richesse (ambivalence again) of the term 'speculation' as it gestures simultaneously to mind and to market; it is thoroughly bound in to economic factors, and so is not quite 'thought', in fact. Adorno sees the same bond between bourgeois thought and the economy but chooses to be ulcered by it: calling this kind of rationalisation 'speculation' and by extension 'imagination' is merely to indulge it. Genuine thought as *ratio* arises only as, curiously enough, something extra to such a supplementary economy – as what Derrida will call a 'gift', something you get 'into the bargain'.[11] Only when the parsimony of the market has been exceeded can dialectical thought appear, as precisely the quasi-aesthetic excess of society over economy. Though at a remove from the market, dialectical thought for both Pocock and Adorno has actually more reality to it. By this, it is meant not only that thought is more quintessentially itself but that it partakes of the real in a more necessary way: in Pocock, precisely because political-intellectual thought abbreviates the social time which has turned into time-as-fantasy; in Adorno, because the dialectic of thought is intrinsically social and 'real'. On the other hand, such a dialecticity, set forth as it is by temporal difference and cultural progress, could hardly be more antithetical to the dialecticity of thought of Pocock's thinkers, which is a reactive fixing of time in plumb configurings, tinged with nostalgia.

This is partly in the nature of a more conservative thinker. It can't be deemed an intellectual fault, then, that the fantasy-time of credit and commerce described by Pocock, so generative of the new, cannot help but seem at once a description of Pocock's own economic times. And the attitude towards it – in this case, it is Pocock embodying it – has endured too, more importantly. It is an attitude concerned to maintain equilibrium, to resist the futures market and futurity *per se*, by for example moderating the bourgeois commercial hysteria prone to the transcendental illusion that it can get along without any empirical anchoring by polity (= thought). Put paradoxically, real time for Pocock is time which, by suppressing futurity, does not change over time; is not temporal. This produces a particularly acute double-bind for the historian whose subject is change over time. With the reduction of excitation at stake, I obviously want to evoke the terms of *Beyond the Pleasure Principle*, such that writing history itself – in its more 'conservative' forms, to draw on all the nuances of this word – can be viewed as a form of credit control, the counter-inflationary policy that has a pathogenesis in keeping the psyche cool. Bourgeois commercialism threatens the albeit ambiguous stasis (ambiguous because the commercialism has to be there in order to be moderated in order to reach stasis . . .). Since in a sense we are talking about the very difference between thought on the Right and thought on the Left, we might be tempted to set Adorno up on the other side of this attitude, saying that for him it was advancement not stasis that was desirable, but we would be deceived: dialectical change affords the medium for equilibrium. For Adorno, advancement is generous equilibrium; as enlightened progress, *ratio* is certainly not rationalisation, but it is *rationality* – proportion, conceived by him in socio-musical time. *Equilibrium* presents itself as the fantasy of dialectical thought. Bourgeois commercialism, liberal capitalism, may be up to a point necessary to achieving that equilibrium, but the stronger reaction to it is the will to its control – a reaction proper to genuine thought.

The curious thing is that, in a recent debate, liberal capitalism has been reframed to answer all by itself just those desiderata of stasis, and so at the expense of dialectics *tout court*. We have come to love Big Brother. I am referring to the debate surrounding Francis Fukuyama's *The End of History and the Last Man*, notably as voiced by Perry Anderson in his own essay, 'The Ends of History'.[12] Anderson relays Fukuyama's thesis that

> after the gigantic conflicts of the twentieth century, 'the unabashed victory of economic and political liberalism' over all competitors means 'not just the end of the Cold War, or the passing of a particular period in history, but the end of history as such: that is the end-point of mankind's ideological evolution and the universalisation of Western liberal democracy as the final form of human government'.[13]

Such flagrant contentiousness will of course not go uncontended, and Anderson reserves his own criticisms until later in the essay. Meanwhile he is content to report the torpedoings of others, for example, the 'chorus of disapproval at the very idea of a historical conclusion, whatever its character':

> The great majority of Fukuyama's commentators in the world's press greeted his argument with incredulity – after all, do not common sense and daily news tell us that there are always fresh and unexpected events, and even that their pace is exponentially quickening, as the sensational close of the decade demonstrates?

But this response is a 'non-sequitur':

> Fukuyama's case allows for any number of further empirical events, as he has pointed out: it simply contends that there is a set of structural limits within which they will now unfold, that has been reached within the OECD zone. Kojève [Anderson picks up a thread from earlier in the essay] replied to this objection in his time, with characteristic vigour: the movement of history was accelerating more and more, but it was advancing less and less – all that was happening was 'the alignment of the provinces'.

The end of history is the stasis of liberal capitalism as practised by democracies in the OECD zone. History itself was a stage on the way to it, and if there are other parts of the world where stasis has not yet been attained it is because they are still trapped within the historical phase that is evidenced pre-eminently by belligerence and revolution. Now it is only a question of ' "the alignment of [these] provinces" '.

As Anderson reminds us, 'the great change that has inspired this version [for it belongs to a tradition] of the end of history is, of course, the collapse of communism'.[14] The globe will gradually come round as a whole to post-history, having shaken all dialecticity off itself, in a kind of quiescent irredentism.

The innovative element within this thesis is that liberal capitalism will have gained a critical level where it can stave itself in, round itself off. Innovative because the creation of capital is usually perceived to be 'exponential', precisely, speculative, creating more of itself out of itself, with an expansionism as its common corollary. That is the quality highlighted by Pocock, and by Weber for that matter, in their very different idioms. For Pocock, speaking through Gibbon, the urge of a successfully commercial state is empire (another factor dragging it further off course from civic republicanism in all its virtue), whereby capital transplants itself abroad, as did 'Britain' in America in the eighteenth century. How to manage this inevitable outcrop, as it were, comes to preoccupy polity all too much, and is likely to corrupt it – which is a secular version of Weber's Protestant capitalism. Yes. Profit must be 'ploughed back' into the enterprise, in a phrase appropriately evocative of *Proverbs*. Only then can increase of capital be a means of magnifying God; otherwise it is external, wasteful, scatological, diabolical, sinful and so on – 'corrupting'. The point is that, as in the Frankenstein myth, the desired excess, the creature of industry, transmogrifies into a burden. Fukuyama shows no such anxiety, but mainly because, one supposes, there is nowhere left for capital to take itself to become monstrous, the profits of it will *de facto* be 'contained' for it has felt out the very limits of the world. The world-as-corporation may magnify itself in paradoxically unchanging form, pulsating, effectively functioning as God. All parts have been touched by its rhetorical hand even if some still have unfinished historical business to get through before they can answer its irresistible call to passivity.

Innumerable objections could still be made to Fukuyama, and Perry Anderson presents an intimidating suite of them, but we want to pursue an alternative agenda. Here we have a version of economy that is no longer temporal-historical, an on the face of it strictly unthinkable proposition to psychoanalysis. It shouldn't be called economy at all, all historicism – the dialecticity of time, and ultimately historical consciousness too – having been effaced from it in its sublimity. Time remains, but has been released from carrying the charge of volition and desire. Its quality of delay therefore makes no sense any more, and a perpetual present penetrates and floods it instead. An immediate fit between wanting and having elides the difference between them, rendering the psychoanalytic subject a theoretic impossibility. That elision must also sublate the distinction between private and public, for that was produced by the exigency upon wish-fulfilment to 'go round the houses', that is, finding a socially acceptable way of gratifying itself. Radically, *radically* democratic subjects will populate the world in the sense that privacy as a meaningful limit to universality will have vanished.

Slavoj Zizek would relish this scene. In a slightly altered form, he has written about it.[15] The not-so-futuristic state is exemplified by a film like *Blade Runner* where the global Corporation owns everything, down to one's memories.

Consequently, these cannot be told apart from products; one's very psyche might be corporately manufactured and the difference between humans and androids becomes a nice point. Again it is a thoroughly Platonic eventuality, termed *anamnesis*, this remembering of what has never been subjectively experienced. The memories have been planted there by the transcendental law. A lateral interpretation might be that a truth about memory has been expressed. Namely, that it is always possible for memory to be expropriated, and cannot be uniquely owned. After all, it is possible to remember after one's turn the memories of another, just as it is possible to memorise fiction – which in principle departs from the *vécu*. Memory is appended to provide the pathos that defined human beings in the historical phase of the world. Human beings *are* this pathos, are this capacity for remembering and forgetting, are, rather, the defectiveness of subjective memorising. The defectiveness is masterfully supplanted by the liberal capitalist technocracy, but then put back into the system to simulate its humanity. In the states envisaged by both Zizek and Fukuyama, memory can then exist apart from experience, just as time continues though no longer receptive to history – always possible, for an expropriatory alterity laminates memory *de jure*, its removability defines it even as it seemed the most inalienably personal faculty a human could have had. The psyche has been invaginated out onto this irenic plateau of conformism which ought by rights to bleach it of all distinctive features, but in fact tolerates an amount of confected 'individuality'. Why? Presumably as the condition under which the universal society can bind 'volitionally', with a semblance at least of coming together, and thus retain its dumb *telos*, rather than existing as a mere aggregate. A techno-Hegelianism has achieved its climax, technology having supervened upon Spirit as the world's immanent Notion while being infinitely capable, since it is technological and nothing but, of mocking up the teleological repletion of Spirit as it chooses. Techno-commerce differs from human, pathetic economic commerce, and has split off from it.

Scintillating a scenario though this be, its typology is somewhat banal in that the old humanist opposition between human and technical has been left intact. It reveals by hindsight that the Enlightenment operates principally as an ideal of being able to determine itself by limiting its own commercially led technological and scientific thrust, thought being that agency that would harness it to the properly defective, the human, the potential for memory that would keep thought's selective dialecticity alive. Memory must be kept just ahead of science; knowledge explodes when technology surpasses it. Perfectibilarian thinking makes sense only against the background of implicit imperfection.

But the human economy, though based on the desire to fulfil wishes and return, and thus deeply moved by memory, as a fact will have induced amnesia: that is sublimation. Wishes go underground. It is only by forgetting that I can get on with living. While the antithesis human/technical has been let lie, even though within it 'human' shrinks to a reference point rather than presenting substantial autotelic opposition, the contrast between the pathos economy of human memory and the Fukuyaman–Zizekian world has less resolution to it than at first sight appears. The 'real' time wherein I get on with my life is just as shallow as the history-repellent time of *post-histoire*. The experiences I have in it, the memories I accrue and the lacunae within or around them are merely the code of ersatz subjectivity that can be translated back into the general legend that is the structure of the psyche. To me it looks like my history, but that is because the memory-economy I am in has forged me in the only form it knows, that of subjectivity. The history is tacit structure. That structure expresses itself in time because temporality inheres in it as delay, as we have seen (the Oedipal phase), not because of any claim over it made by historical phenomenology. The pathos lies in the fact that the subjects who emerge into time from the temporalisation of that structure are bound, because they are subjects (because they now embody the energetic symbiosis of unconscious and conscious), to interpret time as history, that is, the opportunity for memory, humanity, self-expression. And it *is history*, everything we know by that name. It's just that its basis is rather more contorted than usually granted, for its basis is time, which coextends with it but which originates in a structural vortex that has not yet recognised the possibility of an individual and subjective psyche since 'psyche' only refers to an implacable law. This is the law of deferral, competition or economy, of which psychological subjectivity is merely an effect. We can say with equal justification that there is real progress in history and that there is not, that it is as equally life as death. We can also say that any subjective assumption through memory of one's own experiences is just as derivative as in the future-state, for an expropriative, generalising, structural power begets and conditions it.

Subjectively speaking, then, time is history – with all its pathos of commercial-psychological economism, the suffering of negotiation, fortune. Or, subjectivity is the misprism that time is absorbed by history *in toto*, similar to Paul de Man's presentation of subjectivity as what mistakes linguistic, tropological time for the anthropomorphis of history or genetic time (an overestimation of the object, even, to adapt Freud's notation for love). And because memory belongs in with this primary subjectal illusion, thought opens up as well. As sceptical apprehension (our working definition), thought depends on memory as upon its own predicate. For scepticism is not innocence, and relies on knowing something already. One cannot think sceptically without a degree of memory; equally, memory is a constitutive feature of subjectivity. So thought and subjectivity go hand in hand, just as thought fades away in the subjectless realm of the future-state. Can one imagine a theory of thought, an epistemology, that was not at the same time a formula of 'the subject'?

In other words, the psychoanalytic subject certainly does think, it thinks *because it is* a subject, and it thinks *as* a subject, which is to say in relation to its 'own' past no matter how recent or remote: we should say, in relation to itself as related to a particular anteriority taken for its own. There is always some minimal attestation of experience, and a minimal part of thinking is its echo. In this way, through thought-as-memory, the subject perceives itself as individual or having some considerable insularity, living as it does in the channel of its 'own' experience. Even though it is 'wrong' to do so from a structural point of view, the subject is bound to believe in its own individuality, its subjectivity, and thinking primarily is the form of this constitutive belief. The subject exists as a limit; its subjectivity implies experience as limited to a particular form, *finite* experience. We would have no conception of time if we did not also have that of finitude; from a psychoanalytic viewpoint this finitude describes the contours of a private history of desire, memory as it is retained regulatively within the economy of negotiation, that is, bargaining for what we want.

We have now encroached again on the ground whereon thinking and death hold each other in relation. Must not thinking as the subject's experience of its own limit be an intimation of mortality? Well, no: there is no reason to associate the limitation *to* subjectivity with the limitation *of* the subject. On the other hand, the continuous anteriority that shadows all thinking restrains the latter to a necessary regression or 'recidivism', to use Adorno's word again, and for Freud regressiveness is the very meaning of death – the *return* to a simple state. Death comes first, it pre-dates life. For mortals, the absolute past or 'past before the past' is what lies ahead. The movement of life is archaeological, or archaeo-teleo-logical, to be precise. Since this is also the movement of psychoanalysis as a technique whose goal is the retrieval of the lost archaic code (of the psyche), there is some justification for saying that in theorising the death drive psychoanalysis is theorising itself, and through what it itself would call an identification of some kind. For the subject, this movement backwards involves a transition from the finitude of its own subjectivity back to infinity, its dissolution or rather its *generalisation*, the cessation of respect for its speciality. Its finitude means that it will not always be finite, or that its finitude will be finished. And by a peculiarly metacritical logic, this means in turn that the subject will become thinkable again to psychoanalysis, as a phenomenon with attributes susceptible of generalisation. Psychoanalysis can think about the subject only on condition that it be a subject that will die like all others. Mortality would be the subject's promise to leave its specificity behind, to return into the archaeological general origin; and it is on the basis of this promise that psychoanalysis can 'think' the subject.

How do these things tie up with the notion we began with, of thinking as risk-averse repetition? In the economy it participates in (there can be no non-participation), the subject will have occasionally to take risks to get what it wants, and for no other reason than that it is in an economy: for economy implies some diminution of personal control, and therefore the presence of 'chance'. Economy is a risk environment for the subject. Up to a point, such an economy could be contrasted with the achieved economy of Fukuyama in which the anxieties of risk are allayed simply because the economy provides – which, again, barely makes it an economy at all, if economy is, as surely it must be, a form which *can always fail* to provide. Beyond such a point, however, the two types of economy merge again where psychoanalytic subjects can be seen to derive from quite anonymous principles of temporal delay (derived in their turn from the general premise of wish-fulfilment).

Absolute inertia is not an option for the subject which exists only as an economic form. Some life, some risk, some calculation is incumbent upon it. Some thought as the retention of desire must fill at least a part of it; and such thought forms the link with the death which the subject harps back to. Thought necessarily suggests living calculation, the appraisal of opportunity, the estimation of values, all as forms of 'life' – it has its origin in economics (as the epigraph from Nietzsche proposes). But this living risk environment, that of the (by definition) never omniscient subject, is at once nothing but a tension with the death it has pulled away from in order to return to. Death is the realm of no risk (no life). And life is quite literally tension, that is, the apperception of risk, which makes subjective living an *essentially* anxious activity – this is a statement quite proper to psychoanalysis throughout its 'development' as a theory. Whether or not we are compelled to repeat behaviour neurotically later on in life, and whether or not our later thoughts tolerate being translated back into their infantile adumbrations, there exists beforehand a prior link that puts thinking into a necessary relation with death. That is the very meaning of subjectivity. Worse still, the memories that subjects hold as earnests of their individuality themselves hail from a deathly anonymity: the privacy of memory can in principle be deprived from the subject, and individualities traversed by a general law (a 'law of genre', as Derrida would call it) which formally matches the concept of death as I have entertained it here.

NOTES

1. 'The Dream-work Does Not Think', trans. Mary Lydon, in Andrew Benjamin (ed.), *The Lyotard Reader* (Oxford: Basil Blackwell, 1989), pp. 19–55.
2. Friedrich Nietzsche, *On the Genealogy of Morals*, trans. Walter Kaufmann and R. J. Hollingdale (collected with *Ecce Homo*) (New York: Vintage Books, 1969), 3rd essay, §17, p. 131.
3. Walter Benjamin, 'The Work of Art in the Age of Mechanical Reproduction', in *Illuminations*, trans. Harry Zohn (New York: Schocken Books, 1968), pp. 217–51.

4. Theodor Adorno, *Minima Moralia*, trans. E. F. N. Jephcott (London: Verso, 1978), §37, p. 61.

5. Editors' note: in the original publication of this essay, there now follows a more detailed account of Adorno, pp. 62–4.

6. J. G. A. Pocock, *Virtue, Commerce and History* (Cambridge: Cambridge University Press, 1985).

7. Editors's note: in the original publication of this essay, Smith quotes (p. 66) at some length from Pocock, *Virtue, Commerce and History*, pp. 98–9, paragraphs in which Pocock does not balk at using the language of wish-fulfilment himself and in which he talks of 'the probability' of future generations repaying a debt 'at some future date which might never arrive'.

8. Ian Hacking, *The Taming of Chance* (Cambridge: Cambridge University Press, 1990). As for the debate, I refer specifically to Robert Newsom's *A Likely Story: Probability and Play in Fiction* (New Brunswick, NJ and London: Rutgers University Press, 1988); see below.

9. Pocock, p. 99.

10. Max Weber, *The Protestant Ethic and the Spirit of Capitalism*, trans. Talcott Parsons (London and New York: Routledge, 1992), p. 175: ' "I fear, wherever riches have increased, the essence of religion has decreased in the same proportion. Therefore I do not see how it is possible, in the nature of things, for any revival of true religion to continue long. For religion must necessarily produce both industry and frugality, and these cannot but produce riches. But as riches increase, so will pride, anger, and the love of the world in all its branches." '

11. From among many possible references, I choose Derrida's 'Donner la mort', in *L'éthique du don: Jacques Derrida et la pensée du don* (Colloque de Royaumont, December 1990) (Paris: Métailié-Transition, 1992), pp. 11–108.

12. Perry Anderson, *A Zone of Engagement* (London and New York: Verso, 1992), pp. 279–375.

13. Ibid., p. 333.

14. Ibid., p. 332.

15. See ch. 1 of *Tarrying with the Negative* (Durham: Duke University Press, 1993).

Chapter Eleven

'VARIOUS INFINITUDES'
Narration, Embodiment and Ontology in
Beckett's *How It Is* and Spinoza's *Ethics*

Alex Houen

SPINOZA AND THEORY

In *Spinoza and the Origins of Modern Critical Theory* (1990), Christopher Norris declares Spinoza to be the thinker who 'more than anyone saw the need to maintain a clear-cut distinction between knowledge arrived at through experience, sensory acquaintance, and phenomenal intuition', and 'knowledge as established (or produced in thought) through a form of immanent structural critique'.[1] All the most significant developments and debates within modern critical theory have their origin in Spinoza's writings accordingly, Norris argues – whether the critics know it or not – for only by making these distinctions can we conceive of critical thought as producing what Spinoza calls 'adequate knowledge', one which, *à la* Althusser, is unattainable from within the realm of 'ideology, lived experience or the discourses of socially legitimized truth' (p. 164). And this, he asserts, is the 'single most contentious issue in present-day literary critical debate' (ibid.).

These separations, as far as Norris is concerned, are manifest in Spinoza's '*scientia intuitiva*', the third and highest form of knowledge, which is defined in Part 5 of the *Ethics* as the thinking of the body 'under a form of eternity' (*sub specie aeternitatis*). Yet Spinoza denies any possibility of transcendence at many points in the text, declaring at the end that this third kind of knowledge means viewing eternity as determined and known only in particular things: 'the more we understand particular things the more we understand God'.[2] For this reason, Deleuze and Guattari, in *What is Philosophy?* (1991), pose Spinoza as the 'Christ' of philosophers because he 'drew up the "best" plane of immanence'[3] in thinking an incarnation of infinitude. Toni Negri in his Spinozan meditations, *The Savage Anomaly* (1981), concurs, proffering Spinoza as the 'true birthplace of modern and contemporary revolutionary materialism'.[4] Clearly, then, we need to turn briefly to the *Ethics* itself in order to get an adequate idea of the debate.

The conception of an ontological monism of substance which is either God or Nature (*Deus sive natura*) and which involves a totality and infinity of existence is Spinoza's starting point. Substance exists in itself, is conceived through itself (Pt1D3, p. 45), and is thus wholly immanent, for if it were caused by another thing it would no longer be infinite. Consequently, Nature's eternity *is* its existence: 'by eternity I mean existence itself' (Pt1D8, p. 46), and as such it is necessarily offered as the 'indwelling' essence of particular things; what Spinoza calls 'modes'. This immanence of substance is further developed insofar as it is perceived by the intellect as consisting of two 'attributes': thought and extension. While these are thought distinctly, they nevertheless *coexist* through substance like two sides of the same surface: 'substance thinking and substance extended are one and the same substance . . .' (Pt2P7S, p. 86). Here we have the basis for the parallelism that has been attributed to Spinoza, for while it is the case that 'body cannot determine mind to think, and neither can mind determine body to motion or rest' (Pt3P2, p. 131), the order and connection of ideas is the 'same as the order and connection of things' (Pt2P7, p. 86). And once this has been asserted, ideas themselves are presented as existing in strict correlation to particular bodies: 'a mode of extension and the idea of that mode are one and the same thing, though expressed in two ways' (Pt2P7, p. 86). There is no primacy of thought over extension; they have a correlate existence, or *con*sistence through substance. As a result, the essence of God is inseparable from the modes' specificities. Bodies express God in a determinate manner, 'insofar as he is an extended thing' (Pt2Def1, p. 82), and the idea of God affirms of its univocality 'an infinite number of things which follow in infinite ways' (Pt2P4, p. 85).

At this point, though, substance seems to split into two forms. On the one hand, God exists as a series of finite modes, the idea of each involving him 'not insofar as he is infinite, but insofar as he is affected by another idea of a thing actually existing . . . and so on to infinity' (Pt2P9, p. 88). This is an infinitude of finite causes, in which there is no point of transcendence: 'the duration of the body depends on the common order of nature' (Pt2P30S, p. 107), and every body consists of an infinite number of bodies, just as the soul consists of an infinite number of ideas. On the other hand, Spinoza distinguishes eternal essences from modal existence so that we are faced with a very different form of infinity; one that does appear to transcend the other. Modes, he says, 'cannot be or be conceived without God, yet God does not appertain to their essence' (Pt2P10S, p. 90). This must be so, states Spinoza, for if substance were reducible to finite existence, then it could not exist or be conceived as infinite and common to all things (Pt2P37S, p. 109). It appears to have attained a separate status here, and so too does the mind when he declares in Part 5 that it 'cannot be destroyed with the body but there remains of it something which is eternal' (Pt5P23, p. 259).

Two forms of the infinite, then; one in which substance is an atemporal totality, indivisible, and another in which Nature comprises an unlimited series of finite causes and things, where bodies are determined in their existence solely by encounters and engagements, 'distinguished from one another in respect of motion and rest, quickness and slowness and not in respect of substance' (Pt2L1, p. 93).

What is the relation between the two forms? How can we conceive the singular in direct relation to an infinite totality at once, rather than to a series of limited connections?

The problem permeates a number of fields. For Laclau and Mouffe, in a modern theoretical context, the same dichotomy arises when discussing the possibility of analysing the whole social body in terms of specific institutions: does this break with social essentialism, they ask, or merely offer an essentialism of parts? The first position they equate with Spinoza, the latter with Leibniz.[5] Frederic Jameson formulates a similar problem for literary theory when attempting to figure modernist innovation as a 'diachronic' originality labouring against the idea of literary works and traditions as 'timeless substances à la Spinoza'; this opposition forms the basis upon which he proceeds to discuss the historicity of postmodernism in general.[6] In both of these cases, then, Spinoza is aligned with structural essentialism over particularity. But the question remains whether the two do not cohere in the *Ethics* into an altogether different dynamic.

For Norris, the difference is irreconcilable. Arguments can be offered for viewing Spinoza in terms of privileging embodiment, dragging 'theory down to the level of bodily appetites and functions' (p. 56), as he sees Deleuze and Guattari doing in their 'zany' reading of Spinoza in *Anti-Oedipus* (1972) and *A Thousand Plateaus* (1980). Norris attributes this position to postmodern writers in general, including Foucault and Lyotard. Alternatively, we can see Spinoza as Althusser does, he argues; as the thinker who places the 'maximum possible distance between knowledge and lived experience' (p. 122).

In Althusser's outline of theory, in *Reading Capital* (1968), 'thought' produces 'scientific knowledge' not in directly thinking an object's historical time or presence, but in thinking this through the 'synchrony' of social forces and the 'specific relations that exist between the specific elements'.[7] The synchronic 'is eternity in Spinoza's sense', he writes, and has 'nothing to do' with the diachronicity of 'the object as a *real object*' (p. 107). Stability of the structure of theory in its scientificity is thus given because it is not affected by individual 'events'. Only transitions in structures themselves are possible. But what elicits this transition? To what extent are the relations between elements indissociably involved with diachronicity? How can we account for any 'specific elements' within this framework? In other words, *are the two forms of infinity mutually exclusive?*

All of this applies to the distinction between theory and literature itself. Spinoza was the first to have posed the problem of reading and writing, says Althusser, because he was the first to have offered a theory on the difference between the imaginary and the true, as well as objects and their ideas. For Norris, too, fiction is aligned with imagination and phenomenality, which is why we need theory to 'produce a more adequate (theoretically articulated) knowledge of literature's knowledge effects' (p. 248). I will argue, however, that Samuel Beckett, in his novel *How It Is* (1964), takes up precisely these issues through offering an explicit reading of the *Ethics*, and points to the possibility of figuring a direct correlation, *a double genesis*, between the two types of infinity, and between duration and synchrony.[8] In so doing, not only does he offer literature as capable of forming an adequate critique and knowledge of things, he forces us to rethink the distinctions between social structures of mediation and individuals, between thought and corporeality, with the result that the literary text itself must be conceived of in different terms of production.

HOW IT IS: NARRATING BODIES, AND THE TERRAIN OF ONTOLOGY

How It Is is Beckett's translation of his earlier version of the text written in French, *Comment c'est* (1961), the title of which slips from being a statement on the present to an imperative to begin in the infinitive – *commencez, commencer!* The narrative opens with the image of the main character, who is also the narrator, lying face down in a vast expanse of mud, trying desperately to tell of his encounter with a certain Pim: 'how it was I quote before Pim with Pim after Pim how it is three parts I say it as I hear it'.[9] The complication arises immediately here in that the story being recounted is in fact the present of its narrating, and the events also appear coevally with the telling: 'here then part one how it was before pim . . . I quote a given moment long past vast stretch of time' (p. 7). Thus, the narrative splits into two possible directions. Either both narrative and event are referred back indefinitely into the past, and every present is already framed as citation, or everything is *continually* fabricated in the present.

What is at stake here is the possibility of defining limits, a *structure*, in order to have adequate knowledge of events. It is duration itself that causes the problem, as the eponymous protagonist of Beckett's earlier novel, *Molloy* (1955), bemoaned: 'my life, my life, now I speak of it as something over, now as of a joke which still goes on, and it is neither for at the same time it is over and it goes on and is there a tense for that?'[10] If the present exists only in passing instantly, then it must be true that every instant is always already past *and* future as well as present.[11] For the narrator in *How It Is*, narration suddenly involves saying a synthesis of times at once, to the extent that he considers restructuring the parts of his story by dividing 'into three a single eternity for the sake of clarity' (p. 20). The voice he hears speaks a 'vast tract of time' in the present with an 'ancient voice', but it is precisely this immediate unfurling of the moment that prevents him from grasping it within an act of saying. Instead, he experiences himself as both past and present *incessantly*; a 'sudden series' of 'subject object subject object' (p. 11). Moreover, that this dehiscence is absolutely internal to his experience entails that it simultaneously elicits a splitting in the sensation of his body. Before Pim arrives, we find the narrator's corporeality inextricably linked to that of a sack: 'I clutch it it drips in the present but long past gone vast stretch of time the beginning this life first sign very first sign of life' (p. 25). Gradually it is fleshed out, taking on increasingly anthropomorphic characteristics, causing the narrator's feelings for it to burgeon into romantic ardour: 'I take it in my arms talk to it put my head in it rub my cheek on it . . . say to it thou thou' (p. 17), until finally it is replaced by Pim in Part Two.

Knowledge of the body's 'affections' (*affectio*) or 'feelings' is also the first type of knowledge in the *Ethics*: 'the object of the idea constituting the human mind is the body. . . a certain mode of extension which actually exists and nothing else' (Pt2P13, p. 92). Affections *are* modal, for Spinoza, the idea of which involves both the nature of the human body and that of an external body (Pt2P16, p. 98). In itself, the affection is seen as inadequate knowledge, involving only traces and signs of the external thing. These are developed into a more adequate understanding, though, when the affection of the external body is linked to the internal variations of the mode, insofar as these are *experienced* as constituting its own power of existence. Affection becomes 'affect' (*affectus*) accordingly: 'By affect I understand affections of the body by which the body's power is increased or diminished, aided or restrained' (Pt3Def3, p. 130). Because of the correlate existence of thought and extension, the capacity for the mode to affect or be affected is also attributed directly to its power of understanding; there are velocities of both body and thought. With this knowledge, 'common notions' are formed as we recognise a unity of composition *between* modes; that an individual's existence is applicable to and involves Nature in general as a field of forces.[12]

This we see in Part Two of *How It Is*, where Pim arrives and the narrator announces 'the beginnings of our life in common', which consists mostly of the narrator torturing him, inscribing words on his skin with his fingernails and stabbing him with a tin-opener. But he is unable to rid himself of Pim's presence because his own existence is inseparable from that of an Other within this collective time: 'I'll leave him no I'll stay where I am yes glued to him yes tormenting him yes eternally yes' (p. 98). And with the recognition that their

common life is given through time in general, the narrative suddenly acceler-
ates as relations and characters multiply into populations that spread
throughout the mud: 'millions millions there are millions of us and there are
three I place myself at my point of view Bem is Bom Bom Bem let us say Bom
it's preferable Bom then me and Pim me in the middle' (p. 114). Along with
this explosion of Boms, Pims and Bems there is also a parallel parturition of
narrative structure; the organisation into three parts now requires an introduction of other supplementary ones: 'thus need for the billionth time part
three (p. 137). Even the genre of narrative is now ternary, becoming 'refresh-
ing alternations of history, prophesy [sic] and the latest news' (p. 129) all
at once!

From here, the story gets increasingly out of hand as each event, in being
seen as embodying a multiplicity, comes to entail a number of different
modalities in the one breath: 'it's the sack Pim left me without his sack he
left his sack with me I left my sack with Bom I'll leave my sack Bom I left Bem
without my sack to go towards Pim it's the sack' (p. 111). The description
here permutes all tenses and relations of agency, such that each term is constantly open to being made up through an assemblage of different connections.
As a result, the narrator is forced to pose the existence of individual events
and things within an infinitesimal calculus of differentiation:

> as for example our course a closed curve and let us be numbered 1 to
> 1000000 then number 1000000 on leaving his tormentor number
> 999999 instead of launching forth into the wilderness towards an inex-
> istent victim proceeds towards number 1 (p. 117)

The victim/tormentor relation remains static, however, until, with the experience of being organised through the infinite, each individual comes to be
implicated in an entire series of different positions simultaneously:

> linked thus bodily together each one of us is at the same time Bom and
> Pim tormentor and tormented pedant and dunce wooer and wooed
> speechless and reafflicted with speech in the dark in the mud nothing
> to emend here (p. 140)

The subject as mode is thus developed in terms of common notions, and
infinite embodiment emerges in parallel with the collective communication
of events through the transmission of voice. Each individual is incorporated
into a community by virtue of being subject to 'rumour transmissable [sic]
ad infinitum in either direction' (p. 120), and by the repetition of acts.
Multiplicity and singularity are coexistent, then, for as the individual is
imbricated with a univocality of existence, the act of community is made up
singularly with each performance: 'and when on the unpredictable arse for

the millionth time the groping hand descends that for the hand it is the first arse for the arse the first hand' (p. 121). The development that we saw in Spinoza of two forms of the infinite – infinite series of relations of finite causes between modes; univocal totality – is thus attributed a direct correlation by Beckett through the very nature of temporal passage. Eternity and duration *take place* simultaneously.[13]

Now we move towards the construction of a fully ethical plane of narrative, as everyone recognises that his actions and narrations also have a collective significance: 'the same instant always everywhere . . . with the same space between them it's mathematical it's our justice in this muck' (p. 123). Instead of trying to think the infinite between limits and reduce it to finitude, now we think of modal limits only in terms of infinitude. Accordingly as each individual is no longer simply defined through an Other, but is involved singularly in an infinite set of relations, there is no longer a dependence on torture or negation. Denial of another is denial of one's own field of power, as Spinoza asserts (Pt4P18S, pp. 201–2). Individuality thus affirms infinitude at the same time as gaining ontological ratification through it: 'so neither four nor a million . . . nor ten million nor twenty million nor any finite number even or uneven however great because our justice which wills that not one were we fifty million not a single one among us be wronged' (p. 123). In this way, Beckett presents an ethics of singularity as *difference in itself*, rather than a subjectivity thought on the basis of negating difference as Other. '*Non opposita sed diversa*', as Spinoza writes.

Nothing remains to be done now, says the narrator, 'save that of conceiving but no doubt it can be done a procession in a straight line with neither head nor tail in the dark in the mud with all the various infinitudes that such a conception involves' (p. 124). This corresponds to Spinoza's move in the fifth and final part of the *Ethics* from the second type of knowledge, the common notions, to the thinking of the third type, the *scientia intuitiva*, in which God knows himself modally: 'Our mind, in so far as it knows itself and the body under the form of eternity, has to that extent necessarily a knowledge of God, and knows that it is in God, and is conceived through God' (Pt5P30, p. 262). For Norris, this commingling of pure reason with 'concrete sensuous particularity' in Spinoza's *scientia intuitiva* was the most 'problematic' part of the *Ethics*, his solution being to separate out two readings: either bodies or rationality, theory or fiction, rational structure or physical dispersion. Beckett brings the two together in each case, offering a more adequate reading of Spinoza by relating the two forms of infinitude, and giving rise to a *double genesis* involving singular infinities.[14] These particular determinations of essence are, in fact, offered by Spinoza as the most adequate form of knowledge, 'more potent and powerful than the universal knowledge' (Pt5P36C, p. 265). Beckett's innovation, though, is to discover an aesthetics at this very point; the immanence of bodies and narrative through an infinite substance involves the actual production of affects or body-ideas.

A DIFFERENT IMAGE OF LITERARY PRODUCTION: THE 'DIAPHOR'

A constellation of four propositions to conclude.

Proposition I: *A literary text consists of modal affects; singular, corporeal-ideas, as we see in the images of narrative in* How It Is.[15] That the narrative is constructed through a vast mud-voice plane of immanence entails that its images consist of both body – 'I pissed and shat another image' (p. 9) – as well as mind: 'that kind of image not for the eyes made of words not for the ears' (p. 45). The same thing expressed in two ways. Just as bodies are determined in their relations with others, so an image involves and is produced with embodiment, entails a certain praxis. It is not prefabricated. It involves singular productions through corporeal and temporal conjunctions: 'it's me all of me *and* my mother's face I see it from below *it's like nothing I ever saw*' (p. 15, emphases mine). An ethics of reading emerges: the reader is incorporated by the affect, which forms a particular dynamic of relations, at the same time that it is affected by the context of reading. The becoming takes place between them with internal effects for both, according to their particular capacities to affect and be affected – taking into account, for example, gender, age, race and social milieu of a reader, coupled with the genre, style and social milieu embodied in the text.

Deleuze talks of Nietzsche's 'will to power' by way of differential calculus in this sense – though it could equally be applied to Spinozan affects. Every thing as force (Spinoza's speed and slowness of a body) has an essential relation to others: 'the essence of force is its quantitative difference from other forces', and this difference is expressed in terms of a force's 'quality'. But the quantitative force of an individual is not separate from the relation: 'difference in quantity . . . reflects a differential element of related forces – which is also the genetic element of their qualities'.[16] So the Idea of a thing must integrate variation *internally*; not as a function of a constant relation, but as 'a degree of variation of relations themselves'.[17] This is exactly what we see in Beckett's presentation of bodies and narrative as enveloped within a field of infinitesimal differential calculus: the production of 'various infinitudes', which also relates to the image of narrative itself: 'an image in its discontinuity of the journeys of which it is the sum made up' (p. 126). In Beckett's *Ill Seen Ill Said* (1982), the image of this field of composition is further developed to involve a veritable ecology of relations – human, animal and mineral. The figure of a woman whitens with the stones, which themselves whiten 'in the way of animals ovines only', until everything vibrates simultaneously through the same immanent, ontological plane:

> Suffice to watch the grass. How motionless it droops. Till under the relentless eye it shivers. With faintest shimmer from its innermost. Equally the hair . . . And the old body. When it seems of stone ['*calculus*' in Latin is also 'a stone': *OED*]. Is it not ashiver from head to foot?[18]

Proposition II: *The production of body-ideas entails a different image of social production.* Beckett's use of differential calculus to think of the relation between individual things and social fields is similar to Balibar's attempt, in *Reading Capital*, to bring together the synchronic and diachronic in the analysis of capitalism. As Marx shows in the introduction to the *Grundrisse*, economic production itself does not strictly produce social relations. Capitalism, in particular, already depends on distribution, exchange and consumption. It builds itself on immanence; all the more so with post-Fordism, as David Harvey and Frederic Jameson note.[19] Moreover, because it seeks to increase incessantly its circulation, gain control of a global market, at the same time as decreasing the time taken for it to circulate and produce commodities, its tendency to 'eternalise' social relations by reproducing modes of production comes into conflict with the need to continually modify these modes. The resulting tendency to increase production and surplus value leads to a decrease in the value of labour, which Marx cites as the tendency towards a fall in profits: crisis! Capitalism discovers 'immanent barriers'[20] (*immanenten Schranken*), says Marx in *Capital*. That is to say: *immanence problematises capitalism*.

For Balibar, it means that the synchronic always needs to be analysed in terms of the diachronic; the 'peculiar temporality of the productive forces' within a mode of production: 'only this movement can be called a *dynamics* . . . a movement of development *inside* the structure', at the same time that the 'peculiar rhythm and speed [is] determined by the structure' (p. 299). In this way, we can theorise the internal organic composition of capital. It is, he says, a 'differential' concept of history; history as 'problem'. The result is that economics cannot posit itself as ground to the movements of the whole social body. This is where Negri, drawing parallels between capitalist production and a modal production of substance, sees Spinoza as resisting capitalism: 'Spinoza's rejection does not deny the reality of the market . . . It assumes the crisis as an element of the human essence, negates the utopia of the market' (p. 218). Just as 'every singular event of a physical nature is a deter-minate condensation of the cumulative process of being' (p. 224), so we cannot say 'being' except in terms of production, but it is not possible to say production without having to include an 'ecology' of diverse forces: ethical, aesthetic, political, technological, legal, economic and so on.[21]

Proposition III: *The consistence of thought and extension in literary affects implies a different image of textual mediation.* Agamben criticises Adorno for thinking mediation and the economic ground on Hegelian terms: 'All causal interpretations are . . . consistent with Western Metaphysics, and presuppose the sundering of reality into two different ontological terms'.[22] It is precisely this impossibility of transcending or being prior to the social body that *is* the crisis of capitalism, though. So, writes Agamben, the 'only true materialism is one which abolishes this separation, never seeing in concete historical reality the sum of structure and superstructure, *but the direct unity of the two in terms of praxis*' (p. 120, emphasis mine). This does not deny mediation through the total social process. Far from it; all social processes are wholly immanent to bodies and things. Mediation is immediate. But because this necessitates that it be developed on a 'unitary continuous . . . terrain' (Negri), modes pose themselves in an immediate relation to the production of capitalist substance. Consequently, for Agamben, we must approach literary texts differently, not by separating out a historical structure that determines the text. Instead, praxis itself is identified as 'origin' and 'historical structure' (p. 120). Various infinitudes.

Proposition IV: *The tropological capacity of a literary affect also involves a theoretical capacity.* To the extent that literary affects entail distinct multiplicities, must be thought through them, and also produce these multiplicities in specific relations, the notion of metaphor as a transference (*metapherein*; 'to transport') that takes place between two fixed identities is no longer sufficient. We need to think the transference of the singular through an infinite field of relations. This we could call the 'diaphor'.

Difference, in Greek, is *diaphora*. It has several meanings: to tear asunder, to carry over or across, to bear, to *permeate* both space and time.[23] Heraclitus applies it to the concept of Being itself: 'the all is divisible and indivisible' (*einai to pan diaireton adiaireton*), 'agreeing with itself through differing in itself' (*diapheromenon heauto sumpheretai*). An image of the sum of discontinuities. Deleuze discusses *diaphora* as jettisoned by the concept in Aristotle, insofar as it is always the case that specific difference is referred to a presupposed conceptual structure and generality: 'Aristotle's *diaphora* of the *diaphora* is only a false transport: it never shows difference changing in nature . . . which would relate the most universal with the most singular'.[24] This is what Beckett affirms in the affect, thereby placing aesthetics at the heart of the Idea. The production of singular infinities entails a tropology whereby the relation of self and Other proliferates into a variation on the theme of difference and the turnings of its nature ('*trope*' in Greek is a cognate of '*trepo*': 'to turn' or 'put to flight'). So too, with the image of narrative itself, as reading and text interact to elicit something 'like nothing I ever saw', but only to the extent that the act of *poeisis* is always saturated with the dynamics of an entire social field. A theory *of* literature, then (double genitive), as the creation of possible worlds. Not abstract fabulation; rather, the world in its singularity made possible.

NOTES

1. Christopher Norris, *Spinoza and the Origins of Modern Critical Theory* (Oxford: Blackwell, 1990), p. 35.
2. Benedict de Spinoza, *On The Improvement of the Understanding, The Ethics, Correspondence*, trans. R. H. M. Elwes (New York: Dover, 1955), p. 260, Pt5P24. I have adopted the following abbreviations for referring to the text: Pt = part, A = axiom, D = definition, P = proposition, S = scholium, C = corollary, L = lemma.
3. Gilles Deleuze and Félix Guattari, *What is Philosophy?*, trans. Hugh Tomlinson and Graham Burchell (New York: Columbia University Press, 1994), p. 60.
4. Antonio Negri, *The Savage Anomaly: The Power of Spinoza's Metaphysics and Politics*, trans. Michael Hardt (Minneapolis: University of Minnesota Press, 1991), p. 20.
5. Ernesto Laclau and Chantal Mouffe, *Hegemony and Socialist Strategy: Towards a Radical Democratic Politics* (London: Verso, 1993), p. 104.
6. Frederic Jameson, *The Seeds of Time* (New York: Columbia University Press, 1994), p. 134.
7. Louis Althusser and Étienne Balibar, *Reading Capital*, trans. Ben Brewster (London: Verso, 1979), p. 107.
8. Beckett first incorporates Spinoza into his fiction in ch. 6 of *Murphy* (1938; London: Calder & Boyars, 1970), when giving an account of Murphy's mind.
9. Samuel Beckett, *How It Is* (New York: Grove, 1964), p. 7.
10. Samuel Beckett, *The Beckett Trilogy: Malloy, Malone Dies, The Unnameable* (London: Picador, 1979), p. 36.
11. See Deleuze's discussion of passing time and eternity in *Nietzsche and Philosophy*, trans. Hugh Tomlinson (New York: Columbia University Press, 1983), pp. 48–9.
12. Étienne Balibar, in 'Spinoza, the Anti-Orwell: The Fear of the Masses', in *Masses, Classes, Ideas*, trans. James Swenson (London: Routledge, 1994), writes of the affects as constitutive of the 'very concept of the mass': '*It is the process itself*, the affective network cutting across each individual, which soon becomes the true "object" (or the true "subject") . . .' (p. 28).
13. On the relation of eternity to duration in Spinoza, see Martha Kneale, 'Eternity and Sempiternity', in Marjorie Grene (ed.), *Spinoza: A Collection of Critical Essays* (New York: Anchor, 1973), pp. 227–40; also S. Alexander, 'Spinoza and Time', in Grene (ed.), pp. 68–85.
14. Deleuze, in *Expressionism in Philosophy: Spinoza*, trans. Martin Joughin (New York: Zone, 1992), pp. 212–15. Genevieve Lloyd, in *Part of Nature: Self-Knowledge in Spinoza's* Ethics (Ithaca: Cornell University Press, 1994), p. 138.
15. See Deleuze and Guattari's relating of aesthetics to 'affects', 'percepts' and 'sensations' in ch. 7 of *What is Philosophy?* Deleuze, in 'L'Épuisé', published along with Beckett's television pieces, in *Quad et Tro du Fantôme, . . . que nuages . . . , Nacht und Träume, suivi de L'Épuisé* (Paris: Les Éditions de Minuit, 1992), distinguishes between three types of language in Beckett's work which, although

he does not make the parallel, correspond to Spinoza's three types of knowledge (pp. 66–79). For a fuller explication of Spinoza's three knowledges entailing distinct languages, see Deleuze's 'Spinoza et Les Trois Ethiques', in *Critique et Clinique* (Paris: Les Éditions de Minuit, 1994).

16. *Nietzsche and Philosophy*, p. 50. See also Deleuze's *The Logic of Sense*, trans. Mark Lester (New York: Columbia University Press, 1990), pp. 54–5.

17. Gilles Deleuze, *Difference and Repetition*, trans. Paul Patton (New York: Columbia University Press, 1994), p. 173. The connection between a quantitative physics of modal existence and its qualitative power is described in terms of 'longitude' and 'latitude' respectively in Deleuze's 'Spinoza and Us', in *Spinoza: Practical Philosophy*, trans. Robert Hurley (San Francisco: City Lights, 1988), pp. 122–30.

18. Samuel Beckett, *Nohow On: Company, Ill Seen Ill Said, Worstward Ho* (London: Calder, 1992), p. 74.

19. See in particular Jameson's *The Seeds of Time*, pp. 204–5, and Harvey's *The Condition of Postmodernity* (Oxford: Blackwell, 1990), pp. 173–89, 338–43.

20. Karl Marx, *Capital, Volume 3*, trans. Samuel Moore and Edward Aveling (London: Lawrence & Wishart, 1974), p. 245.

21. On the 'ecological' field of production, see Negri's *The Politics of Subversion: A Manifesto for the Twenty-First Century*, trans. James Newell (Cambridge: Polity, 1989), pp. 89–115.

22. Giorgio Agamben, *Infancy and History*, trans. Liz Heron (London: Verso, 1993), p. 119.

23. H. G. Liddel and R. Scott, *A Greek-English Lexicon* (Oxford: Clarendon, 1996), pp. 418–19.

24. *Difference and Repetition*, p. 32. Laclau and Mouffe, in *Hegemony and Socialist Strategy*, write of the need to see 'synonymy, metonymy and metaphor' as 'part of the primary terrain itself in which the social is constituted' (p. 110), once the strict dualisms of base/superstructure and thought/reality are rejected and replaced by 'historical blocs' of organic coexistence. They do not, however, propose a concomitant transformation of tropological categories themselves.

Chapter Twelve

EDWARD SAID AFTER THEORY: THE LIMITS OF COUNTERPOINT

Charles Forsdick

[I]l y a peut-être, du voyageur au spectacle, un autre choc en retour dont vibre ce qu'il voit. . . . [N]'est-ce pas à un cran plus haut, de dire, non pas tout crûment sa vision, mais par un transfert instantané, constant, l'écho de sa présence.[1]

As a student of exoticism, I approach Said with my understanding of such a compromised notion informed by Victor Segalen's early twentieth-century theorisation and critique of western approaches to radical otherness. In the light of such apparent ahistoricity, two principal questions have concerned me: how should one read a 'colonial' author in a self-consciously postcolonial age, and how practicable are strategies of reading which propose a contrapuntal approach to texts, balancing metropolitan and extra-metropolitan elements, implicit and explicit? Unlike, in their varying fields, Jean Baudrillard, James Clifford, Abdelkebir Khatibi and Edouard Glissant, Said refers rarely to Segalen. This chapter is inspired, nevertheless, by traces of Victor Segalen discovered in the writings of Edward Said: actual traces in the form of fleeting (and often critical) references, as well as suggested resonances between Said's critique of Orientalism and Segalen's earlier commentary on the allied representational practices inherent in western exoticism.

EXILE AND IDENTITY

In his [Said's] quite entertaining but intellectually insignificant *Orientalism*, . . . [t]he ex officio disqualification of 'orientalists' goes hand in hand with an endorsement or preferential treatment of those privileged and enlightened, those who see the problem 'from within his subject'. Such a privileged insider view seems to be acquired primarily by origin, or sometimes by political stance. This self-glorification appears to be extended even to those who, like Said himself, though perhaps Easterners by origin, are in fact fully naturalized and perfectly assimilated citizens of Woody Allen-land.[2]

Included in Ernest Gellner's penultimate contribution to the increasingly hostile debate over his critical review of Said's *Culture and Imperialism*, this wilful misreading and associated barbed accusation drove its target to a splenetic extreme. Resorting to folklore (to the realms of which their exchange would soon be elevated), Said retorted: 'Ernest Gellner is an academic Rumpelstiltskin, stamping his little feet when he doesn't get his way . . . [He] can only resort to the puerile anti-American joke and the piffling trivia of the Common Room.'[3] What became one of the principal academic feuds of the early 1990s, rivalled in intensity only by Said's earlier exchanges with Bernard Lewis over *Orientalism* in the *New York Review*, had begun with sober debate about the nature of Empire, its relation to industrialisation and the role of culture in its propagation. There was rapid descent, however, via polemic, into the invective of personal abuse and apparent encroachment of the biographical fallacy into the territory of theory.

Rigorous foundation of criticism in lived experience is, however, central to an understanding of Said's thought, for this is predicated on the author's self-identification as interstitial intellectual, both hybrid and unlocatable, not so much crossing borders as straddling them, a product of cultural displacements and of elaborate historical forces. Said's writings, like the texts he studies in them, are accordingly to be perceived as 'protean things . . . tied to circumstances and to politics large and small'.[4] As a result, the committed and individual nature of his work – as that of an 'organic' intellectual – is treated in turn with praise and with scorn, depending on the reader's sympathies. Ferial J. Ghazoul – author of one of the 'hagiographic' contributions to Michael Sprinker's *Critical Reader* – claims that Said attempts to 'bring together the two aspects of himself in a tentative project of self-fulfilment', whereas Peter Conrad, in *The Observer*, sneeringly called his *Culture and Imperialism* 'autobiography by other means, analysing the mutual incomprehension of the two worlds he [Said] bestraddles'.[5]

What for Gellner was little more than a fleeting attempt to debunk such paradigmatically 'exilic' status had been developed more rigorously by Aijaz Ahmad in his essay '*Orientalism* and After' where he interrogates Said's self-description as 'Oriental subject' and studies his idiosyncratic – or perhaps, rather, ambivalent – use of the first-person plural pronoun:

[A]ny careful reading of the whole of his work would show how strategically he employs words like 'we' and 'us' to refer, in various contexts, to

Palestinians, Third World Intellectuals, academics in general, humanists, Arabs, Arab-Americans, and the American citizenry at large.[6]

This valency of reference – implicit in such pronominal shifts and their subsequent ambiguity – is central to a number of the issues linked to the cultural politics of contemporary postcolonial criticism: choice of object of study, relevance of site of production, position of target audience and identity of practitioner. Gellner touched a raw nerve, however, in parodying, minimising and debasing the essential topography of Said's work, the root of which – what Said has called 'the crippling sorrow of estrangement' inherent in exile – the two men actually shared.[7] Aware of the risks of romanticising or trivialising the horrors of such displacement, he views the trope of exile 'not as a privilege, but as as an *alternative* to the mass institutions that dominate modern life'.[8] Countering the misdiagnosed and essentialist *occidentosis* misconstrued by some critics as the root of *Orientalism*, Said considers the permeability as opposed to the hermeticism of cultures, and casts '[e]xile, immigration, and the crossing of boundaries' as 'experiences that can therefore provide us with new narrative forms, or with *other* ways of telling'.[9]

As prototype of such modern transgressions, Said cites the work of Jean Genet as that of an 'exceptional visionary figure'.[10] Genet, like Said himself, is (in JanMohamed's terms) a 'specular' as opposed to a 'syncretic' exile, refusing to be at home in any of the cultures to which he travels or in which he dwells.[11] Said's concern with exile, however, is most clearly manifested in his regular return to two allied texts which, in the context of his work, have acquired talismanic status: Hugo of St Victor's *Didascalicon* and Erich Auerbach's *Mimesis*. He is drawn to Hugo's 'exilic credo' that perfection depends on a process of othering of the entire world: 'perfecto vero cui mundus totus *exilium* est' (my emphasis).[12] Said applies this paradigm of adoption of the earth as 'philological home' to a concrete instance of literary criticism: the exiled Auerbach's writing of his study of 'the representation of reality in Western literature' in the refuge of wartime Istanbul. The production of this text, according to Said, constituted an 'act of cultural, even civilizational, survival of the highest importance', for Auerbach not only rejected the risk of exile (i.e. the possibility of not writing) but also thus challenged the contemporary threat to Romania which had caused his own exile.[13] Said's adherence to *Mimesis*, this pre-theoretical, profoundly Humanist text, illustrates the contradictory precariousness of his own work as literary critic which seemingly perpetuates the tradition of Auerbach and Spitzer while by implication undermining the Eurocentric bases of that very tradition by acknowledgement of extra-European and postcolonial languages and literatures. For it is these very languages and literatures which Auerbach views with dread in the postwar essay 'Philologie der *Weltliteratur*'. 'Romania', Said comments in *Culture and Imperialism*, 'is under threat' (p. 530).

THE AMBIGUITIES OF HUMANISM: SAID *AFTER* THEORY

For Said, the ambivalence of personal identity, as signalled by Ahmad in his analysis of fluid use of pronominal shifters, is linked not merely to cultural but also to methodological location: he vacillates between Palestinian and North American, but also between Humanist and Theorist. The study of colonial discourse inaugurated by *Orientalism* may have its foundations in exclusively *western* critical practice – and is based clearly on a Foucauldian notion of power wielded through dominant discourse, allied (despite apparent contradictions) to a Gramscian concept of hegemony – but its implications of resistance ally it rather with postcolonial theory of which it is often cast as the first stage, a point of departure in both senses of that phrase.[14] It is important to situate the text within an understanding of postcolonial theory which stresses that the Empire Writing Back poses a challenge to the centre. For it is tempting to view postcolonialism as one of a series of posts, each of which lays claim to the status of 'Last Post' which the debate surrounding the post-theoretical often seems to imply.[15] Certain devices and techniques which appear to characterise postmodern and postcolonial texts – such as discontinuity, parody, polyphony, problematisation of representation – are, in fact, put to very different, even divergent uses. These strands of postcolonial criticism are more a response to than a fragment of such post-theoretical aporia. Here, the implications of its prefix suggest movement beyond, super-session of the outmoded.

There is then inevitable animosity between this *post* (of the postcolonial) and that of modern, Eurocentric Critical Theory. Claiming to respond to the epithet 'humanist' with 'contradictory feelings of affection and revulsion', Edward Said as theorist positions himself explicitly at the cleavage between European and extra-European theory, rejecting what he calls the New New Criticism and asserting the 'worldliness' or 'circumstantial reality' of the text.[16] Said's role as postcolonial critic is ambivalent (some might say suspect), for, as I have suggested, his notion of 'Orientalism' is fundamentally indebted to a highly personal reading of what he describes significantly as Foucault's 'scrupulously ethnocentric' undertaking;[17] but despite the status of Said's work as landmark and point of reference in the theorisation of the mechanics and articulation of means of oppression, his hostility to Theory is vehement. Said, it would seem, has been *after* Theory for a long time now. He describes, for instance, in an interview with Raymond Williams (whose work's 'stubborn Anglocentrism' he had commented on elsewhere), '[t]he great horror I think we should all feel towards systematic or dogmatic orthodoxies of one sort or another that are paraded as the last word of high Theory still hot from the press'.[18] Such antipathy has become increasingly marked and is clearly stated in one of the numerous interviews which Said has given. He describes to Michael Sprinker a loss of interest in the metacritical, and classes

Deconstruction as 'completely exhausted' and New Historicism as 'an orthodoxy of some sort'.[19] Since *Orientalism*, his initially sympathetic reading of
Foucault has turned to hostility as he casts him as a *'scribe* of power' who
pays little attention to the 'continuing attraction of libertarian struggle'.[20]

This reassessment of Foucault clearly reveals more about Said himself, for
his interest is retained by what he classes as 'novel attempts to do something
from an historical point of view, across lines in often transgressive ways'.[21]
Said claims in *Culture and Imperialism*, however, that Critical Theory not
only operates in 'a timeless vacuum, so forgiving and permissive as to deliver
the interpretation directly into a universalism free from attachment, inhibition,
and interest' (p. 66), but has also avoided 'the major, I would say determining,
political horizon of modern Western culture, namely imperialism' (p. 70). He
concludes that the failing of western theoreticians is not only their
Eurocentrism, their propensity to carry on 'churning out theories of Marxism,
language, psychoanalysis, and history with an implied applicability to the
whole world', but also their lack of *engagement* which suggests for him the
equation of guild membership with 'choosing items from a menu'.[22] Said
casts himself as an organic intellectual espousing a 'critique engagée', and
contrasts his own methods with those of the incestuous and hermetically
sealed 'interpretative communities' described in 'Opponents, Audiences,
Constituencies and Community': 'People who write specialized, advanced
(i.e. New New) criticism faithfully read each other's books. . . . A nice little
audience had been built and could be routinely mined' (p. 136).

It would be easy to dismiss the evidence as anecdotal and oversimplistic,
for it casts the 'difficult to read' as arcane and ignores the (often inevitable)
exclusivity of specifically academic discourse. In accusing the western theorist of hermeticism, however, Said does make a substantive point about
geography and introspection. The subtext evokes Wole Soyinka's notion of
a 'second epoch of colonization', namely his understanding of the reimposi-
tion of Euro-American conceptual patterns onto non-metropolitan cultural
production via what Derek Wallcott has called the 'dead fish of French
criticism'. Such a critique is a demand for justification of the status of First
World tertiary institutions as site for the production of universal meanings.
Said's most recent work – and in particular the afterword to the new edition
of *Orientalism* – is an approving statement of how a number of his acolytes
and various postcolonial theorists have challenged theoretical statements of
(often unwitting) critical universality and proposed new openings for transgressive rereadings.

In a perceptive essay on the pitfalls of the term 'postcolonialism', Anne
McClintock, one of Said's former students, has attempted to locate the post
of the epithet 'postcolonial' within what she calls a wider 'global crisis in
ideologies of the future, particularly the ideology of "progress"', manifested
in the proliferation of 'afters' which the title of this collection presupposes.[23]

Rejecting the idea of a movement forward, she perceives rather the threat of the stasis of foreclosure: 'the risk of gazing back, spellbound, at the epoch behind us, in a perpetual present marked only as "post"'.[24] Said's counterpoint is an attempt to circumvent this risk, to bypass the pre-contrapuntal, single, unaccompanied line of Theory, to present a 'different and innovative paradigm for humanistic research'.[25]

COUNTERPOINT AND POST-THEORETICAL APORIA

Said presents himself in self-exile, sealed from the threat of Theory. Indeed, counterpoint can be viewed as the intersection of these two allied impulses: it is significant that the first sustained use of the notion is in the early 1980s essay 'Reflections on Exile' where he foregrounds 'contrapuntal juxtapositions that diminish orthodox judgement and elevate appreciative sympathy' (p. 366). This position is of course partially disingenuous: even counterpoint retains traces – the reversal of margin and periphery in his critical practice, especially in the reading of *Mansfield Park*, contains clear hints of deconstructionist reading. Practical exercises in the contrapuntal approach appear to avoid deliberately, however, exhaustive footnoting and linguistic obliquities. This response to a post-theoretical aporia, seeking new modes of approach, begins to illuminate the nature of the *post* in the concept of post-Theory. The current sense of aporia is accepted uncritically by Said as a development of the fears he has been voicing since the publication of *Literature and Society* in 1980. The understanding of this *post*, in the light of his work, is not only temporal but also conceptual – that is, extra-Theoretical. For Said, the postcolonial is not a subset of the postmodern: challenging the lingering imperial understanding of centre and periphery, it is the context from which the latter has emerged.

In *Culture and Imperialism*, Said responds to his earlier critics and acknowledges the role in the formation of culture of those dissenting voices silenced or ignored by the monolith of *Orientalism*. The innovation proposed by *Culture and Imperialism* is its attempt at synthesis in what Said casts as a contrapuntal reading informed by an awareness of the 'overlapping territories and intertwined histories' embedded in the colonial and postcolonial text. It seems tempting to dismiss this seemingly anti-Manichaean middle course, 'alternative both to a politics of blame and to the even more destructive politics of confrontation and hostility' (p. 19), as a synthetic, cosmopolitan, carnivalesque approach to cultures which veers towards the postmodern in its failure to distinguish between hybridity and hierarchy. It is significant, however, that in developing this musical elaboration, Said distances himself from earlier models of comparative literature by avoiding analogy with the synthetic symphony of *Weltliteratur* and describing his own reading practice of contrapuntal analysis as based on the 'atonal ensemble' (p. 386), recognising and

accepting cultural diversity as opposed to homogenising it. Cultural difference exists within the text as a condition of pluralism without being
absorbed into it. The critical methodology of *Culture and Imperialism* is a
patent response to the partisan critics of *Orientalism* who saw Said's unwill-
ingness to provide an alternative to what he attacked as an inability to move
beyond expiation of empire.

Saidian counterpoint is, then, a response to and a *potential* movement
beyond restrictive binary versions of the colonial encounter.[26] It is rooted in
a varied series of precursors: Arab-Islamic thought; Commonwealth literary
criticism; the Fanonian desire to force Europe to consider its own history
together with that of the colonies; Fernando Ortiz's study of transculturation
(the neologism he coined) in *Cuban Counterpoint*, whose lyrical study of
tobacco and sugar is in turn at the heart of Mary Louise Pratt's *Imperial
Eyes: Travel Writing and Transculturation*; Segalen's notion of exoticism,
the extreme of which is a 'contact zone' experience of autoscopy in which
identities of traveller and travellee, of western self and Tibetan other, seem
to merge.[27] James Clifford's understanding of this latter programme of exoticism as 'both an epitome and a critique of the white man's relentless quest
for himself' is eloquent, for it can be contrasted with Said's reading of
Segalen in *Culture and Imperialism*.[28] *Orientalism* had already contained a
cursory reference to Segalen. Said absorbs the latter into a heterogeneous list
ranging from Yeats to Claudel and then describes Segalen's textualisation of
China as a 'secondhand abstraction . . . viewed with the mistrust with which
[the west's] learned attitude to the Orient had always been freighted'.[29]

The equation of Segalen with Claudel into a seamless tradition ignores
fundamental differences in the pair's sinological knowledge and textual practice. Moreover, the implicit criticism in the accusation of 'secondhand
abstraction' ignores the problematics of textual representation of otherness
(and, of course, of representation in general) which cannot but depend on
the absence of what is represented. Said's persistence, in *Culture and
Imperialism*, in allying Segalen with an orthodox colonial exoticism, however,
points to a lingering adherence to monolithic discourse. Focusing on a
number of renegade border intellectuals whose marginality allows them to
'cross to the other side' (p. xxii), he cites, as I've shown, Jean Genet (sited on
the peripheries with Palestinians and Black Panthers) as a specific French
example of such a figure.[30] It is striking that in a study of 'internationalisme
littéraire', Abdelkebir Khatibi similarly cites Genet as an author for whom
cultural hybridity became a vocation.[31] For Khatibi, however, the paradigm
for such a figure remains the *exote* Segalen himself. Said nevertheless persists
in his reduction of Segalen, absorbing him into a catalogue of authors who
domesticated the imperial space within the metropolitan tradition of the
novel: 'Loti, the early Gide, Daudet, Maupassant, Mille, Psichari, Malraux,
the exoticists like Segalin [sic], and of course Camus [who] project a global

concordance between the domestic and imperial situations' (p. 85). He then proceeds to ally Segalen and Gide as authors for whom 'Algeria is an exotic locale in which their own spiritual problems ... can be addressed and therapeutically treated' (p. 222). Such positioning is fallacious – and not only in terms of geography (for in his work Segalen scupulously avoids the principal topoi of French New Imperialist literature: North Africa and Indo-China). To focus on these seemingly minor weak points in Said's argument is an indication neither of excessive pedantry on the part of the reader nor of careless scholarship on that of a bold and polymathic critic. It is rather an indication of the restrictions and inevitable misrepresentations implicit in the reading of texts of exoticism and colonialism which subsume the potential resistance of the individual into the orthodoxy of the collective.[32]

As I have already suggested, the contrapuntal reading practices proposed in *Culture and Imperialism* are in part a response to this call for a new critical consciousness and for an engagement with the taxonomy and hegemony implicit in western epistemology. However, this call for a movement beyond is to be found already in Segalen. Precocious critic of the Orientalist notion of the 'Yellow Peril' and the homogenising generalities of early twentieth-century travel guides to China, Segalen rejects the prevailing modes of engagement with otherness and suggests a shift *au-delà*. Segalen's exoticism attempts maintenance of the exotic in its radical otherness and avoids the assimilation implicit in *exotisme colonial*. It foregrounds the impenetrability of other cultures and avoids absorption and domestication of difference in textual *chinoiseries* by endeavouring to refuse to exploit representation as (what Said calls) 'a way of controlling the redoubtable Orient'.[33] Lexical innovation, formal experimentation and a self-conscious poetics of representation all reveal Segalen's marked rejection of Orientalist tropes. Such a concern for writing otherness is manifest especially in the collection of poems which is perhaps Segalen's best known work, the bilingual *Stèles*, which combines French text and Chinese form and epigraph to suggest polyphonic, fragmented images of cultural contact focusing on the slippage and overlap in the interstices. *Stèles* is neither an exercise in juxtaposition nor a total absorption of the ideogram into western aesthetics. It is part of Segalen's ongoing attempt to present a new poetics of exoticism which a recent critic has described as a *poétique du métissage*.[34] Said's reading of Segalen tends not only to downplay but also to dismiss the theoretical significance of such an engagement with orthodoxy and the possible existence not merely of germs of resistance within the dominant metropolitan discourse of empire, but even of heterogeneity and equivocation. The discursive giant of empire continues to crush the dwarf of anti-colonial counterdiscourse whose resistance is no more than derisory, pathetic.

This is my final point, an attempt to tease out the limits of counterpoint. As a response to the perceived impasse of colonial discourse, purported offspin

of *Orientalism*, such a critical approach offers a way beyond. As Said's reading
of Segalen suggests, however, indifference to textual gaps and ambivalences
threatens the ability to recover 'counter-voices that limit or contest the discourse of mastery'.[35] Counterpoint is a divided metaphor, visual and aural,
whose representation as distinct lines of the musical score signals a need to
resist fusion and to recognise the 'combination of two or more melodic lines,
so that the expressive power of each is enhanced'.[36] It risks becoming a
matter of continued separation rather than interplay and ultimately bypasses
recognition of the ambivalent dynamics and dialogues of the postcolonial
'contact zone' it initially appears to survey.

Avoidance of this fixity of Manichaeanism through the grasping of self as
the other's other, a commonplace in contemporary, postcolonial ethnographic
fieldwork, was the mainstay of Segalen's aesthetic of diversity. Such an
awareness of the contrapuntal nature of contact of colonialism and the resul-
tant cultural hybridity is dependent on a reversal of the traditional polarities
of exoticism, and subsequent foregrounding of the exotic.[37] Segalen's theorisation of exoticism in *Essai sur l'exotisme* either complements or nuances
post-Saidian, postcolonial theory for which it is serving increasingly as a
point of reference. Abdelkebir Khatibi, the Moroccan critic, draws on Segalen's
work in his consideration of orality and of 'internationalisme littéraire', and
develops his notion of the tensions of contrapuntal cultural contact leading
not only into the *bi-langue* of his fictional work but also into the sociological
double-critique (described in *Maghreb pluriel*) which rejects the respective
epistemologies of both western imperialism and Maghrebi fundamentalist
theocracy.[38] A similarly reserved ambivalence is forged by the Martiniquan
Edouard Glissant to whose writings – anti-colonial and postcolonial – Segalen
has been central for the past forty years. For Glissant, Segalen is 'en avant'
and his texts and conception of *exotisme* are precursory to his own notions
of *opacité* and *la Relation*.[39] Glissant and Khatibi, postcolonial critics who
have avoided the pitfalls of metanarrative by concentrating on regionally
specific models of *antillanité* and *Maghreb pluriel*, were both drawn to
Segalen in the 1950s when his work was largely unknown outside a narrow
group of initiates. Both stress the role of his exoticism not only in their initial
mapping of cultural and linguistic location, but also through its continued
importance in their more recent writings. What I am trying to stress is the
inverse of this debt: the rich implications of Glissant and Khatibi's writings
for an understanding of Segalen's work which (chronologically) postcolonial
readings have liberated from restriction to a hazy post-symbolism. The
potentials of contrapuntal reading advocated in *Culture and Imperialism* are
not realised by Said in his treatment of Segalen, the consideration of whose
work within the concept of colonial discourse fails to advance far beyond
the historically imposed label of *littérature coloniale*. Khatibi delineates his
own uneasy relationship to Segalen in an interview with Jean Scemla: 'We

must distance ourselves from Segalen whilst devouring him, that is to say whilst absorbing him magically'.[40] Together with Glissant, he nevertheless reveals the potential of achronological appropriation of metropolitan voices towards the former periphery. These models of postcolonial consumption offer a way beyond the limits of counterpoint.

NOTES

1. Victor Segalen, *Essai sur l'exotisme* (Fontfroide: Fata Morgana, 1978), pp. 17–18. 'From the traveller to what he sees there is perhaps another, reciprocal impact with which what is seen vibrates. Rather than saying quite bluntly what you see, is it not more sophisticated to describe the echo of your presence by means of a spontaneous and constant process of transference?' (my translation).

2. Ernest Gellner, 'Letters to the Editor', *Times Literary Supplement*, 9 April 1993, p. 15.

3. Edward Said, 'Letters to the Editor', *Times Literary Supplement*, 4 June 1993, p. 17. The vitriolic public dispute became journalistic folklore in its own right. See, for example, Brian Cathcart, 'An academic row turns personal', *The Independent on Sunday*, 6 June 1993, p. 7.

4. *Culture and Imperialism* (London: Chatto and Windus, 1993), p. 385.

5. See Ferial J. Ghazoul, 'The Resonance of the Arab-Islamic Heritage in the Work of Edward Said', in Michael Sprinker (ed.), *Edward Said. A Critical Reader* (Oxford: Blackwell, 1992), pp. 157–72 (p. 157); Peter Conrad, 'Empires of the Senseless', *The Observer*, 7 February 1993, p. 23. The assessment of Sprinker's collection as hagiography was made by Bart Moore-Gilbert in 'Which Way Postcolonial Theory? Current Problems and Future Prospects', *History of European Ideas*, 18:4 (1994), 553 60 (p. 553).

6. Aijaz Ahmad, *In Theory* (London: Verso, 1992), p. 171.

7. Edward Said, 'Reflections on Exile', in Russell Ferguson (ed.), *Out There: Marginalization and Contemporary Cultures* (New York: New Museum of Contemporary Art, 1990), pp. 357–66 (p. 357).

8. Ibid., p. 365.

9. Edward Said, 'Representing the Colonized: Anthropology's Interlocutors', *Critical Inquiry*, 15 (1989), 205–25 (p. 225).

10. Ibid. See also *Culture and Imperialism*, p. xxii.

11. For a discussion of Said and the exilic, see Abdul R. JanMohamed, 'Worldliness without World, Homelessness-as-Home: Toward a Definition of the Specular Border Intellectual', in Michael Sprinker (ed.), *Edward Said. A Critical Reader*, pp. 96–120.

12. See *Culture and Imperialism* (London: Chatto and Windus, 1993), p. 407; 'Reflections on Exile', p. 365; and 'Secular Criticism', in *The World, the Text and the Critic* (London: Vintage, 1991), p. 7.

13. *The World, the Text and the Critic*, p. 6.

14. The incompatibility of Foucault and Gramsci is signalled in Dennis Porter's 'Orientalism and its Problems', in Francis Barker (ed.), *The Politics of Theory* (Colchester: University of Essex, 1983), pp. 179–93, and James Clifford, 'On

Orientalism', in idem, *The Predicament of Culture* (Cambridge, Massachusetts: Harvard University Press, 1988), pp. 255–76.

15. This idea is developed in Ian Adam and Helen Tiffin (eds), *Past the Last Post* (New York: Harvester Wheatsheaf, 1991).

16. See 'Opponents, Audiences, Constituencies and Community', in Hal Foster (ed.), *Postmodern Culture* (London: Pluto, 1985), pp. 135–59 (p. 135); Edward Said (ed.), *Literature and Society* (Baltimore: Johns Hopkins University Press, 1980), p. ix; *The World, the Text and the Critic*, p. 34.

17. I quote this from Benita Parry, 'Overlapping Territories, Intertwined Histories', in Michael Sprinker (ed.), *Edward Said. A Critical Reader*, pp. 19–47 (p. 20).

18. See 'Narrative, Geography and Interpretation', *New Left Review*, 180 (1990), 81–97 (p. 83); *The Politics of Modernism* (London: Verso, 1989), p. 182.

19. Michael Sprinker, 'Interview with Edward Said', in idem (ed.), *Edward Said. A Critical Reader*, p. 248.

20. See 'Orientalism and After. An Interview with Edward Said', *Radical Philosophy*, 63 (1993), 22–32 (p. 25); 'Foucault and the Imagination of Power', in David Couzens Hoy (ed.), *Foucault: A Critical Reader* (Oxford: Blackwell, 1986), pp. 149–55 (p. 153).

21. Ibid.

22. *Culture and Imperialism*, pp. 336, 389.

23. See Anne McClintock, 'The Angel of Progress: Pitfalls of the Term "Postcolonialism"', in Francis Barker (ed.), *Colonial Discourse/Postcolonial Theory* (Manchester: Manchester University Press, 1994), pp. 253–67 (p. 262).

24. Ibid.

25. *Culture and Imperialism*, p. 565.

26. See Stuart Hall, 'When was "the post-colonial"? Thinking at the Limit', in Iain Chambers and Lidia Curti (eds), *The Post-Colonial Question* (London: Routledge, 1996), pp. 242–60 (p. 247).

27. See Ferial J. Ghazoul, op. cit. n. 5 above; Bart Moore-Gilbert, *Postcolonial Theory. Contexts, Practices, Politics* (London: Verso, 1997), p. 180; Fernando Ortiz, *Cuban Counterpoint* (New York: Knopf, 1947); Louise Pratt, *Imperial Eyes: Travel Writing and Transculturation* (London: Routledge, 1992).

28. James Clifford, *The Predicament of Culture*, p. 163.

29. *Orientalism* (Harmondsworth: Penguin, 1991), p. 252.

30. See also Michael Sprinker, 'Interview with Edward Said', p. 249.

31. See *Figures de l'étranger* (Paris: Denoël, 1987), pp. 129–200.

32. See also 'Afterword to the 1995 Printing' in the most recent re-edition of *Orientalism* (Harmondsworth: Penguin, 1995): '[F]or artists like Nerval and Segalen, the word "Orient" was wonderfully, ingeniously connected to exoticism, glamour, mystery and promise' (p. 341).

33. *Orientalism*, p. 60.

34. See Carol Lee Wilson, *Exotica: Narratives of the Exotic Body and the Fin-de-siècle* (unpublished doctoral thesis, Brown University, 1993), p. 26.

35. Benita Parry, op. cit., p. 26.

36. Edmund Rubbra, *Counterpoint. A Survey* (London: Hutchinson University Library, 1960), p. 14.

37. See Victor Segalen, *Essai sur l'exotisme* (Fontfroide: Fata Morgana, 1978), pp. 17–18.
38. *Maghreb pluriel* (Paris: Denoël, 1983).
39. See Edouard Glissant, *Le Discours antillais* (Paris: Seuil, 1981); *L'Intention poétique* (Paris: Seuil, 1969); *Poétique de la Relation* (Paris: Gallimard, 1990).
40. Jean Scemla, 'Entretien avec Khatibi', *Bulletin de l'Association Victor Segalen*, 2 (1989), 9–10 (p. 10) (my translation).

Chapter Thirteen

GROUNDING THEORY
Literary Theory and the New Geography

Julian Murphet

The spectacular fortunes of what came to be called 'Theory' after the pivotal year of 1968 hinged not only on the decline in political power of the European and American working class (as Perry Anderson once speculated), but also on a momentous internal revolution specific to philosophical discourse itself: namely, the abandonment of the dialectic and the production paradigm, and the arcane turn towards linguistics.[1] No doubt the two are in some sense related ('in the last instance' perhaps), but the semi-autonomy of the latter development will require extensive analysis and critique in coming years, as the inevitable backlash is now well under way. To anatomise our 'post-theoretical' moment – our emergent dissatisfaction with orthodoxical post-structuralisms of all stripes, our sense of being both after theory and in the theory of the 'post' – it will be essential to come to grips with the suddenness of the philosophical break from Marxian and Hegelian social science, and its consequences at the level of 'thick description' of social and cultural phenomena. The mantras of Theory ('the unconscious is structured like a language', 'the subject is an effect of power', 'play is the disruption of pres-ence'), having worn thin over time, no longer seem quite to quell the episte-mological questions they left to linger: what is the nature of our social system? What relates its heteronomous parts? How does it change? How do cultural forms engage with social ones? If it were permissible to hazard a prediction, it would not seem outrageous to suggest that the dialectic is today set for a resurgence, if only according to the law of alternating intellectual energies. Either that or the triumph of radical Deleuzian thought, its proliferating rhizomatic free particulars, seems ready to fill the vacuum left by the exhausted language paradigm; or perhaps both Deleuze *and* Hegel, circling each other like irreducible and incompatible Forms in the night sky of the conceptual cosmos, will beat together the arrhythmic tempi of our immediate theoretical future.

In any event, this chapter tests the proposition (*pace* Geoffrey Bennington) that the dialectic is an inexhaustible, if not immutable, mode of theoretical engagement with our social system (namely, capitalism), and that the circumstances of Theory's rise and rise forced upon it a certain tactical detour and reorientation, a *ruse of reason*, which is today receiving widespread acknowledgement and application throughout the humanities. For at the very moment that Marxian and Hegelian thought was being unceremoniously ditched from sociology, philosophy and cultural theory, it found refuge in most unlikely and unpromising quarters: the disciplinary hinterland of geography. Here a radical hypothesis took root. What if production today no longer referred simply to the production of 'things' (goods, commodities, products) but to the total horizon of social space itself? To our cities, our interlinked spatial networks of production, distribution and consumption, our states, our very planet and its ecological limits? If this is correct, if we are now in a historical period defined by the *production of space*, then a new possibility for dialectical thought has arisen: the possibility of a unitary critical theory dedicated to this problematic of space. The principal theoretician of this reinvention of dialectical thought, Henri Lefebvre, once asked us to imagine that the dialectic '*is no longer attached to temporality*',[2] but to space and spatiality. This lateral leap suddenly exonerates the dialectic from all the tedious charges that have accumulated around both Hegel's and Marx's successive-stage-models of social systems, and their supposed ideology of 'progress' and perfection. Instead, we are obliged to think the dialectic 'horizontally', in already familiar terms of centre and periphery, body and city, the simultaneously non-simultaneous, everyday life and state control, place and space, and to see these all intranimating in a total dialectical process of spatial production, consumption, control and appropriation, according to one, abiding economic logic.

If the discipline of human geography has been the breeding-ground of these spatial dialectics over the last twenty years, my own interest is in somehow adapting this reassertion of space to a theory of literary production similarly grounded in the rich textures of produced space. Such a development would not only assist in overcoming some of the weaknesses of the geography: namely, its incipient philistinism, and its inevitable distance from the individual and from the body, from storytelling and from sensuous-practical being; but it might also effect a radical rupture within the still overly formalist discipline of literary studies itself, in ways that have already been prefigured in architecture, film theory, media theory, urbanism and world-systems analysis – disciplines associated with concrete spatial forms.[3] Later I will suggest some tactics for initiating this redefinition, and suggest why the taboo subject of 'lived experience' looks likely to re-enter literary studies in powerful new ways. But to begin with, an overview of the major recent developments in human geography is probably in order.

Let us begin in the early 1970s, with the publication of major works by the prominent Marxist geographers, Manuel Castells and David Harvey: respectively, *The Urban Question* (1975) and *Social Justice and the City* (1973). Here, for the first time in the geographical discipline, was articulated the central thesis developed by all the work that was to follow, the so-called 'socio-spatial dialectic'. Social relations, according to this hypothesis, do not constitute themselves in a void or an abstract realm of academic discourse, but very precisely *in space*; and this constitution in space in turn modifies and partially determines the social relations. It matters that, say, feudalism was structured not simply by a politically regulated economic order of production and accumulation, but equally by a complex integration of peasant agrarian space, town and market space, bureaucratic space, religious and monastic space, aristocratic space, and the symbolic spaces of death and carnival; without this tissue of spatial orders, the system could not have functioned and most certainly could not have reproduced itself. By becoming indistinguishable from the environment it required, by *producing* its own space, feudalism, like ancient society, absolutism and capitalism, facilitated its own duration, its necessary appearance of immortality and inexorability. And indeed, this progressive-regressive 'socio-spatial' hypothesis grew out of a renewed attempt to address the old Marxian problem of the relations of production, the shell encasing the explosive dynamism of the productive forces. The leading question for Castells and Harvey was how and why capitalist social relations should have reproduced themselves so effectively, after a rather gruelling and one would have thought inherently destabilising century of World Wars, a world Depression, the abiding Communist alternative, and the many radicalisms of the 1960s. To each of these aspects of the overarching question, it appeared, the resounding answer was: *space*.

The international relations of production were recognised for the first time as having achieved determinate spatial forms. Principally, of course, the mid-twentieth century saw the global consolidation of the nation state as the geographico-political dominant, with all of the bureaucratic, technical, managerial, militarist, administrative rationality of the modern state in tow; confined henceforth to strict borders and no longer spread out across huge colonial empires. Along with the state came its symbolic and material centre, the city. More than ever, the city dominated its surrounding regions, evolving typical spatial forms: its core Central Business Districts, gentrified downtowns, surrounding industrial districts, working-class areas and ethnic ghettos, and outer rims of suburban middle-class autopia. Mobility and relations between regions were rationalised by new transport and information technologies. New surveillance techniques increasingly pried open the spaces of everyday life to constant supervision. Very clear patterns of international exploitation emerged, and along with them a rhetoric of 'Third World' nationality, wedged between the competing bourgeois and Communist State blocs. To reap the rewards of this new global space, opened up by the omnipotent logic of the market, new forms of multinational corporation exploited the vast differentials between labour markets and consumer markets. The long and historic haul out of pre-capitalism had been completed; the super-states held planetary sway; and as certain contemporary prophets have not failed to recognise, Hegel was thus ultimately proved right: History, or the great period of capitalist expansion and wars of conquest, was over. In its stead, however, space could justifiably be said to have become the repository of his dialectic, of politics and of contradiction. Space, which has uprooted and exiled the very sense of time and of experience in postmodern society, is our inexorable social horizon, as such is wholly saturated with ideology and politics. Space is at once the *field* of production and the ultimate *goal* of production, for an economic mode hell-bent on perpetuating itself *ad infinitum*. New strategies of domination and new contradictions to undermine them are thereby opened up for critical, theoretical scrutiny.

The 'socio-spatial dialectic' paved many avenues for critical work. Since 1973, this theoretical vein has been mined by geographers like Derek Gregory, Edward Soja, Doreen Massey, Neil Smith, Linda MacDowell, Mike Featherstone, Nigel Thrift and many others.[4] There has been a renaissance of the geographical imagination: admitting semiotics and anthropology into the van of a push towards 'cultural geography'; allowing for an urgent feminist critique of the masculine scopic regimes dominating the discipline; introducing radical ecology through the thesis of geographically uneven development. One of the most significant of the theoretical innovations in this field has been the complication of the socio-spatial dialectic by a *local–global dialectic*, an insistence upon the contradictory claims of global economic space and the intimate spaces of locality and identity, in all present-day practice. Neil Smith has elaborated a seven-stage 'scaling' of the production of space: 'body, home, community, urban, region, nation, global',[5] each with its own logic of social manifestation and resistance, yet all strangely articulated within the total process of capitalist consolidation. Harvey himself has gone on to become one of the leading theorists of postmodernism, his concept of cultural *time-space compression* and its determinate links to flexible accumulation effectively transforming that particular field of inquiry.[6]

What I would like to draw out of this new geography for literary studies, first of all, is the consistency and rigour of its application of the concept of space. We have all been made aware of the metaphorisation of space in much recent literary theory, tropes such as 'mapping', 'location', 'sites', 'travel' and 'theoretical space'; much of which tends to leave everything just where it was found. But the materiality of the production paradigm, as protected and developed by the new geography, marks a substantial improvement over this fashionable rhetoric, as it strives to elucidate the complex determinations of socially produced space on all practice. Second, these complex determinations are no longer to be sought (as they once were) simply in the abstract realms of 'ideology' or 'discourse', but very precisely in the grounded and interani-mating practices of the billions of bodies whose organised everyday life reproduces the spaces in question. In a word, 'everyday life' and 'lived experience' are very much at issue once again, no longer as the insipid baggage of liberalism, but as the material force-field of the dialectic between locality and globalisation, the body and the state, class and race, production and consumption: the social and spatial structures of our world. Culture is intimately and materially bound up with these practices, these dialectics, strung out over their contradictions. Henceforth, as Jody Berland has reminded us, the production of culture 'cannot be conceived outside of the production of diverse and exacting spaces'.[7]

In order to give some idea of how one might go about implementing such concepts and paradigms in cultural and literary theory, it will be useful to turn to Lefebvre's 1974 magnum opus, *The Production of Space* itself. Countless hints are contained therein of how to re-establish aesthetics after the ideologies of semiology, all of which turn on the ascendancy of spatial problems in late capitalism. Primarily, Lefebvre sees culture emerging out of the conflict between what he calls 'representations of space' and 'representational spaces', opposed representational practices which interact dynamically with the 'spatial practice' of everyday life. By 'representations of space' Lefebvre means all of the abstract, pseudo-logical, codified practices which confer 'knowledge', 'science' and mastery – in a word, all the epistemologies of power: *savoir*, in Foucault's sense. Lefebvre's twist is to present these as the knowledge/power *of space* – the organs and tools of spatial domination by the state and capital. 'Ideology *per se*', he says, 'might well be said to consist primarily in a discourse upon social space.'[8] These representations inform technology, architecture, urban planning, politics and all of the techniques which dominate daily life; they enable and are subject to historical change. Dialectically opposed to these instrumentalities of abstraction and power are the pockets of residual 'representational spaces': those imagined spaces where the body reasserts its playful and sensuous being, in some ritual or aesthetic form.

> Redolent with imaginary and symbolic elements, they have their source in history – in the history of a people as well as in the history of each individual belonging to that people . . . Representational space is alive: it speaks. It has an affective kernel or centre: Ego, bed, bedroom, dwelling, house; or, square, church, graveyard. It embraces the loci of passion, of action and of lived situations, and thus immediately implies time.[9]

We need only think of the conflict between the claims to traditional land of indigenous peoples and the state bureaucracies and multinationals seeking to administer and profit from this land to get a clear idea of what Lefebvre has in mind. It is between these opposed representative practices, between abstract epistemologies and concrete affective phenomenologies, each of them contingent upon the mode of production in which they obtain, that culture emerges as such. Art and literature constitute a society's fraught attempt to bridge the gaps between them in the name of an imaginary consensus; or alternatively, to blast them asunder in the name of differential bodily freedoms – in either case seeking to modify blind, routinised 'spatial practice'.

To put this in a different register, Lefebvre argues that, at the level of the body, this spatial triad of 'representations of space', 'representational spaces' and mundane 'spatial practices' is matched by a triad of modes of subjectivity: the *conceived* (epistemology), the *lived* (the fugitive domain of experience in a world increasingly without experience) and the *perceived* (*habitus*, everyday actions and sensations). From this perspective, cultural production might be seen as the work of 'mapping' the contradictory space of the mode of production *onto* the subject, through these three categories.[10] If the processes of modernity and postmodernity have ushered in an escalating estrangement of the conceived, the perceived and the lived – what we 'know' doesn't match up with what we 'sense' and do, and neither of these squares with what little we 'live' or truly experience any more – then culture today has the impossible task of somehow opening up paths between them, glossing over or exposing their contradictions. Individual works or texts may then be scrutinised for the labour they perform in programming social subjects for their social space – but I can only indicate here how *narrative* studies might profit from such a spatial theory.[11]

The level of 'spatial practice' is 'perceived' in the text via the banal narrative conventions whereby representative forms of social action (entering through doors, riding in a carriage, mounting stairs, buying a banana and so on) are articulated: Barthes called this the 'proairetic' code, by which he meant the standardised and conventional patterns of narrative progression which broke down into completely reliable sequences of mini-actions within one whole, articulated event.[12] What we should add to his account is that such codes are in essence historically and spatially variable, and that the task of narrative is precisely to normalise and naturalise (or, alternatively, to 'estrange') them against possible historical alternatives. Narrative exists, in part, to normalise spatial habits that are in reality in a constant state of flux, to give them an appearance of immortality and inevitability. Meanwhile, the level of Lefebvre's 'representations of space' is 'conceived' in the text through the received wisdom and assumed knowledge, as well as all the structures and codes of narrative form itself, with which the text projects itself as part of the 'modern' world – not prey to superstitions, but enlightened, transparent and realistic: Barthes called this the 'cultural code'. This is the level at which the work feeds parasitically off the 'representations of space' which dominate and homogenise society. Where the text is 'conceived', there too it is divorced from the affective contents of myths, rituals and bodily rhythms, a fact which makes it at once powerfully enlightening and deleteriously abstract. At this level – unless it is critical, comic or satirical – the literary work subordinates its vocation to the tasks of social reproduction, and rejoins the governing codes.

Finally, then, the level of 'representational space' is 'lived' in the text at those moments where 'content', 'affect' and 'experience' radiate some buried and well-nigh forgotten memory of what it might have been like to 'live', of what it still might be like to live today. That literature still continues to harbour these glimmerings of bodily differentation and sensuousness, is borne out by the aesthetic theory of Deleuze and Guattari: works of art produce (or, better yet, *are*) *affects*, material complexes of representational intensity wherein the body strives to become other, to break free from abstraction and domination and freely appropriate some affective space for its own sensuous uses.[13] In their various affects, what Adorno called their mimetic impulse, art and literature contest social reproduction by refusing rationality, and embody utopian and libidinal urges that exceed every governing principle of the state. One thinks, for instance, of Gregor Samsa's paradigmatic metamorphosis into a giant bug; or, in a more contemporary example, of the narrator 'Sammy' in Kelman's *How Late It Was, How Late* (1994), whose initial blinding by the police cancels a stroke the conventional spatial practices and representations of modern life in Glasgow, and obliges him to rediscover the informal knowledge of his other senses. These affects, however, must also be understood historically and relative to the social space they distort and 'deturn'; for affects are not as transhistorical as they seem, and must be construed as symptomatic of the historical space in which they are produced.

To sum up this schematic spatial literary theory: literary works have the social function of producing what Fredric Jameson called 'cognitive maps' for social subjects. They mediate dialectically between modes of conception, perception and affection, programming the bodies of historical human beings for the spatial trials of their 'unrepresentable' mode of production. These programs, however, are clearly highly variable in quality and political purpose – for you can intervene narratively in the interests of socio-spatial cohesion, reform, reaction or revolution, and you can do any of these with varying degrees of cultural competence and performative interest. What matters then, in the spatial analysis of a literary work, is (first) establishing the dialectical character of its mediations of conceived, perceived and lived, relative to the historical mode of production in which it emerges and the literary codes it has inherited from previous modes of production; and then deciding the value of this work according to (a) the complexity and dexterity of these mediations, and to (b) the overall political cause served by the cognitive map the work offers to social subjects, the fortunes of its reception, and so on.

Of course, there are road-signs and trial runs of such a spatial literary criticism in the history of the discipline: Benjamin's work on Baudelaire; Bakhtin's on the 'chronotope'; de Certeau's 'spatial stories'; and, at a different level, Bachelard's work on intimate spatial phenomenology. But crucial consequences of the detour of the dialectic through human geography await their application. In the last twenty years, the new geography has transformed the very image of society, from one shaped by abstract social 'structures' to one firmly grounded and active in the social production of space: thus at once more relative to the contingent, fragmentary pressures of the local and of bodies, but also more subject to the ceaseless processes of homogenisation, devastation, waste and abstraction of purified global capitalism. My conviction is that literary studies would do well to immerse itself in these lessons. For 'culture', the mass media or Culture Industry, is of course one of the principal instruments of capital's homogenisation of the lifeworld, its reduction to a sterile but libidinal logic of visualisation and spectacle. The same film or sitcom or news story is now seen everywhere and at once, collapsing local differences and the full sensorium of the body into a single imposed image of Utopia, whose nether side is a body in chains, the senses sealed off, local communities gutted, structural unemployment, what have you. It is not stretching the imagination too far to appreciate that literary narratives today are actively responding to these dominating processes at work in culture and space: that, say, Irvine Welsh's affect of a heroin-addicted, bodily appropriation of council-estate space is a critical symbolic act in Scottish 'culture' which resonates across all derelict council-estate space and strikes against the representations of planners, politicians and jurists – even though it may be aesthetically uninteresting and doomed to a short period of resonance. Or that cyberpunk achieved its vitality by its affect of the becoming-body of the information machine, in an age and a space typified by the becoming-machine of the human body itself. Or that Pynchon's *Vineland* (1990) worked by producing an anachronistic affect of the family on the farm, in an American 1984 presided over by televisions, entertainment, the FBI and Reagan's Cold War. And so on. Literature, while programming us to live and move in our own mutating historical space, also retains the occasional task of allowing certain, possible 'representational spaces' to squeeze through the gates of an abstract and iterable discourse. Only a dialectical theory of spatial production will enable us to understand just how and why this happens.

NOTES

1. See Jürgen Habermas, 'On the Obsolescence of the Production Paradigm', in *The Philosophical Discourse of Modernity*, trans. Frederick Lawrence (Cambridge: Polity, 1990), pp. 75–82; and Jean-François Lyotard, *The Postmodern Condition:*

A Report on Knowledge, trans. Brian Massumi (Manchester: Manchester University Press, 1984).

2. Henri Lefebvre, *The Survival of Capitalism: Reproduction of the Relations of Production*, trans. Frank Bryant (London: Allison & Busby, 1976), p. 17.

3. See Fredric Jameson, *Postmodernism, or, The Cultural Logic of Late Capitalism* (London: Verso, 1991), and *The Geopolitical Aesthetic: Cinema and Space in the World System* (London: BFI, 1992), for substantial treatments of architecture and cinema vis-à-vis the production of space.

4. See Derek Gregory, *Ideology, Science and Human Geography* (London: Hutchinson, 1978), and *Geographical Imaginations* (Oxford: Blackwell, 1994); Edward Soja, *Postmodern Geographies: The Reassertion of Space in Critical Social Theory* (London: Verso, 1989); Doreen Massey, *Spatial Divisions of Labour: Social Structures and the Geography of Production* (London: Macmillan, 1985), and *Space, Place and Gender* (Cambridge: Polity, 1994); and Neil Smith, *Uneven Development: Nature, Capital and the Reproduction of Space* (Oxford: Blackwell, 1990).

5. Neil Smith, 'Homeless/Global: Scaling Places', in Jon Bird et al. (eds), *Mapping the Futures: Local Cultures, Global Changes* (London: Routledge, 1993), p. 101.

6. David Harvey, *The Condition of Postmodernity* (Oxford: Blackwell, 1989).

7. Jody Berland, 'Angels Dancing: Cultural Technologies and the Production of Space', in Lawrence Grossberg, Cary Nelson and Paula A. Treichler (eds), *Cultural Studies* (London: Routledge, 1992), pp. 38–51 (p. 39).

8. Lefebvre, *The Production of Space*, trans. Donald Nicholson-Smith (Oxford: Blackwell, 1991), p. 44.

9. Ibid., pp. 41-2.

10. For an excellent illustration of a textual analysis carried out in the name of such a mapping of social space onto social body, see Fredric Jameson, 'The Realist Floorplan', in Blonsky (ed.), *On Signs* (Baltimore: Johns Hopkins University Press, 1985), pp. 373–83.

11. To see suggestive work on how Lefebvrian thought might be adapted to poetic analysis, see the wonderful book by Kristin Ross, *The Emergence of Social Space: Rimbaud and the Paris Commune* (Houndmills, Basingstoke: Macmillan, 1988).

12. Barthes, *S/Z*, trans. Richard Miller (Oxford: Blackwell, 1993), pp. 19ff.

13. Gilles Deleuze and Félix Guattari, *What is Philosophy?*, trans. Hugh Tomlinson and Graham Burchell (London: Verso, 1994), pp. 163–99.

POST-WORD

Hélène Cixous

Editors' note: The text presented here is a letter sent by Hélène Cixous in response to a request by the editors for a short epilogue to this collection. As Cixous explains below, this is an impossible task, and the question of 'Post-Theory' demands a more rigorous and expansive place for thought. In other words, what 'Post-Theory' requires is the essays in this collection. However, the editors feel that this letter exceeds what might have been thought possible in the space of a 'post-word', and, with the kind permission of the author, we have reproduced it here. Perhaps it will inaugurate a short-lived but innovative academic genre.

The Letter which I would have Preferred
not to See Myself Write to my Friend
Martin McQuillan

Paris, 15 January 1998

Dear Martin,

On the very first possible day of this year I have read – carefully – everything you sent to me.

I found the whole volume extremely striking – powerful, inspired.

I enjoyed your piece enormously, I do think it is a creation, it is so clever and informed and inventive.

Then I started thinking about how to inscribe 'myself' (is there any?) in the field you have ploughed.

Then I sat early in the morning at my desk and I started trying to begin starting to write a something not unworthy of you (you = Martin my friend).

What came out was a number of puns and fables which I immediately judged totally inadequate, jarring with the harmony of the whole, and obviously bound and promised to a sentence of rejection and misconstruction. It has to do with:

209

1. the magnitude of the subject, which deserves and demands the most thorough type of consideration;
2. so as not to feel shamefully dishonest I would have to write a book-length book in order to, minimum-wise, at least make the necessary preliminary distinctions between *Theory* (a concept in an Anglo-Saxon context) and *Théorie*, which does not refer at all to the same country of meaning.

I, as a writer, relate (*negatively*) to *théorie* in France. Whereas *Theory* is a battlefield in England and the USA where I would of course side with all of you who have to defend what is construed under that name against the Philistines.

Then, I am a *poet* – you know things come to me (thought-things that is) under the guise of birds, clouds, and the sea washing herself in her shores, and where? where do I situate all my visions but on that blade-thin region where Life casts a quick glance at her death and sees for the first and last time how beautiful she is (Life that is), in this instant. There and then there is simply no time for Theory, only time for Thee, then, out brief candle.

I would have called my 'contribution' *Avantposte*. You know what that means, dear Martin? It is the post before the post where the army-general posts the soldiers who are supposed to watch and get killed first. They see-before and shout first, and die-before. It would have had four sections.

The first section runs like this:

For *Post*, see postallion, postconditional postequities posthumour, postlove postcoïtumcoyness postmartem postoomany yet impostible postoral i.e. impostscriptum, postprandial postreintroducing Prepost-seriousness postwartem potspottery etcaetery . . .
> > > > *in* H. C. *in* FW, J. Joyce's hyposthumious pot of prijudicious
> > > > hystheorical processes.

The second section runs:

Théorie:
1. In French (not pronounced at all like *Theory* in English) is pronounced: Thé au riz. Can also be read: Théo rit.
2. Feminine noun like *Philosophie*.
3. Name of the god of Humour often represented as the cat of a great philosopher.
4. Fiction.
5. Additional word that had ambiguous fortunes during the twentieth century in English-speaking countries.

Since the 1960s this term has belonged to the lexicon of the intra-academic ideological war. It is employed with a pejorative and even phobic connotation in the Universities the press and the media that fuss over the Humanities by all those who talk about writing which is to say what is called with prudence and hesitation literature or text. Or else with a positive one by those who write.

N.B.: It should be noted that the active Agents of literature, producers of texts, poets playwrights, authors of fictions in all genres who are the objects and the hostages of the conflict and are not inhabitants of Academia care little about the word and its implications, interpretations and exegeses. Under the rain of arrows that whistle over their head, they write. Most of them do not know that the battle rages regarding their past and future works.

I think of Clarice Lispector, the greatest woman writer of this century in my opinion, whose work stands equal to Kafka's, who preferred to go to the market, who did not frequent the hermeneutic circles and never dreamed of enclosing the *agua viva* white-water of her immense philosophicopoetical meditations in a net. Of all those, poets, who are *the prophets of the instant* and who, at lightning speed, want to write, write, *before*, in the still-boiling time before the cooled fall-out of the narrative when we feel and it is not yet called such-and-such, this, him or her. Tempest before the immobilisation, the capture, the concept. Where there is already the murmur of words but not yet proper-name-words. In the time when God is only yet a forename of God.

The third does not actually run but rather crawls:

Une Théorie de Fourmis

It was in the days when I watched.

I watched at length the clouds. And with velocity they did not watch me, they charged at the slow speed of boats.

It was in the days when I watched the sea wash herself and I listened to the sea caress herself moaning at night with great tail-strokes on the rocky shore.

The child I was in the Garden of the *Cercle Militaire* in Oran. She is three years old. Her father lieutenant-doctor is on the war front. She sees this:

The doors of the Law were opened yesterday for her to enter into the Garden. It is her first Garden. This is where she learns in three strokes of time all she will know later . . . : the Evil in the Good, men's hate of men which is the mark of mankind, the rottenness already in young hearts, all that she *does not know* yet and that has no name, will happen to her in the Garden. And the selfless love for what is living.

A body, legs, a good nose come to her. She crawls, she smells, she tastes. She gathers leaves, she tries all the plants with her mouth. I still remember their tastes the acrid, the tangy, the honeyed. She makes her living acquaintances [*ses connaissances vivantes*]. Without number. Without gender. She remains for hours lying flat neighbouring a motionless lizard. They watch each other.

Across a path, here is a single-file line of ants. The ants carry burdens on their backs. The child sees the relationship and the resemblance: procession of indigenous porters in the bush and the maquis. One cannot say who resembles whom exactly. There is reciprocity. She herself an isolated ant on the sand, but not forever: a line of porters is formed in the paths of her dream: it is her first discontinuous continuous line. The words move, take turns, go around each other, climb.

It is her first theory.

At that time she still lives things according to things. No separation. It happens before *I*. Before *Them*. Before 'she'. Before Knowledge. Here, at the terrestrial *Avantposte*.

The fourth would have been a prosopopoeia of Theoria
(I have not written it)

I am telling you about this not to tantalise you, but to give you the proof that I do not want to resign out of laziness and indifference. I have done the work and I have judged it incompatible with the collection of dedicated and passionate essays you have gathered. I cannot bear playing the role of the firecracker – which is exactly how my three or four pages sound.

Dear Martin, when I glimpsed my *Avantposte* I felt that I could expect nothing else from my 'inspiration' and that this was so out of place, it might even be perceived as *désinvolte* or offensive I am afraid. I don't want to take the two risks, the risk of being called disrespectful; the risk of hurting the feelings of the scholars I regard and intellectually love.

I beg you humbly to absolve me. I feel guilty because you have been generous, patient, and because I would give anything not to disappoint you, except what I call my honour. I feel strongly it would be a mistake if I listened to the voice of my affection for you instead of listening to the wisdom of my reluctance.

Do absolve and forgive me or try to later. I shall write something for you in more suitable circumstances. I know I am right in giving up. It would do neither of us two, and none of us all any good if I stood miserably at this worthy *avantposte*.

Let me not give you more explanations (there are dozens more). Put it all on the account of my intuition: I feel I am not powerful enough to sum up all I should have to say on this huge issue. There are questions and places I avoid or try to avoid because I know I would express myself as a usurper there.

My dear friend, if you feel it would help you disentangle the situation with the press, you can show them (whoever they are) my letter.

Please do not worry and do not rue. The book is just wonderful. It certainly doesn't need my poor pinch of spice.

Lovingly,

Hélène

Translated Eric Prenowitz

NOTES ON CONTRIBUTORS

Catherine Belsey is Professor of English and Chair of the Centre for Critical and Cultural Theory at the University of Cardiff, Wales. Her publications include *Critical Practice* (1980), *The Subject of Tragedy* (1985) and *Desire* (1994).

Geoffrey Bennington is Professor of French and Director of the Centre for Modern French Thought at the University of Sussex. His publications include *Lyotard: Writing the Event* (1988), *Jacques Derrida* (1993) and *Legislations* (1994).

Hélène Cixous is Director of Studies at the Centre d'Études Féminines at the Université de Paris VIII. Her recent publications in English translation include *Rootprints* (1997), *FirstDays of the Year* (1998), and *Stigmata* (1998).

Patricia Duncker is Senior Lecturer in the Department of English at the University of Wales (Aberystwyth). Her publications include *Sisters and Strangers* (1992) and the acclaimed fiction *Hallucinating Foucault* (1996).

Antony Easthope is Professor of English and Cultural Studies at Manchester Metropolitan University. His publications include *British Post-Structuralism* (1988), *Literary into Cultural Studies* (1991), and *Englishness and National Culture* (1999).

Charles Forsdick is a Lecturer in French at the University of Glasgow.

Alex Houen is writing his Ph.D., 'Exploding Literature: Writing Terrorism from R. L. Stevenson to Don Delilo', in English Literature at Kings College, University of Cambridge.

214

Lorna Hutson is Professor of English Literature at the University of Hull. Her publications include *Thomas Nashe in Context* (1989) and *The Usurer's Daughter* (1994).

Ernesto Laclau is Professor of Politics and Chair of the Centre for Theoretical Studies at the University of Essex. His publications include *Hegemony and Socialist Strategy* (1985) with Chantal Mouffe, *New Reflections on the Revolution of Our Time* (1990) and *Emancipations* (1996).

Jeremy Lane is a Lecturer in French at the University of Aberdeen.

Julian Murphet is a Junior Research Fellow at St John's College, University of Oxford.

Christopher Norris is Professor of Philosophy at the University of Cardiff, Wales. His publications include *Uncritical Theory* (1992), *Resources of Realism* (1997), and *Against Relativism* (1997).

Eric Prenowitz is affiliated with the Centre d'Études Féminines at the Université de Paris VIII. He is an acclaimed translator of Hélène Cixous and Jacques Derrida.

Nicholas Royle is Reader in English Studies at the University of Stirling. His publications include *Telepathy and Literature* (1991) and *After Derrida* (1995).

Robert Smith is a former Prize Fellow at All Souls College, University of Oxford. His publications include *Derrida and Autobiography* (1995).

Eric Woehrling wrote his Ph.D., 'Tragic Eikonografy: A Conceptual History of Mimesis, from Plato to T. S. Eliot', in English Literature at the University of Liverpool.

EDITORS

Graeme Macdonald and Robin Purves are each completing a Ph.D. in English Literature at the University of Glasgow. Dr Stephen Thomson teaches Children's Literature at the University of Reading. Dr Martin McQuillan is a Lecturer in Literature at Staffordshire University.

INDEX